2008 CASE AND STATUTORY SUPPLEMENT

COX, BOK, GORMAN AND FINKIN

CASES AND MATERIALS

LABOR LAW

FOURTEENTH EDITION

by

ROBERT A. GORMAN
Kenneth W. Gemmill Professor of Law Emeritus
University of Pennsylvania

MATTHEW W. FINKIN
Albert J. Harno and Edward W. Cleary Chair in Law
University of Illinois

FOUNDATION PRESS

© 2001, 2004 FOUNDATION PRESS
© 2005, 2006 THOMSON REUTERS/FOUNDATION PRESS
© 2008 By THOMSON REUTERS/FOUNDATION PRESS
                              395 Hudson Street
                              New York, NY 10014
                              Phone Toll Free 1–877–888–1330
                              Fax (212) 367–6799
                              foundation–press.com
Printed in the United States of America

ISBN 978–1–59941–549–9

TEXT IS PRINTED ON 10% POST
CONSUMER RECYCLED PAPER

PREFACE

Since the Fourteenth Edition was published in May 2006, the world of labor law has been in turmoil. The intimation of the direction the NLRB would take under President George W. Bush's appointees can be seen in some of the decisions discussed or set out for discussion in the Fourteenth Edition: *Brown University* (2004), at p. 96, holding graduate assistants to be statutory non-employees; *Harborside Healthcare* (2004), at p. 119, limiting the role of statutory supervisors when they speak out favorably on unionization; *Martin Luther Memorial Home, Inc.* (2004), at p. 124, loosening restrictions on general rules of conduct that might be read to restrict union expression; *North Hills Office Services, Inc.* (2005), at p. 143, extending a property owner's property-based right to exclude union organizers to a contractor's employment-based right to prohibit employees to talk to those organizers; *Oakwood Healthcare Center* (2004), at p. 309, making it virtually impossible for employees in trilateral employment networks to unionize; *Flying Food Group, Inc.* (2004), at p. 409, allowing employers to continue to campaign against unionization even as they bargain with the union; *Hollings Press, Inc.* (2005), at p. 544, finding an employee's solicitation of co-workers' help in perfecting a sexual harassment claim to be unprotected for want of statutory "mutual aid or protection"; *IBM Corp.* (2004), at p. 546, abandoning the right of an employee in a disciplinary interrogation at a non-unionized workplace to have a co-worker present; and more. Since then and accelerating in 2007, the NLRB has handed down perhaps two dozen decisions divided along party lines, either 3-2 for full Board decisions or 2-1 for panel decisions, abandoning doctrine — some of considerable vintage — or modifying it, few of which to the advantage of unions.

The pattern of these decisions is such that on December 13, 2007, a joint hearing of the Senate and House labor subcommittees was held to inquire into the Board's conduct of office. The more salient of these decisions are set out in text or for discussion in this Supplement.

Meanwhile, the turmoil continues apace: the judicial reception to Board decisions has been less than deferential in several cases treated in this Supplement; bills to require "card check" certification and to narrow the scope of the supervisory exemption have been introduced with strong Congressional support; and the Labor Board has been reduced to two sitting members.

In other words, this is an interesting time for students—and teachers—to address labor law. The intensification of the NLRB's politicization presses to the fore the role of the NLRB and of presidential appointments in the fashioning of national labor policy. These events necessarily raise the larger substantive questions of what national labor policy ought to be—and whether a statute that received its last major legislative reconsideration in 1947 is capable of addressing the world of work sixty years on.

June 15, 2008

ANALYTICAL TABLE OF CONTENTS

v

TABLE OF CASES

Principal cases are in bold type. Non-principal cases are in roman type. References are to Pages.

2008 CASE AND STATUTORY SUPPLEMENT

CASES AND MATERIALS

LABOR LAW

*

PART ONE

THE EVOLUTION OF LABOR RELATIONS LAWS

IV. LEGISLATIVE & CONSTITUTIONAL PROTECTIONS

Page 66. After the discussion of *Burlington Northern RR.*:

The Second Circuit, relying on the special features of the Railway Labor Act, held that the Norris–La Guardia Act does not constrain the power of a district court to enjoin a strike by airline employees to secure better terms than those approved by a bankruptcy court. *Northwest Airlines Corp. v. Association of Flight Attendants*, 483 F.3d 160 (2d Cir. 2007).

VIII. JURISDICTION, ORGANIZATION AND PROCEDURE OF THE NLRB

Page 89. Item 3 ("Excluded Employees"), after the discussion of *Sure–Tan, Inc.* and *Hoffman Plastics*:

A panel of the Court of Appeals for the District of Columbia Circuit has sustained the NLRB's position that the Immigration Reform and Control Act (IRCA), passed after *Sure–Tan*, making it unlawful to hire undocumented aliens, did not supersede *Sure–Tan* to exempt undocumented aliens from coverage of the Labor Act. *Agri Processor Co., Inc. v. NLRB*, 514 F.3d 1 (D.C. Cir. 2008). One judge concurred noting the anomaly created by the juxtaposition of the IRCA and the Labor Act, i.e., workers whose hiring was made unlawful by the former would nevertheless be protected by the latter in their right to workplace representation; but that anomaly called for legislative correction. A third member of the panel agreed with the company's argument.

Page 94. After the discussion of *Kentucky River*:

In *Oakwood Healthcare, Inc.*, 348 NLRB No. 37 (2006), the Board, by a 3–2 vote, set out the basic framework for deciding whether an employee who has authority effectively to recommend the assignment of work to others is a supervisor. On March 22, 2007, H.R. 1644, the "Re–Empowerment of Skilled and Professional Employees and Construction Tradeworkers (RESPECT) Act" was introduced with 160 sponsors. It would redefine a supervisor as "any individual having authority, in the interest of the employer *and for a majority of the individual's work time*, to hire, transfer, suspend, lay off, recall, promote, discharge, [assign], reward, or discipline other employees, [or responsibly to direct them], or to adjust their grievances" the rest remaining as it is in § 2(11). The new language is in italics, existing language to be excised in brackets. It was reported out of committee on Sept. 19, 2007, by a 26–20 note.

Page 108. At the end of *Representation Cases*:

The NLRB has proposed a new form of expedited consent election—one initiated by joint submission of the employer and the union without requiring a showing of interest. The comments on this proposal, published in the February 28, 2008 *Federal Register*, are posted at http://www.nlrb. gov/research/frequentlyrequested_documents.aspx.

PART TWO

THE ESTABLISHMENT OF THE COLLECTIVE BARGAINING RELATIONSHIP

I. PROTECTION OF THE RIGHT OF SELF-ORGANIZATION

Page 121. After *Harborside Healthcare*:

In *Madison Square Garden CT*, 350 NLRB No. 8 (2007), a 2–1 decision, several supervisors, clothed with authority to recommend discipline, were vocal union supporters—active in circulating union designation cards and speaking at pro-union meetings. They resisted their employer's demand to support its anti-union campaign or, at least, to remain neutral. They circulated a flyer to the staff, "Just Ask Us," in response to several staff meetings called by the General Manager, Mr. Brooks, to explain to the staff the employer's opposition to the union. It read:

> We, the undersigned Event Staff supervisors, take offense at the recent assertions by Mr. Brooks about our thoughts on the subject of unionization. We are all adults, and are fully capable of speaking for ourselves. Regardless of whether we support the Union organizing campaign, we think it is wrong for Mr. Brooks to speak for us. If you want to know what we think, JUST ASK US!

The union won the election, 27 to 22. The Board set the election aside. Member Liebman dissented, in part on the ground that *Harborside* was wrongly decided, and in part on the ground that its criteria were misapplied in this case.

Page 124. End of Problem 8:

The Board's disposition on remand in the *Lee* case is at 346 NLRB No. 59 (2006).

Page 132.   Add to the end of the Problems for Discussion:

What if the policy provided:

> *We honor confidentiality.* We recognize and protect the confidentiality of any information concerning the company, its business plans, its partners [apparently the company's appellation for its employees], new business efforts, customers, accounting and financial matters.

Is the maintenance of this policy—which refers to no section 7 activity, has never been applied by the company to any section 7 activity, and for which there is no evidence that any employee has interpreted the prohibition to apply to section 7 activity—an unfair labor practice? See Cintas Corp. v. NLRB, 482 F.3d 463 (D.C. Cir. 2007).

2.   The UC Corporation, a non-unionized firm, has promulgated an employee-policy handbook. All employees are required to sign an acknowledgement, a copy of which is returned to the company, that the handbook sets forth the employee's terms and conditions of employment. One section of the handbook sets out the "UC Agreement to Arbitrate" [UCAA] which the employee is required separately to sign. It establishes an arbitration procedure to be administered by a neutral outside agency. In terms of coverage the UCAA provides in pertinent part that it

> ... applies to all UC employees, regardless of length of service or status and covers all disputes relating to or arising out of an employee's employment with UC or the termination of that employment. Examples of the type of disputes or claims covered by the UCAA include, but are not limited to, claims for wrongful termination of employment, breach of contract, fraud, employment discrimination, harassment or retaliation under the Americans With Disabilities Act, the Age Discrimination in Employment Act, Title VII of the Civil Rights Act of 1964 and its amendments, the California Fair Employment and Housing Act or any other state or local anti-discrimination laws, torts claims, wage or overtime claims or other claims under the Labor Code, or any other legal or equitable claims and causes of action recognized by local, state or federal law or regulations.

Another section of the handbook is headed "What about Unions?" It provides in pertinent part that the company prefers to remain union-free. It concludes with a paragraph headed "Resolution Opportunity Program":

> We know that you want to express your problems, suggestions, and comments to us so that we can understand each other better. You have that opportunity here at UC. This can be done without having a union involved in the communication between you and the company. Here you can speak up for yourself at all levels of management. We will listen, and we will do our best to give you a responsible reply. *Furthermore, you should understand that if your problem is not resolved to your satisfaction through the Appeal process, you are expected to see me.* [Emphasis in original.]

The section is signed by UC's president whose photograph appears on the facing page. A fuller multi-level procedure for employees to bring their grievances forward is set out.

Does the maintenance of either or both of these provisions violate the National Labor Relations Act? See *U–Haul Co. of California*, 347 NLRB No. 34 (2006). Assume the Resolution Opportunity Program included the following:

> Each employee using the Resolution Opportunity Program must represent his or her self in the process—no employee may represent, appeal, or speak on behalf of another employee during the process except as a witness as needed by the investigating manager. There is no retaliation or reprisal for an employee who uses the Resolution Opportunity Program.

Would it violate the National Labor Relation Act? See *Cast–Matic Corp.*, 350 NLRB No. 94 (2007). Assume the UCAA precluded any "group claim or class action" from being allowed to be brought in the arbitration procedure. Would that preclusion, coupled with the substitution of arbitration for civil litigation, be violative of the Act?

Page 142. End of the first note after *Lechmere*:

Justice Thomas notes that Lechmere's employees were "accessible"— that "a substantial percentage" had been contacted via mailings, home visits, and phone calls. It is not obvious how the union was able to secure their names, mailing addresses, and telephone numbers. The Court noted that the union was able to get that information concerning about 20% of the workforce by recording their license-plate numbers and securing that identifying information from the state's Department of Motor Vehicles. That often-used technique is now foreclosed by the federal Driver's Privacy Protection Act. See Pichler v. Unite, 457 F.Supp.2d 524 (E.D. Pa. 2006).

Page 142. End of the second note after *Lechmere* discussing California Law:

In *Fashion Valley Mall, LLC v. NLRB*, 42 Cal.4th 850, 69 Cal.Rptr.3d 288, 172 P.3d 742 (2007), the California Supreme Court addressed a question certified to it by the U.S. Court of Appeals for the District of Columbia Circuit. The Mall maintained a rule, Rule 5.6.2., forbidding expressive activity on the premises "Urging, or encouraging in any manner, customers, not to purchase the merchandise or services offered by one or more of the stores or merchants in the shopping center." Unionized employees of a local newspaper were forbidden by the Mall to leaflet at one of the paper's advertisers, located in the Mall, urging customers to call the newspaper's CEO. The leafleting posed no hindrance to customer traffic. The D.C. Circuit affirmed the NLRB's decision that the leafleting would be protected if California law would accord an expressive easement for such speech on the Mall's premises and so certified that question to the California court. The state court answered the question—"Under California law may Fashion Valley maintain and enforce against the Union its Rule 5.6.2.?''—in the negative, by a four-to-three vote:

> A shopping mall is a public forum in which persons may reasonably exercise their right to free speech guaranteed by article I, section 2 of the California Constitution. Shopping malls may enact and enforce reasonable regulations of the time, place and manner of such free expression to assure that these activities do not interfere with the normal business operations of the mall, but they may not prohibit certain types of speech based upon its content, such as prohibiting speech that urges a boycott of one or more of the stores in the mall.

Page 144.   End of Problem 5:

In *Toering Elec. Co.*, 351 NLRB No. 18 (2007), by a 3–2 decision, the Board held that in order for the General Counsel to prevail in a § 8(a)(3) claim for refusal to hire "salted" applicants, the General Counsel must prove that the applicant was "genuinely interested" in establishing an employment relationship with the employer. In the view of the majority, it was not sufficient to warrant the shelter of the NLRA that an individual, denied employment undeniably and solely because of his union membership, had applied for a job and thus was apparently an "employee" within the Supreme Court rulings in *Phelps Dodge Corp. v. NLRB* [casebook p. 260] and *NLRB v. Town & Country Elec. Co.* [casebook p. 144]. The majority interpreted those two seminal decisions extremely narrowly and read the "genuine interest" requirement into the definition of "employee" in NLRA § 2(3) in an unprecedented fashion. Citing the Supreme Court's 1953 decision in *Jefferson Standard Broadcasting* [casebook p. 574], the majority opined:

> Clearly, employers are not to be immunized from lawful economic pressure resulting from labor disputes. However, there is a meaningful distinction between direct economic warfare between parties to labor disputes and the subversion of the Board's processes by one party for the objective of inflicting economic injury on the other. The Board does not serve its intended statutory role as neutral arbiter of disputes if it must litigate hiring discrimination charges filed on behalf of disingenuous applicants who intend no service and loyalty to a common enterprise with a targeted employer. Instead, the Board becomes an involuntary foil for destructive partisan purposes. . . .
>
> We seek to discourage cases where unfair labor practice allegations of hiring discrimination are filed for this objective. We therefore believe that a change in law is warranted so as to better insure against it. We find that this result is better achieved by shifting the focus with respect to an applicant's genuine job interest from the employer's proof of a motivational defense to the General Counsel's proof that an applicant is entitled to the protected status of a statutory employee. Thus, we will abandon the

implicit presumption that anyone who applies for a job is protected as a Section 2(3) employee.

(a) Is the Board a "neutral arbiter of disputes"? *See* Clyde W. Summers, *Politics, Policy Making, and the NLRB,* 6 Syr. L. Rev. 92 (1954):

> The critical issues before the Board represent underlying disputes between unions and management. No matter how the Board decides these issues, it cannot avoid aiding one and hindering the other. Impartiality is impossible. There can be no impartial rules governing the relationship between a tree and the woodsman's ax, even though we let the chips fall where they may.

(b) The majority states in *Toering Electric* that it will not litigate "hiring discrimination charges filed on behalf of disingenuous applicants." Does the General Counsel act "on behalf" of an injured party? As the dissent noted, under the Act the General Counsel must act upon a charge, but the charge need not be filed by any person even arguably injured or aggrieved by the alleged unfair labor practice. On whose behalf in such a case does the General Counsel act?

(c) Elsewhere in the decision the majority opines that "Hiring discrimination under the Act simply cannot occur unless the individual was actually seeking an employment opportunity with the employer." Is this true? If an employer has a policy or practice of refusing to hire employees who would be interested in union representation—and that policy is revealed because "testers" who have no interest actually in taking the job have been seen to sound out whether such a policy or practice is in effect—would the employer be in violation of § 8(a)(1) irrespective of the General Counsel's failure to prove a § 8(a)(3)? Under *Toering Electric,* could the General Counsel pursue such a case, *i.e.,* one resulting in a cease and desist order and posting of notice, even if not an order to hire or pay backpay?

Page 147. Following Problem for Discussion:

Guard Publishing Company D/B/A The Register–Guard
351 NLRB No. 70 (2007).

■ Chairman Battista and Members Schaumber and Kirsanow:

In this case, we consider several issues relating to employees' use of their employer's e-mail system for Section 7 purposes. First, we consider whether the Respondent violated Section 8(a)(1) by maintaining a policy prohibiting the use of e-mail for all "non-job-related solicitations." Second, we consider whether the Respondent violated Section 8(a)(1) by discriminatorily enforcing that policy against union-related e-mails while allowing some personal e-mails, and Section 8(a)(3) and (1) by disciplining an employee for sending union-related emails. Finally, we consider whether the Respondent violated Section 8(a)(5) and (1) by insisting on an allegedly illegal bargaining proposal that would prohibit the use of e-mail for "union business."

After careful consideration, we hold that the Respondent's employees have no statutory right to use the Respondent's e-mail system for Section 7 purposes. We therefore find that the Respondent's policy prohibiting employee use of the system for "non-job-related solicitations" did not violate Section 8(a)(1).

With respect to the Respondent's alleged discriminatory enforcement of the e-mail policy, we have carefully examined Board precedent on this issue. As fully set forth herein, we have decided to modify the Board's approach in discriminatory enforcement cases to clarify that discrimination under the Act means drawing a distinction along Section 7 lines. We then address the specific allegations in this case of discriminatory enforcement in accordance with this approach.

Finally, we find that the Respondent did not insist on its bargaining proposal prohibiting the use of e-mail for "union business." Therefore, we dismiss the allegation that the Respondent insisted on an illegal subject in violation of Section 8(a)(5) and (1).

I. BACKGROUND

On February 21, 2002, Administrative Law Judge John J. McCarrick issued the [decision below].... On January 10, 2007, the National Labor Relations Board issued a notice of oral argument and invitation to the parties and interested amici curiae to file briefs. The notice requested that the parties address specific questions concerning employees' use of their employer's email system (or other computer-based communication systems) to communicate with other employees about union or other Section 7 matters. The Board's questions included, among other things, whether employees have a Section 7 right to use their employer's e-mail system to communicate with one another, what standard should govern that determination, and whether an employer violates the Act if it permits other nonwork-related e-mails but prohibits e-mails on Section 7 matters.

The General Counsel, the Charging Party, the Respondent, and various amici filed briefs.[1] On March 27, 2007, the Board held oral argument.

The Board has considered the decision and the record in light of the exceptions, briefs, and oral argument and has decided to affirm the judge's rulings, findings, and conclusions in part, to reverse them in part, and to adopt the recommended Order as modified and set forth in full below.

II. FACTS

A. The Respondent's Communications Systems Policy

The Respondent publishes a newspaper. The Union represents a unit of about 150 of the Respondent's employees. The parties' last collective-

---

1. .... Amicus briefs were filed by the Council on Labor Law Equality, Employers Group, the HR Policy Association, the Minnesota Management Attorneys Association, Proskauer Rose LLP, the National Employment Lawyers Association, the National Workrights Institute, and the United States Chamber of Commerce.

bargaining agreement was in effect from October 16, 1996 though April 30, 1999. When the record closed, the parties were negotiating, but had not yet reached a successor agreement.

In 1996, the Respondent began installing a new computer system, through which all newsroom employees and many (but not all) other unit employees had e-mail access. In October 1996, the Respondent implemented the "Communications Systems Policy" (CSP) at issue here. The policy governed employees' use of the Respondent's communications systems, including e-mail. The policy stated, in relevant part:

> Company communication systems and the equipment used to operate the communication system are owned and provided by the Company to assist in conducting the business of The Register–Guard. Communications systems are not to be used to solicit or proselytize for commercial ventures, religious or political causes, outside organizations, or other non-job-related solicitations.

The Respondent's employees use e-mail regularly for work-related matters. Throughout the relevant time period, the Respondent was aware that employees also used e-mail to send and receive personal messages. The record contains evidence of e-mails such as baby announcements, party invitations, and the occasional offer of sports tickets or request for services such as dog walking. However, there is no evidence that the employees used e-mail to solicit support for or participation in any outside cause or organization other than the United Way, for which the Respondent conducted a periodic charitable campaign.

B.   Prozanski's E–Mails and Resulting Discipline

Suzi Prozanski is a unit employee and the union president. In May and August 2000, Prozanski received two written warnings for sending three e-mails to unit employees at their Register–Guard e-mail addresses. The Respondent contends that the e-mails violated the CSP.

1.   May 4, 2000 e-mail

The first e-mail involved a union rally that took place on the afternoon of May 1, 2000. Earlier that day, Managing Editor Dave Baker sent an e-mail to employees stating that they should try to leave work early because the police had notified the Respondent that anarchists might attend the rally. Employee Bill Bishop sent a reply e-mail to Baker and to many employees. Bishop's email message also attached an e-mail the Union had received from the police stating that the Respondent had notified the police about the possibility of anarchists. Thus, Bishop's e-mail implied that Baker was mistaken or untruthful when he told employees that the police had notified the Respondent about the anarchists.

The rally took place as scheduled. Afterward, Prozanski learned that certain statements in Bishop's e-mail had been inaccurate. On May 2, Prozanski told Baker that she wanted to communicate with employees to "set the record straight." Baker told her to wait until he talked to Human Resources Director Cynthia Walden. On May 4, Prozanski had not heard back from management about her request, so she told Baker that she was going to send an e-mail response. Baker said, "I understand." Prozanski then sent an e-mail entitled, "setting it straight." She composed the e-mail on her break but sent it from her work station. A few hours later, Baker told Prozanski that she should not have used company equipment to send the e-mail.

Prozanski's e-mail began: "In the spirit of fairness, I'd like to pass on some information to you. . . . We have discovered that some of the information given to you was incomplete. . . . The Guild would like to set the record straight." The e-mail then set forth the facts surrounding the call to police about anarchists attending the rally. The e-mail was signed, "Yours in solidarity, Suzi Prozanski."

On May 5, Baker issued Prozanski a written warning for violating the CSP by using e-mail for "conducting Guild business."

2.   E–Mails on August 14 and 18, 2000

Prozanski received a second written warning on August 22, 2000, for two e-mails sent on August 14 and 18. The August 14 e-mail asked employees to wear green to support the Union's position in negotiations. The August 18 e-mail asked employees to participate in the Union's entry in an upcoming town parade. As with the May 4 email, Prozanski sent these e-mails to multiple unit employees at their Register–Guard e-mail addresses. However, this time she sent the e-mails from a computer in the Union's office, located off the Respondent's premises. Prozanski testified she thought that the May 5 warning was for using the Company's equipment to send the message, and that there would be no problem if she sent e-mails from the Union's office instead. On August 22, however, Walden issued Prozanski a written warning, stating that Prozanski had violated the CSP by using the Respondent's communications system for Guild activities. The warning quoted the CSP's prohibition on "nonjob-related solicitations."

C.   Respondent's Bargaining Proposal Concerning E–Mail Use

About October 25, 2000, during bargaining, the Respondent presented the Union with "counterproposal 26," which proposed the following contract language:

> The electronic communications systems are the property of the Employer and are provided for business use only. They may not be used for union business.

. . . . On November 16, 2000, the Union stated that it would not respond to the proposal because the Union viewed the proposal as illegally restricting Section 7 rights. On November 30, 2000, the Union filed a charge alleging that the Respondent violated Section 8(a)(5) by proposing counterproposal 26. The Region dismissed the charge on March 31, 2001.

In April 2001, the Union requested, and the Respondent provided, additional information on the scope of counterproposal 26. On April 21, the parties also discussed the proposal at the bargaining table. The Union's lead negotiator, Lance Robertson, noted that the Union's unfair labor practice charge had been dismissed. Although Robertson continued to press for additional clarification of the proposal, he also told the Respondent: "I'm here to bargain a proposal." At the hearing, he testified that the Union's position as of April 21 was that it "neither accepted nor rejected" counterproposal 26. The Union never made a counterproposal. The parties stipulated that counterproposal 26 has been the Respondent's position since October 25, 2000.

On April 24, 2001, the Union filed a new charge alleging that the Respondent had proposed and "refus[ed] to withdraw" counterproposal 26. On August 13, 2001, the Region revoked its dismissal of the previous charge.

. . . .

V. DISCUSSION

For the reasons set forth below, we agree with the judge that the Respondent did not violate Section 8(a)(1) by maintaining the CSP. We also agree with the judge that the Respondent's enforcement of the CSP with respect to Prozanski's May 4 e-mail was discriminatory and therefore violated Section 8(a)(1). Likewise, the written warning issued to Prozanski for the May 4 e-mail violated Section 8(a)(3) and (1).

However, we reverse the judge and dismiss the allegations that the Respondent's application of the CSP to Prozanski's August 14 and 18 e-mails was discriminatory. We also find no 8(a)(3) violation as to Prozanski's discipline for those e-mails. Finally, we reverse the judge and dismiss the allegation that the Respondent violated Section 8(a)(5) and (1) by insisting on counterproposal 26.

A. Maintenance of the CSP

The CSP, in relevant part, prohibits employees from using the Respondent's e-mail system for any "non-jobrelated solicitations." Consistent with a long line of cases governing employee use of employer-owned equipment, we find that the employees here had no statutory right to use the Respondent's e-mail system for Section 7 matters. Therefore, the Respondent did not violate Section 8(a)(1) by maintaining the CSP.

An employer has a "basic property right" to "regulate and restrict employee use of company property." Union Carbide Corp. v. NLRB, 714 F.2d 657, 663–664 (6th Cir. 1983). The Respondent's communications system, including its e-mail system, is the Respondent's property and was purchased by the Respondent for use in operating its business. The General Counsel concedes that the Respondent has a legitimate business interest in maintaining the efficient operation of its e-mail system, and that employers who have invested in an e-mail system have valid concerns about such issues as preserving server space, protecting against computer viruses and dissemination of confidential information, and avoiding company liability for employees' inappropriate e-mails.

Whether employees have a specific right under the Act to use an employer's e-mail system for Section 7 activity is an issue of first impression. In numerous cases, however, where the Board has addressed whether employees have the right to use other types of employer-owned property—such as bulletin boards, telephones, and televisions—for Section 7 communications, the Board has consistently held that there is "no statutory right ... to use an employer's equipment or media," as long as the restrictions are nondiscriminatory. Mid–Mountain Foods, 332 NLRB 229, 230 (2000) (no statutory right to use the television in the respondent's breakroom to show a prounion campaign video), enfd. 269 F.3d 1075 (D.C. Cir. 2001). See also Eaton Technologies, 322 NLRB 848, 853 (1997) ("It is well established that there is no statutory right of employees or a union to use an employer's bulletin board."); Champion International Corp., 303 NLRB 102, 109 (1991) (stating that an employer has "a basic right to regulate and restrict employee use of company property" such as a copy machine); Churchill's Supermarkets, 285 NLRB 138, 155 (1987) ("[A]n employer ha[s] every right to restrict the use of company telephones to business-related conversations...."), enfd. 857 F.2d 1474 (6th Cir. 1988), cert. denied 490 U.S. 1046 (1989); Union Carbide Corp., 259 NLRB 974, 980 (1981) (employer "could unquestionably bar its telephones to any personal use by employees"), enfd. in relevant part 714 F.2d 657 (6th Cir. 1983); cf. Heath Co., 196 NLRB 134 (1972) (employer did not engage in objectionable conduct by refusing to allow prounion employees to use public address system to respond to antiunion broadcasts).

Our dissenting colleagues, however, contend that this well-settled principle—that employees have no statutory right to use an employer's equipment or media for Section 7 communications—should not apply to e-mail systems. They argue that the decisions cited above involving employer telephones—*Churchill's Supermarkets* and *Union Carbide*—were decided on discriminatory enforcement grounds, and therefore their language regarding an employer's right to ban nonbusiness use of its telephones was dicta. The Board, however, reaffirmed *Union Carbide* in *Mid-Mountain Foods*, supra, citing it for the specific principle that employees have no statutory right to use an employer's telephone for nonbusiness purposes. See 332 NLRB at 230.

Nevertheless, our dissenting colleagues assert that the issue of employees' use of their employer's e-mail system should be analyzed under Republic Aviation v. NLRB, 324 U.S. 793 (1945), by balancing employees' Section 7 rights and the employer's interest in maintaining discipline, and that a broad ban on employee non-work-related e-mail communications should be presumptively unlawful absent a showing of special circumstances. We disagree and find the analytical framework of *Republic Aviation* inapplicable here.

In *Republic Aviation*, the employer maintained a general rule prohibiting all solicitation at any time on the premises. The employer discharged an employee for soliciting union membership in the plant by passing out application cards to employees on his own time during lunch periods. The

Board found that the rule and its enforcement violated Section 8(a)(1), and the Supreme Court affirmed. The Court recognized that some "dislocation" of employer property rights may be necessary in order to safeguard Section 7 rights. See 324 U.S. at 802 fn. 8. The Court noted that the employer's rule "entirely deprived" employees of their right to communication in the workplace on their own time. Id. at 801 fn. 6. The Court upheld the Board's presumption that a rule banning all solicitation during nonworking time is "an unreasonable impediment to self-organization . . . in the absence of evidence that special circumstances make the rule necessary in order to maintain production or discipline." Id. at 803 fn. 10. Otherwise, employees would have no time at the workplace in which to engage in Section 7 communications.

In contrast to the employer's policy at issue in *Republic Aviation*, the Respondent's CSP does not regulate traditional, face-to-face solicitation. Indeed, employees at the Respondent's workplace have the full panoply of rights to engage in oral solicitation on nonworking time and also to distribute literature on nonworking time in nonwork areas, pursuant to *Republic Aviation* and *Stoddard-Quirk*. What the employees seek here is use of the Respondent's communications equipment to engage in additional forms of communication beyond those that *Republic Aviation* found must be permitted. Yet, "Section 7 of the Act protects organizational rights . . . rather than particular means by which employees may seek to communicate." Guardian Industries Corp. v. NLRB, 49 F.3d 317, 318 (7th Cir. 1995); see also NLRB v. United Steelworkers (Nutone), 357 U.S. 357, 363–364 (1958) (The Act "does not command that labor organizations as a matter of law, under all circumstances, be protected in the use of every possible means of reaching the minds of individual workers, nor that they are entitled to use a medium of communications simply because the Employer is using it."). *Republic Aviation* requires the employer to yield its property interests to the extent necessary to ensure that employees will not be "entirely deprived," 324 U.S. at 801 fn. 6, of their ability to engage in Section 7 communications in the workplace on their own time. It does not require the most convenient or most effective means of conducting those communications, nor does it hold that employees have a statutory right to use an employer's equipment or devices for Section 7 communications.[10] Indeed, the cases discussed above, in which the Board has found no Section 7 right to use an employer's equipment, were decided long after *Republic*

---

10. The Board recently distinguished *Republic Aviation* in a case involving employee use of an employer's personal property. In Johnson Technology, Inc., 345 NLRB 762, 763 (2005), the Board found that the respondent did not violate Sec. 8(a)(1) by prohibiting an employee from using the employer's scrap paper to prepare a union meeting notice. The Board emphasized that "it is not unlawful for an employer to caution employees to restrict the use of company property to business purposes." Rejecting the General Counsel's reliance on *Republic Aviation*, the Board further noted: "The issue in *Republic Aviation* was whether an employer's right to control the activities of employees lawfully on its premises was subject to limitations to accommodate the employees' Sec. 7 rights, such as to engage in prounion solicitations. Here, the question is whether an employee can take and use the employer's personalty, without its consent, to engage in a nonwork-related purpose such as a Sec. 7 activity." Id. at 763 fn. 8.

Aviation and have been upheld by the courts. See, e.g., NLRB v. Southwire Co., 801 F.2d 1252, 1256 (11th Cir. 1986) (no statutory right to use an employer's bulletin board); Union Carbide Corp. v. NLRB, 714 F.2d 657, 663 (6th Cir. 1983) ("As recognized by the ALJ, Union Carbide unquestionably had the right to regulate and restrict employee use of company property.") (emphasis in original).

The dissent contends that because the employees here are already rightfully on the Respondent's premises, only the Respondent's managerial interests—and not its property interests—are at stake. That would be true if the issue here concerned customary, face-to-face solicitation and distribution, activities that involve only the employees' own conduct during nonwork time and do not involve use of the employer's equipment. Being rightfully on the premises, however, confers no additional right on employees to use the employer's equipment for Section 7 purposes regardless of whether the employees are authorized to use that equipment for work purposes.[11]

The dissent contends that e-mail has revolutionized business and personal communications and that, by failing to carve out an exception for it to settled principles regarding use of employer property, we are failing to adapt the Act to the changing patterns of industrial life. The dissent attempts to distinguish use of e-mail from other communication equipment based on e-mail's interactive nature and its ability to process thousands of communications simultaneously.

We recognize that e-mail has, of course, had a substantial impact on how people communicate, both at and away from the workplace. Moreover, e-mail has some differences from as well as some similarities to other communications methods, such as telephone systems. For example, as the dissent points out, transmission of an e-mail message, unlike a telephone conversation, does not normally "tie up" the line and prevent the simultaneous transmission of messages by others. On the other hand, e-mail messages are similar to telephone calls in many ways. Both enable virtually instant communication regardless of distance, both are transmitted electronically, usually through wires (sometimes the very same fiber-optic cables) over complex networks, and both require specialized electronic devices for their transmission. Although the widespread use of telephone systems has greatly impacted business communications, the Board has never found that employees have a general right to use their employer's telephone system for Section 7 communications.

---

11. Testimony in the record that sending or receiving a simple "text" e-mail does not impose any additional monetary cost on the Respondent is of no consequence to our inquiry here. The Respondent's property rights do not depend on monetary cost. Cf. Johnson Technology, supra at 763 ("[T]he issue is whether the [employees'] use of the property was protected, not how much the property is worth."). Moreover, although the dissent, noting that "the Respondent does not own cyberspace," seems to question the very existence of Respondent's property interest in its e-mail system, it is beyond doubt that the Respondent has a property interest in its servers that host its e-mail system and in the software on which it operates, as well as its computers on which the employees access e-mail.

In any event, regardless of the extent to which communication by e-mail systems is similar to or different from communication using other devices or systems, it is clear that use of the Respondent's e-mail system has not eliminated face-to-face communication among the Respondent's employees or reduced such communication to an insignificant level. Indeed, there is no contention in this case that the Respondent's employees rarely or never see each other in person or that they communicate with each other solely by electronic means. Thus, unlike our dissenting colleagues, we find that use of e-mail has not changed the pattern of industrial life at the Respondent's facility to the extent that the forms of workplace communication sanctioned in *Republic Aviation* have been rendered useless and that employee use of the Respondent's e-mail system for Section 7 purposes must therefore be mandated. Consequently, we find no basis in this case to refrain from applying the settled principle that, absent discrimination, employees have no statutory right to use an employer's equipment or media for Section 7 communications.[12]

Accordingly, we hold that the Respondent may lawfully bar employees' nonwork-related use of its e-mail system, unless the Respondent acts in a manner that discriminates against Section 7 activity.[13] As the CSP on its face does not discriminate against Section 7 activity, we find that the Respondent did not violate Section 8(a)(1) by maintaining the CSP.

B.   Alleged Discriminatory Enforcement of the CSP

The judge found that the Respondent violated Section 8(a)(1) by discriminatorily enforcing the CSP to prohibit Prozanski's union-related e-mails while allowing other nonwork-related e-mails. We affirm the violation as to Prozanski's May 4 e-mail, but reverse and dismiss as to her August e-mails. In doing so, we modify Board law concerning discriminatory enforcement.[14]

---

12.   Contrary to the dissent, in reaching this conclusion, we are not applying an "alternative means of communication" test appropriate only for questions of nonemployee access. See Lechmere, Inc. v. NLRB, 502 U.S. 527 (1992). Rather, we are merely examining whether, as asserted by the dissent, e-mail has so changed workplace communication that the Board should depart from settled precedent and order that the Respondent must permit employees to use its e-mail system to communicate regarding Sec. 7 matters. Such an analysis necessarily requires examination of whether the face-to-face solicitation and distribution permitted under *Republic Aviation* no longer enable employees to communicate. As we find controlling here the principle that employees have no statutory right to use an employer's equipment or media for Sec. 7 communications, neither *Republic Aviation* nor *Lechmere* is applicable.

13.   We do not pass on circumstances, not present here, in which there are no means of communication among employees at work other than e-mail.

14.   The Respondent contends that all allegations regarding enforcement of the CSP are time-barred by Sec. 10(b), which states in relevant part that "no complaint shall issue based upon any unfair labor practice occurring more than 6 months prior to the filing of the charge with the Board." The Respondent argues that the 10(b) period runs from 1996, when the CSP was promulgated.... We find no merit in the Respondent's argument ... The Board considers each instance of disparate enforcement of a policy to be a separate and independent act for purposes of Sec. 10(b). Norman King Electric, 334 NLRB 154, 162 (2001)....

1. The appropriate analysis for alleged discriminatory enforcement

In finding that the Respondent discriminatorily enforced the CSP, the judge relied on evidence that the Respondent had permitted employees to use e-mail for various personal messages. Specifically, the record shows that the Respondent permitted e-mails such as jokes, baby announcements, party invitations, and the occasional offer of sports tickets or request for services such as dog walking. However, there is no evidence that the Respondent allowed employees (or anyone else) to use e-mail to solicit support for or participation in any outside cause or organization other than the United Way, for which the Respondent conducted a periodic charitable campaign.

Citing Fleming Co., 336 NLRB 192 (2001), enf. denied 349 F.3d 968 (7th Cir. 2003), the judge found that "[i]f an employer allows employees to use its communications equipment for nonwork related purposes, it may not validly prohibit employee use of communications equipment for Section 7 purposes." We agree with the judge that the Board's decision in *Fleming* would support that proposition. However, having carefully examined current precedent, we find that the Board's approach in *Fleming* and other similar cases fails to adequately examine whether the employer's conduct discriminated against Section 7 activity.

In *Fleming*, the Board held that the employer violated Section 8(a)(1) by removing union literature from a bulletin board because the employer had allowed "a wide range of personal postings" including wedding announcements, birthday cards, and notices selling personal property such as cars and a television. There was no evidence that the employer had allowed postings for any outside clubs or organizations. Id. at 193–194. Likewise, in Guardian Industries, 313 NLRB 1275 (1994), enf. denied 49 F.3d 317 (7th Cir. 1995), the Board found an 8(a)(1) violation where the employer allowed personal "swap and shop" postings but denied permission for union or other group postings, including those by the Red Cross and an employee credit union.

The Seventh Circuit denied enforcement in both cases. Fleming, supra, 349 F.3d at 968; Guardian, supra, 49 F.3d at 317. In *Guardian*, the court started from the proposition that employers may control the activities of their employees in the workplace, "both as a matter of property rights (the employer owns the building) and of contract (employees agree to abide by the employer's rules as a condition of employment)." Id. at 317. Although an employer, in enforcing its rules, may not discriminate against Section 7 activity, the court noted that the concept of discrimination involves the unequal treatment of equals. See id. at 319. The court emphasized that the employer had never allowed employees to post notices of organizational meetings. Rather, the nonworkrelated postings permitted by the employer consisted almost entirely of "swap and shop" notices advertising personal items for sale. The court stated: "We must therefore ask in what sense it might be discriminatory to distinguish between for-sale notes and meeting announcements." Id. at 319. The court ultimately concluded that "[a] rule banning all organizational notices (those of the Red Cross along with meetings pro and con unions) is impossible to understand as disparate treatment of unions." Id. at 320.

In *Fleming*, the court reaffirmed its decision in *Guardian* and further stated:

> Just as we have recognized for-sale notices as a category of notices distinct from organizational notices (which would include union postings), we can now add the category of personal postings. The ALJ's factual finding that Fleming did not allow the posting of organizational material on its bulletin boards does not support the conclusion that Fleming violated Section 8(a)(1) by prohibiting the posting of union materials.

349 F.3d at 975.

We find that the Seventh Circuit's analysis, rather than existing Board precedent, better reflects the principle that discrimination means the unequal treatment of equals. Thus, in order to be unlawful, discrimination must be along Section 7 lines. In other words, unlawful discrimination consists of disparate treatment of activities or communications of a similar character because of their union or other Section 7–protected status. . . .

For example, an employer clearly would violate the Act if it permitted employees to use e-mail to solicit for one union but not another, or if it permitted solicitation by antiunion employees but not by prounion employees.[17] In either case, the employer has drawn a line between permitted and prohibited activities on Section 7 grounds. However, nothing in the Act prohibits an employer from drawing lines on a non-Section 7 basis. That is, an employer may draw a line between charitable solicitations and noncharitable solicitations, between solicitations of a personal nature (e.g., a car for sale) and solicitations for the commercial sale of a product (e.g., Avon products), between invitations for an organization and invitations of a personal nature, between solicitations and mere talk, and between business-related use and nonbusiness-related use. In each of these examples, the fact that union solicitation would fall on the prohibited side of the line does not establish that the rule discriminates along Section 7 lines.[18] For example, a rule that permitted charitable solicitations but not noncharitable solicitations would permit solicitations for the Red Cross and the Salvation Army, but it would prohibit solicitations for Avon and the union.[19]

17. On the other hand, an employer may use its own equipment to send antiunion messages, and still deny employees the opportunity to use that equipment for prounion messages. As noted above, employees are not entitled to use a certain method of communication just because the employer is using it. See Nutone, supra at 363–364.

18. Of course, if the evidence showed that the employer's motive for the line-drawing was antiunion, then the action would be unlawful. There is no such evidence here. . . .

19. Indeed, the Board has already recognized that allowing limited charitable solicitations does not necessarily require an employer to allow union solicitations. See Hammary Mfg. Corp., 265 NLRB 57 (1982) (an employer will not violate Sec. 8(a)(1) by "permitting a small number of isolated 'beneficent acts' "—such as solicitation for a United Way campaign—as "narrow excep-

The dissent contends that our analysis is misplaced because, in 8(a)(1) cases, discrimination is not the essence of the violation. Rather, the dissent asserts that discrimination is relevant in 8(a)(1) cases merely because it weakens or exposes as pretextual the employer's business justification for its actions. In our view, the dissent . . . too readily writes off discrimination as the essential basis of many 8(a)(1) violations.

. . . . [T]he dissent fails to acknowledge that many decisions require actual discrimination. For example, as the Board noted in Salmon Run Shopping Center, 348 NLRB No. 31 (2006), the Supreme Court has held that "an employer violates 8(a)(1) of the Act by prohibiting nonemployee distribution of union literature if its actions 'discriminate against the union by allowing other distribution.'" Id., slip op. at 1, quoting NLRB v. Babcock & Wilcox Co., 351 U.S. 105, 112 (1956). After determining that the employer's decision to deny the union access was based "solely on the Union's status as a labor organization and its desire to engage in labor-related speech," the Board found in *Salmon Run* that "[s]uch discriminatory exclusion" violated Section 8(a)(1). Salmon Run Shopping Center, above, slip op. at 2.

Similarly, in Enloe Medical Center, 348 NLRB No. 63 (2006), the Board found that the employer violated Section 8(a)(1) by sending employees a message stating that "it is not appropriate for union literature to be . . . placed in our breakroom." The Board found that the message was discriminatory, and therefore unlawful, because it "barred only union literature, and no other, from being placed in the breakroom." Id., slip op. at 1.

To be sure, the cases on which the dissent relies include language suggesting that the employers' unlawful, discriminatory conduct tended to undermine their asserted business justifications. However, the presence of such language in those cases does not negate the many cases that find discriminatory conduct violative of Section 8(a)(1) purely on the basis of the conduct's discriminatory nature.

We therefore adopt the position of the court in *Guardian* and *Fleming* that unlawful discrimination consists of disparate treatment of activities or communications of a similar character because of their union or other Section 7–protected status, and we shall apply this view in the present case and in future cases.[21] Accordingly, in determining whether the Respondent discriminatorily enforced the CSP, we must examine the types of e-mails allowed by the Respondent and ask whether they show discrimination along Section 7 lines.

2.   Application of the standard

Prozanski's August 14 e-mail urged all employees to wear green to support the Union. Her August 18 e-mail urged employees to participate in

tions" to a no-solicitation rule, while prohibiting union solicitation).

21. Accordingly, we overrule the Board's decisions in *Fleming, Guardian*, and

other similar cases to the extent they are inconsistent with our decision here. . . .

the Union's entry in a local parade. Both messages called for employees to take action in support of the Union. The evidence shows that the Respondent tolerated personal employee e-mail messages concerning social gatherings, jokes, baby announcements, and the occasional offer of sports tickets or other similar personal items. Notably, however, there is no evidence that the Respondent permitted employees to use e-mail to solicit other employees to support any group or organization.[23] Thus, the Respondent's enforcement of the CSP with respect to the August 14 and 18 e-mails did not discriminate along Section 7 lines, and therefore did not violate Section 8(a)(1).[24]

Prozanski's May 4 e-mail, however, was not a solicitation. It did not call for action; it simply clarified the facts surrounding the Union's rally the day before. As noted above, the Respondent permitted a variety of nonwork-related e-mails other than solicitations. Indeed, the CSP itself prohibited only "non-job-related solicitations," not all non-job-related communications. The only difference between Prozanski's May e-mail and the e-mails permitted by the Respondent is that Prozanski's e-mail was union-related. Accordingly, we find that the Respondent's enforcement of the CSP with respect to the May 4 e-mail discriminated along Section 7 lines and therefore violated Section 8(a)(1).

C.   The 8(a)(3) Allegations

  .... Here, the May 5 warning stated that Prozanski "used the company's e-mail system expressly for the purpose of conducting Guild business" and that this violated the CSP. Thus, it is clear from the warning itself that the Respondent disciplined Prozanski for sending a union-related e-mail. The issue is whether Prozanski lost the protection of the Act by using the Respondent's e-mail system to send the message. With respect to the May 4 e-mail, she did not. As explained above, although there is no Section 7 right to use an employer's e-mail system, there is a Section 7 right to be free from discriminatory treatment. See St. Joseph's Hospital, supra at 95. The Respondent acted discriminatorily in applying the CSP to Prozanski's May 4 e-mail. Accordingly, the May 5 warning to Prozanski for sending that e-mail violated Section 8(a)(3) and (1).

However, we reverse the judge and dismiss the allegation that the August 22 warning violated Section 8(a)(3) and (1). That warning was

---

23. The sole exception is the limited use of e-mail in connection with the Respondent's United Way campaign, which does not establish discriminatory enforcement. Hammary Mfg. Corp., 265 NLRB 57 (1982) (an employer does not violate 8(a)(1) "by permitting a small number of isolated 'beneficent acts' as narrow exceptions to a no-solicitation rule").

24. The dissent asserts that there is no clear evidence that the Respondent ever enforced the CSP against anything other than union-related messages. However, there is no evidence that any employee had ever previously sent e-mails soliciting on behalf of any groups or organizations. Accordingly, given the absence of evidence that the Respondent permitted employees to use e-mail to solicit support for groups or organizations, we decline to find that the Respondent's barring of e-mail solicitation on behalf of the Union constituted disparate treatment of activities or communications of a similar character....

issued in response to Prozanski's August 14 and 18 e-mails. We have found above that the Respondent's application of the CSP to prohibit those e-mails did not discriminate along Section 7 lines. Prozanski's conduct was therefore unprotected, and the August 22 discipline was lawful.

D.   The 8(a)(5) Allegation

The judge found that the Respondent violated Section 8(a)(5) and (1) by insisting on counterproposal 26, which the judge found was an unlawful bargaining proposal. We reverse. In doing so, we find it unnecessary to decide whether counterproposal 26 was unlawful on its face. Rather, we find the evidence insufficient to show that the Respondent insisted on the proposal.

A party violates its duty to bargain in good faith by insisting on an unlawful proposal. See, e.g., Teamsters Local 20 (Seaway Food Town), 235 NLRB 1554, 1558 (1978); Thill, Inc., 298 NLRB 669, 672 (1990), enfd. in rel. part 980 F.2d 1137 (7th Cir. 1992). However, a party does not necessarily violate the Act simply by proposing or bargaining about an unlawful subject.... Rather, what the Act prohibits is "the insistence, as a condition precedent of entering into a collective bargaining agreement," that the other party agree to an unlawful provision....

Here, contrary to the dissent, we find no proof of such insistence . . . . . In these circumstances, especially given the initial dismissal of the Union's 8(a)(5) charge and the Union's subsequent statements that it was prepared "to bargain a proposal" and that it "neither accepted nor rejected" the Respondent's proposal, we find the evidence insufficient to establish that the Respondent insisted on the proposal as a condition of entering into an agreement, or that the proposal impeded negotiations on lawful subjects. Accordingly, we find no 8(a)(5) violation.

■ MEMBERS LIEBMAN and WALSH, dissenting in part.

Today's decision confirms that the NLRB has become the "Rip Van Winkle of administrative agencies." NLRB v. Thill, Inc., 980 F.2d 1137, 1142 (7th Cir. 1992). Only a Board that has been asleep for the past 20 years could fail to recognize that e-mail has revolutionized communication both within and outside the workplace. In 2007, one cannot reasonably contend, as the majority does, that an e-mail system is a piece of communications equipment to be treated just as the law treats bulletin boards, telephones, and pieces of scrap paper.

National labor policy must be responsive to the enormous technological changes that are taking place in our society. Where, as here, an employer has given employees access to e-mail for regular, routine use in their work, we would find that banning all nonwork-related "solicitations" is presumptively unlawful absent special circumstances. No special circumstances have been shown here. Accordingly, we dissent from the majority's holding that the Respondent's ban on using e-mail for "nonjob-related solicitations" was lawful.

We also dissent, in the strongest possible terms, from the majority's overruling of bedrock Board precedent about the meaning of discrimination as applied to Section 8(a)(1). Under the majority's new test, an employer does not violate Section 8(a)(1) by allowing employees to use an employer's equipment or media for a broad range of nonwork-related communications but not for Section 7 communications. We disagree, and therefore would also affirm the judge's finding that the Respondent violated Section 8(a)(3) and (1) by issuing written warnings to employee Suzy Prozanski for sending union-related emails. Finally, we dissent from the majority's finding that the Respondent did not insist on a bargaining proposal that codified the Respondent's unlawful discriminatory practice of prohibiting union-related e-mails while allowing other nonwork-related e-mails.

. . .

II. DISCUSSION

A. Maintenance of the CSP

1. Legal framework governing Section 7 communications by employees in the workplace

The General Counsel contends that the CSP's prohibition on "non-job-related solicitations" is unlawfully overbroad and violates Section 8(a)(1). The judge dismissed that allegation, and the majority affirms the dismissal. We dissent.

The issue in an 8(a)(1) case is whether the employer's conduct interferes with Section 7 rights. If so, the employer must demonstrate a legitimate business reason that outweighs the interference. See, e.g., Caesar's Palace, 336 NLRB 271, 272 fn. 6 (2001); Jeannette Corp., 532 F.2d 916, 918 (3d Cir. 1976).

It is intuitively obvious that the workplace is "uniquely appropriate" for Section 7 activity. NLRB v. Magnavox Co. of Tennessee, 415 U.S. 322 (1974). In cases involving employee communications at work, the Board's task is to balance the employees' Section 7 right to communicate with the employer's right to protect its business interests. Beth Israel Hospital v. NLRB, 437 U.S. 483, 494 (1978). Limitations on communication should not be "more restrictive than necessary" to protect the employer's interests. Id. at 502–503.

Republic Aviation Corp. v. NLRB, 324 U.S. 793 (1945), is the seminal case balancing those interests with respect to oral solicitation in the workplace. The employer in *Republic Aviation* maintained a rule prohibiting solicitation anywhere on company property and discharged an employee for soliciting for the union during nonworking time. The Board adopted a presumption that restricting oral solicitation on nonworking time was unlawful, absent special circumstances. The Supreme Court affirmed the Board's finding that the employer's rule and its enforcement violated Section 8(a)(1). Although the solicitation occurred on the employer's property, the Court found that an insufficient justification to allow the employer to prohibit it. Rather, the Court endorsed the Board's reasoning that "[i]t is not every interference with property rights that is within the Fifth Amendment.... Inconvenience or even some dislocation of property rights, may be necessary in order to safeguard the right to collective bargaining." 324 U.S. at 802 fn. 8. Although an employer may make and enforce "reasonable rules" covering the conduct of employees on working time, "time outside working hours ... is an employee's time to use as he wishes without unreasonable restraint, although the employee is on company property." Id. at 803 fn. 10 (emphasis supplied). The Court upheld the Board's presumption that a rule banning solicitation during nonworking time is "an unreasonable impediment to self-organization ... in the absence of evidence that special circumstances make the rule necessary in order to maintain production or discipline." Id. at 803 fn. 10.

Thus, the presumption adopted in *Republic Aviation* vindicates the right of employees to communicate in the workplace regarding Section 7 matters, subject to the employer's right to maintain production and discipline. Although the majority correctly notes that the rule in *Republic Aviation* itself involved a complete ban on solicitation on the employer's premises, the Board and courts have long since applied *Republic Aviation*'s principles to lesser restrictions on employee speech. See, e.g., Beth Israel, 437 U.S. at 492 (rule prohibiting solicitation and distribution in the hospital's patient-care and public areas; employer permitted those activities in employee locker rooms and restrooms); Times Publishing Co., 240 NLRB 1158 (1979) (rule prohibiting solicitation in "public areas" of the building), affd. 605 F.2d 847 (5th Cir. 1979); Bankers Club, Inc., 218 NLRB 22, 27 (1975) (rule banning solicitation in "customer areas" of the respondent's restaurant).

The Supreme Court struck quite a different balance in cases involving nonemployees seeking to communicate with employees on the employer's premises. In a case involving distribution of union literature on an employer's property by nonemployee union organizers, the Court emphasized that "[a]ccommodation" between Section 7 rights and employer property rights "must be obtained with as little destruction of one as is consistent with the maintenance of the other." NLRB v. Babcock & Wilcox, 351 U.S. 105, 112 (1956). The Court held that an employer "may validly post his property against nonemployee distribution of union literature if reasonable efforts by the union through other available channels of communication will enable it to reach the employees with its message and if the employer's notice or order does not discriminate against the union by allowing other distribution." Id. (emphasis supplied). Distinguishing *Republic Aviation* on the basis that it involved communications by employees, the Court emphasized that "[t]he distinction [between employees and nonemployees] is one of substance. No restriction may be placed on the employees' right to discuss self-organization among themselves, unless the employer can demonstrate that a restriction is necessary to maintain production or discipline. But no such obligation is owed nonemployee organizers." Id. at 113; see also Hudgens v. NLRB, 424 U.S. 507, 521 fn. 10 (1976) ("A wholly different balance [is] struck when the organizational activity was carried on by employees already rightfully on the employer's property, since the employer's management interests rather than his property interests were there involved.'').

In short, the Board and courts have long protected employees' rights to engage in Section 7 communications at the workplace, even though the employees are on the employer's "property."

2. The Respondent's prohibition on all "non-jobrelated solicitations" violated Section 8(a)(1)

Applying the foregoing principles, the General Counsel contends that employer rules restricting employee email use must be evaluated under *Republic Aviation*, and that broad bans on employee e-mail use should be presumptively unlawful. The General Counsel emphasizes that e-mail has become the "natural gathering place" for employees to communicate in the workplace, and that e-mail sent and received on computers issued to employees for their use is not analogous to employer "equipment" such as bulletin boards, photocopiers, and public address systems.

The majority, however, finds the *Republic Aviation* framework inapplicable. Emphasizing the employer's "property" interest in its e-mail system, the majority reasons that, absent discriminatory treatment, employees have no Section 7 right to use employer personal property such as bulletin boards, television sets, and telephones. According to the majority, *Republic Aviation* ensures only that employees will not be "entirely deprived" of the ability to engage in any Section 7 communications in the workplace, but otherwise does not entitle employees to use their employer's equipment. Here, the majority asserts, the employees had other means of communication available.

We disagree. Indeed, we find that the General Counsel's approach is manifestly better suited to the role of email in the modern workplace. "The responsibility to adapt the Act to changing patterns of industrial life is entrusted to the Board." NLRB v. J. Weingarten, 420 U.S. 251, 266 (1975). The majority's approach is flawed on several levels. . . .[6]

E-mail has dramatically changed, and is continuing to change, how people communicate at work. According to a 2004 survey of 840 U.S. businesses, more than 81 percent of employees spent at least an hour on e-mail on a typical workday; about 10 percent spent more than 4 hours. About 86 percent of employees send and receive at least some nonbusiness-related e-mail at work. Those percentages, no doubt, are continuing to increase. "Even employees who report to fixed work locations every day have seen their work environments evolve to a point where they interact to

---

6. We also disagree with the majority's characterization of our approach as "carv[ing] out an exception" to precedent. Our analysis is hardly novel. Rather, as explained below, we apply the decades-old principles that employees have a right to communicate in the workplace, that the Board must balance that right with the employer's right to protect its business interests, and that interference with employees' Section 7 rights is unlawful unless outweighed by a legitimate business interest. Republic Aviation, supra, 324 U.S. at 803 fn. 10; Beth Israel, supra, 437 U.S. at 494; Jeannette Corp., supra, 532 F.2d at 918.

an ever-increasing degree electronically, rather than face-to-face. The discussion by the water cooler is in the process of being replaced by the discussion via e-mail."[9]

Given the unique characteristics of e-mail and the way it has transformed modern communication, it is simply absurd to find an e-mail system analogous to a telephone, a television set, a bulletin board, or a slip of scrap paper. Nevertheless, that is what the majority does, relying on the Board's statements in prior cases that an employer may place nondiscriminatory restrictions on the nonwork-related use of such equipment and property. None of those "equipment" cases, however, involved sophisticated networks designed to accommodate thousands of multiple, simultaneous, interactive exchanges. Rather, they involved far more limited and finite resources. For example, if a union notice is posted on a bulletin board, the amount of space available for the employer to post its messages is reduced. See, e.g., Sprint/United Management Co., 326 NLRB 397, 399 (1998) (employer "may have a legitimate interest in ensuring that its postings can easily be seen and read and that they are not obscured or diminished in prominence by other notices posted by employees"). If an employee is using a telephone for Section 7 or other nonworkrelated purposes, that telephone line is unavailable for others to use. Indeed, in Churchill's Supermarkets, 285 NLRB 138, 147 (1987), enfd. 857 F.2d 1471 (6th Cir. 1988), cert. denied 490 U.S. 1046 (1989), cited by the majority, the judge noted that the employer's "overriding consideration has always been that an employee should not tie up the phone lines" for personal use.[11]

Here, in contrast, the Respondent concedes that text e-mails impose no additional cost on the Respondent. At the time of the hearing in 2000, the Respondent's system was receiving as many as 4000 e-mail messages per day. One or more employees using the e-mail system would not preclude or interfere with simultaneous use by management or other employees. Furthermore, unlike a telephone, e-mail's versatility permits the sender of a message to reach a single recipient or multiple recipients simultaneously; allows the recipients to glimpse the subject matter of the message before deciding whether to read the message, delete it without reading it, or save it for later; and, once opened, allows the recipient to reply to the sender and/or other recipients, to engage in a realtime "conversation" with them, to forward the message to others, or to do nothing. Neither the telephone nor any other form of "equipment" addressed in the Board's prior cases shares these multidimensional characteristics.

9. Martin H. Malin & Henry H. Perritt Jr., "The National Labor Relations Act in Cyberspace: Union Organizing in Electronic Workplaces," 49 U. Kan. L. Rev. 1, 17 (Nov. 2000).

11. In any event, the statements in *Churchill's*, supra, and Union Carbide Corp., 259 NLRB 974, 980 (1981), enfd. in rel. part 714 F.2d 657 (6th Cir. 1983), that an employer may bar all personal use of its telephones were dicta. In both of those cases, the Board found that the employer had discriminatorily prohibited union-related telephone calls while allowing other personal calls. Therefore, the Board was not faced with the issue of whether a nondiscriminatory ban on personal use was lawful. . . .

The majority relies on the employer's ownership of the computer system as furnishing a "basic property right" to regulate e-mail use. But ownership, simpliciter, does not supply the Respondent with an absolute right to exclude Section 7 e-mails. The Respondent has already provided the computers and the e-mail capability to employees for regular and routine use to communicate at work. Thus, the employees are not only "rightfully" on the Respondent's real property, the building itself; they are rightfully on (using) the computer system.... Moreover, an e-mail system and the messages traveling through it are not simply "equipment"; the Respondent does not own cyberspace....

As the discussion above demonstrates, the existence of a "property right" does not end the inquiry—rather, it only begins it. The Respondent has not demonstrated how allowing employee e-mails on Section 7 matters interferes with its alleged property interest. To repeat, the Respondent already allows the employees to use the computers and e-mail system for work—and, for that matter, for personal messages. Additional text e-mails do not impose any additional costs on the Respondent. And e-mail systems, unlike older communications media, accommodate multiple, simultaneous users.

Common law involving computer "trespass," on which the Respondent relies, harms its case rather than helping it. Trespass cases illustrate that the mere use of a computer system to send e-mails does not interfere with the owner's property interest, absent some showing of harm to the system....

As stated, the majority also reasons, based on the particular facts of *Republic Aviation*, that the Respondent need not yield its "property interests" here, because employees have alternative means to communicate in the workplace, such as oral in-person communication. In 2007, however, that train has already left the station: that is not how the courts and the Board have applied *Republic Aviation*, and the availability of alternative means is not relevant when dealing with employee-to-employee communications. See, e.g., Babcock & Wilcox, supra at 112–113; Helton v. NLRB, 656 F.2d 883, 896–897 (D.C. Cir. 1981) (collecting cases). The alternative-means test applies only to activity by nonemployees on the employer's property. See Babcock & Wilcox, supra at 112; Lechmere, Inc. v. NLRB, 502 U.S. 527 (1992). The distinction between employee and nonemployee activity is "one of substance." Babcock & Wilcox, supra at 113. If the absence of alternative means to communicate in the workplace were a prerequisite to employees' right to engage in Section 7 activity on employer property, presumably an employer could ban oral solicitation by employees in "work areas," or even everywhere except an employee breakroom, without any showing of special circumstances, because the employer would not have "entirely deprived" employees of the right to communicate on the premises. Of course, neither the Board nor the Supreme Court has ever placed such limits on Section 7 communication.[15]

---

15. See, e.g., Stoddard–Quirk Mfg. Co., 138 NLRB 615, 621 (1962) ("the right of employees to [orally] solicit on plant premises must be afforded subject only to the restric-

For all of the foregoing reasons, we reject the majority's conclusion that e-mail is just another piece of employer "equipment." Where, as here, the employer has given employees access to e-mail in the workplace for their regular use, we would find that banning all nonwork-related "solicitations" is presumptively unlawful absent special circumstances. This presumption recognizes employees' rights to discuss Section 7 matters using a resource that has been made available to them for routine workplace communication. Because the presumption is rebuttable, it also recognizes that an employer may have interests that justify a ban. For example, an employer might show that its server capacity is so limited that even text e-mails would interfere with its operation. An employer might also justify more limited restrictions on nonwork-related e-mails—such as prohibiting large attachments or audio/video segments—by demonstrating that such messages would interfere with the efficient functioning of the system. In addition, rules limiting nonwork-related e-mails to nonworking time would be presumptively lawful, just as with oral solicitations.[17]

Here, the Respondent has shown no special circumstances for its ban on "non-job-related solicitations," which on its face would prohibit even solicitations on nonworking time, without regard to the size of the message or its attachments, or whether the message would actually interfere with production or discipline. Accordingly, we would reverse the judge and find that the Respondent violated Section 8(a)(1) by maintaining the portion of the CSP that prohibits employees from using e-mail for "non-job-related solicitations."

B. The Respondent's Enforcement of the CSP

Even assuming the maintenance of the CSP were lawful, the judge correctly found that the Respondent violated Section 8(a)(1) by discriminatorily enforcing it. The majority does not dispute that this result was correct under Board precedent. Instead, the majority overrules that precedent and announces a new, more limited conception of "discrimination," based on two decisions from the Seventh Circuit.[18]

As explained below, we respectfully but emphatically disagree with the Seventh Circuit's analysis.[19] But even assuming we did not, the majority's

---

tion that it be on nonworking time"; in contrast, distribution of flyers and other printed material may be limited to nonworking time and nonworking areas).

17. As with oral solicitations, however, if an employer has no rule in place that limits nonwork-related e-mails to nonworking time, the employer must show an actual interference with production or discipline in order to discipline employees for e-mails sent on working time. See, e.g., Union Carbide, supra at 979 . . . . .

18. Fleming Co. v. NLRB, 349 F.3d 968 (7th Cir. 2003); Guardian Industries Corp. v. NLRB, 49 F.3d 317 (7th Cir. 1995).

19. As the Seventh Circuit itself has observed, it is not the obligation of the Board to "knuckle under to the first court of appeals (or the second, or even the twelfth) to rule adversely to the Board. The Supreme Court, not this circuit . . . is the supreme arbiter of the meaning of the laws enforced by the Board. . . ." Nielsen Lithographing Co. v. NLRB, 854 F.2d 1063, 1066 (1988). Rather, the court continued, the duty of the Board when faced with adverse circuit precedent is application of its new test is flawed. Accordingly, we would affirm the judge's conclusion that the Respondent violated Section 8(a)(1) by discriminatorily enforcing the CSP to all three of Prozanski's union-related e-mails.

1. The Respondent violated Section 8(a)(1) under longstanding precedent

Section 7 grants employees the right "to engage in ... concerted activities for the purpose of collective bargaining or other mutual aid or protection...." An employer violates Section 8(a)(1) by "interfer[ing] with, restrain[ing], or coerc[ing] employees" in the exercise of that right. In particular, and in accord with the decades-old understanding of discrimination within the meaning of the National Labor Relations Act, the Board has long held that an employer violates that section by allowing employees to use an employer's equipment or other resources for nonwork-related purposes while prohibiting Section 7–related uses. See, e.g., Vons Grocery Co., 320 NLRB 53, 55 (1995) (bulletin board); Honeywell, Inc., 262 NLRB 1402 (1982), enfd. 722 F.2d 405 (8th Cir. 1983) (bulletin board); Union Carbide, supra at 980 (telephone). As recently as 2005, the Board applied this principle to employee use of e-mail. See Richmond Times–Dispatch, 346 NLRB No. 11, slip op. at 3 (2005) (employer violated Sec. 8(a)(1) by permitting a "wide variety of e-mail messages unrelated to the Respondent's business" but prohibiting union-related messages), enfd. 225 Fed. Appx. 144 (4th Cir. 2007), cert. denied 128 S.Ct. 492 (2007); see also E. I. du Pont de Nemours & Co., 311 NLRB 893, 919 (1993) (employer violated Sec. 8(a)(1) by permitting the "routine use" of e-mail by employees "to distribute a wide variety of material that has little if any relevance to the Company's business," but prohibiting the use of e-mail to distribute union literature).

Here, the record makes plain that the Respondent allowed employees to use e-mail for a broad range of nonwork-related messages, including e-mails requesting employees to participate in nonwork-related events. For example, employees and supervisors used e-mail to circulate jokes, baby announcements, and party invitations; to offer sports tickets; to seek a dog walker; to organize a poker group; and to make lunch plans. Yet, the Respondent enforced the CSP against Prozanski for sending three union-related messages. This is a clear 8(a)(1) violation under longstanding precedent.

2. The majority's standard

The majority defines "unlawful discrimination" as "disparate treatment of activities or communications of a similar character because of their union or other Section 7–protected status." According to the majority, the employer "may draw a line between charitable solicitations and non-charitable solicitations, between solicitations of a personal nature ... and solicitations for the commercial sale of a product ..., between invitations for an organization and invitations of a personal nature, between solicita-

"to take a stance, to explain which decisions it agree[s] with and why, and to explore the possibility of intermediate solutions.... We do not follow stare decisis inflexibly; if the Board gives us a good reason to do so, we shall be happy to reexamine [our decisions]."

tions and mere talk, and between business-related use and non-business-related use." Applying that standard to the record here, the majority finds that the Respondent permitted nonwork-related e-mails other than solicitations, but had never permitted solicitations to support any group or organization. Therefore, the majority concludes, the Respondent discriminated along Section 7 lines in applying the CSP to Prozanski's May 4 email about the union rally (which was not a solicitation), but did not discriminate in applying the CSP to Prozanski's August 14 and 18 e-mails (which the majority finds were solicitations).

a.   The *Fleming* and *Guardian* decisions

The majority decision is based on two Seventh Circuit cases: Fleming Co. v. NLRB, 349 F.3d 968 (7th Cir. 2003), denying enf. to 336 NLRB 192 (2001), and Guardian Industries Corp. v. NLRB, 49 F.3d 317 (7th Cir. 1995), denying enf. to 313 NLRB 1275 (1994). In *Guardian*, the Board found an 8(a)(1) violation where the employer allowed personal "swap and shop" postings advertising items for sale, but denied permission for union or other group postings, including those by the Red Cross and an employee credit union. In *Fleming*, the Board held that the employer violated Section 8(a)(1) by removing union literature from a bulletin board. Although the employee handbook stated that the bulletin boards were "for company business purposes only," the employer had allowed "a wide range of personal postings," including wedding announcements, birthday cards, and notices selling personal property such as cars and a television. There was no evidence that the employer had allowed postings for any outside clubs or organizations. 336 NLRB at 193–194. According to the credited testimony, an employee had asked permission to post a church announcement, which the employer denied. Id. at 202–203. Thus, the employer had affirmatively excluded at least one "organizational" posting other than union postings.

The Seventh Circuit denied enforcement in both cases. In *Guardian*, the court stated that discrimination "is a form of inequality" and that a person claiming discrimination "must identify another case that has been treated differently and explain why that case is 'the same' in the respects the law deems relevant or permissible as grounds of action." See id. at 319 . . . . . [T]he *Guardian* court noted that the employer had never allowed employees to post notices of organizational meetings. The court acknowledged that a practice of tolerating notices for anything but unions would be "antiunion discrimination by anyone's definition," id. at 321, but "[a] rule banning all organizational notices (those of the Red Cross along with meetings pro and con unions) is impossible to understand as disparate treatment of unions." Id. at 320. Accordingly, the court found that the employer's refusal to post union notices was not unlawful. Id. at 322.

In *Fleming*, the court reaffirmed *Guardian*. 349 F.3d at 975. The court noted that Fleming did not enforce its written "company use only" policy, but that "Fleming consistently excluded any posting of group or organizational notices." Id. at 974. Therefore, the court reasoned, "Fleming's actual practice of permitting personal postings, but not organizational ones, was consistently enforced." Id. at 975. The court then held: "Just as we have recognized for-sale notices as a category of notices distinct from organizational notices (which would include union postings), we can now add the category of personal postings." Id.

b. The Seventh Circuit's analysis is inappropriate in the context of the NLRA

In analyzing whether union postings were "equal to" "swap and shop" notices, the *Guardian* court relied on case law and hypotheticals involving the First and Fourteenth Amendments and ADEA [Age Discrimination in Employment Act]. See 49 F.3d at 320. Thus, the court implicitly assumed that the "discriminatory" enforcement of a rule in violation of Section 8(a)(1) is analogous to "discrimination" in other contexts. Cf. Rebecca Hanner White, Modern Discrimination Theory and the National Labor Relations Act, 39 Wm. & Mary L. Rev. 99, 115 (Oct. 1997) (the *Guardian* court "mistakenly ... imported Title VII's disparate treatment approach into Section 8(a)(1)").

The hypotheticals posed by the court, however, are not analogous to an 8(a)(1) analysis. Unlike antidiscrimination statutes, the Act does not merely give employees the right to be free from discrimination based on union activity. It gives them the affirmative right to engage in concerted group action for mutual benefit and protection.... [I]n evaluating whether an employer's conduct violates Section 8(a)(1), the Board examines whether the conduct reasonably tended to interfere with those affirmative Section 7 rights. If so, the burden is on the employer to demonstrate a legitimate and substantial business justification for its conduct. Caesar's Palace, 336 NLRB 271, 272 fn. 6 (2001); Jeannette Corp., 532 F.2d 916, 918 (3d Cir. 1976). Motive is not part of the analysis. Section 8(a)(3) separately prohibits discrimination with the motive to encourage or discourage union support.[21]

Therefore, by focusing on what types of activities are "equal" to Section 7 activities, the majority misses the point. In 8(a)(1) cases, the essence of the violation is not "discrimination." Rather, it is interference with employees' Section 7 rights. The Board's existing precedent on discriminatory enforcement—that an employer violates Section 8(a)(1) by allowing nonwork-related uses of its equipment while prohibiting Section 7 uses—is merely one application of Section 8(a)(1)'s core principles: that employees have a right to engage in Section 7 activity, and that interference with that right is unlawful unless the employer shows a business justification that outweighs the infringement. Discrimination, when it is

---

21. On that basis alone, we would have to reject the majority's definition of 8(a)(1) discriminatory enforcement as "disparate treatment of activities or communications of a similar character because of their union or other Section 7–protected status" (emphasis supplied). This improperly suggests that discriminatory motive is required—something even the Seventh Circuit does not propose.

present, is relevant simply because it weakens or exposes as pretextual the employer's business justification.[22] . . . .[24]

. . . . [U]nder the basic Section 8(a)(1) principles discussed above, if an employer wants to "draw a line" between permitted and prohibited e-mails—or, for that matter, between permitted and prohibited bulletin board postings, telephone calls, or other uses of employer equipment or media—based on whether the employees are urging support for "groups" or "organizations," the employer must show some legitimate business reason for drawing that particular line, and that business justification must outweigh the interference with Section 7 rights. Otherwise, the employer's rule is completely antithetical to Section 7's protection of concerted activity. The Seventh Circuit and majority fail to engage in this analysis. In any event, the Respondent has not offered any such justification here.

Taken to its logical extreme, the majority's holding that an employer need only avoid "drawing a line on a Section 7 basis" is a license to permit almost anything but union communications, so long as the employer does not expressly say so.[26] It is no answer to say that a rule prohibiting all

22. See, e.g., Honeywell, 722 F.2d at 407 (an employer's decision to allow other bulletin board postings "minimize[d] its managerial concerns"); Sprint/United Management Co., supra, 326 NLRB at 399 (1998) (where the employer had "already ceded the locker space to the personal use of the employees to whom the lockers are assigned," the employer "has clearly already assumed the risk" that the presence of other materials in the lockers could cause notices the employer places there to be overlooked; "[t]hus, the [employer] cannot legitimately claim that concern as a reason for refusing to allow employees to put union literature into the lockers"); Churchill's, 285 NLRB at 156 ("When an employer singles out union activity as its only restriction on the private use of company phones, it is not acting to preserve use of the phones for company business. It is interfering with union activity . . . ."); White, supra at 111 ("Under a [S]ection 8(a)(1) balancing approach, an employer that permits solicitation by employees during working time for nonunion activities is hard-pressed to stand on its managerial interests in production and discipline when the working time solicitation is on behalf of the union.") (citations omitted).

24. The Board decisions cited by the majority are also inapposite. In Salmon Run Shopping Center, 348 NLRB No. 31 (2006), the Board found that the employer's exclusion of nonemployee union organizers from the premises was discriminatorily motivated.

Because *Salmon Run* involved access by nonemployees, it implicated the employer's property interests, not just its managerial interests. See id., slip op. at 1. Even aside from that distinction, the fact that the employer in *Salmon Run* had a discriminatory motive for excluding the union does not mean that proof of such a motive is *required* in order to find a violation.

Enloe Medical Center, 348 NLRB No. 63 (2006), involved a facially discriminatory rule (barring union literature, but nothing else, from the breakroom), not a facially neutral rule that was discriminatorily applied. In any event, the fact that a rule will violate Sec. 8(a)(1) if it expressly singles out union activity does not establish that an express "singling out" is *required* in order to find a violation. In short, *Salmon Run* and *Enloe* are examples of particularly clear-cut and obvious violations, but nothing in those decisions suggests that they limit the circumstances under which a violation may be found, redefine "discrimination," or otherwise modify the Board's longstanding precedent.

26. For example, an employer might prohibit all nonwork-related solicitations by membership organizations. Such a rule would extend privileges to employee solicitations on behalf of any commercial enterprise and many charities and other activities, but not to employee solicitations on behalf of the union representing the employees—the entity noncharitable solicitations or all solicitations for a group or organizations is not discriminatory because it would also prohibit selling Avon or Amway products. The Act does not protect against interference with those activities; it does protect against interference with Section 7 activity. Accordingly, we would adhere to precedent, which properly reflects that principle.

3. The Respondent violated Section 8(a)(1) even under the majority's standard

In any event, even under the majority's standard, the Respondent's enforcement of the CSP was unlawful with respect to all three of Prozanski's e-mails: the May 4 email "setting the record straight" about the union rally, the August 14 e-mail urging employees to wear green to support the Union, and the August 18 e-mail urging participation in the Union's entry in a town parade.

First, assuming that Prozanski's August 14 and 18 emails were "solicitations" and that the Respondent could lawfully draw a line between "solicitations to support any group or organization" and other messages, as the majority contends, that is not the line the CSP drew. By its terms, the CSP barred all "non-job-related solicitations," whether or not they urge support for a "group or organization." Yet, the Respondent allowed other personal "solicitations"—which violated the terms of the CSP—while disallowing Prozanski's union-related "solicitations."

Second, even the Seventh Circuit recognized that if an employer allowed notices for anything except unions, "that is anti-union discrimination by anyone's definition." Guardian, supra at 321. In *Fleming*, the employer had denied an employee's request to post a church announcement. 336 NLRB at 202–203. In *Guardian*, the employer routinely excluded all "organizational" requests. Here, there is no clear evidence that the Respondent ever enforced the CSP against anything other than union-related messages. That is unlawful discrimination "by anyone's definition." Guardian, supra at 321.

B. The Respondent's Discipline of Prozanski Violated Section 8(a)(3) and (1)

. . . . [With respect to the written warnings to Prozanski on May 5 and August 22 for sending union-related e-mails], we would find both warnings unlawful.

First, we would find that the CSP's prohibition on using e-mail for any "non-job-related solicitations" was unlawful on its face. Therefore, the

through which the employees have chosen to vindicate their Sec. 7 right to engage in concerted activity. In other words, the rule would permit employees to solicit on behalf of virtually anything except a union. Yet, on its face, this policy would not "draw the line" on Sec. 7 grounds, and would therefore be lawful. Such a result stands labor law on its head.

The majority notes that a line drawn out of antiunion motive will still be unlawful. As noted above, however, motive is not an element of this type of 8(a)(1) violation.

discipline of Prozanski on May 5 and August 22 pursuant to that policy was unlawful . . . . .

Alternatively, even assuming the policy was lawful, we agree with the majority that it was discriminatorily enforced with respect to the May 4 e-mail. Therefore, the Respondent's May 5 discipline of Prozanski for sending that e-mail violated Section 8(a)(3) and (1). As explained above, we would also find that the CSP was discriminatorily enforced with respect to the August 14 and 18 e-mails. Accordingly, the second, August 22 warning for sending those e-mails also violated Section 8(a)(3) and (1). See St. Joseph's Hospital, 337 NLRB 94, 95 (2002) (warning for displaying union-related screen saver violated Sec. 8(a)(3) where employer allowed other nonwork-related screen savers), enfd. 55 Fed. Appx. 902 (11th Cir. 2002).

D.   The Respondent's Insistence on an Illegal Bargaining Proposal

The judge found that the Respondent violated Section 8(a)(5) and (1) by insisting on the proposal known as counterproposal 26, which stated that the Respondent's electronic communication systems could not be used for "union business." The majority reverses the judge, finding that the evidence fails to show "insistence" on the proposal. The majority finds it unnecessary to pass on whether the proposal was unlawful. We dissent.

First, we agree with the judge that counterproposal 26 was an illegal codification of the Respondent's discriminatory practice of allowing e-mail use for a broad range of nonwork-related messages, but not for union-related messages. Second, for the reasons stated below, we disagree with the majority's finding of no "insistence." . . . . If the Respondent had any doubt about the Union's position after the April 21 bargaining session, the filing and service of the charge put it on notice that the Union did not want to discuss counterproposal 26. Nevertheless, the Respondent still did not withdraw the proposal.

Under the above circumstances, we find that the Union communicated a "clear and express refusal" to bargain over counterproposal 26, and that the Respondent nevertheless continued to insist on the proposal. Accordingly, we would adopt the 8(a)(5) violation.

III.   CONCLUSION

The majority decision, particularly those portions addressing the maintenance and enforcement of the CSP, does damage to employee Section 7 rights on multiple levels. First, the majority fails to heed the Supreme Court's instruction that the Board must "adapt the Act to changing patterns of industrial life"—here, the explosion of electronic mail as a primary means of workplace communication. Second, the majority erroneously treats the employer's asserted "property interest" in e-mail—a questionable interest here, in any event—as paramount, and fails to give due consideration to employee rights and the appropriate balancing of the parties' legitimate interests. Third, the majority blurs the "distinction of substance" between the rights of employees and those of nonemployees. Finally, the majority discards the Board's longstanding test for discriminatory enforcement of a rule, replacing it with a standard that allows the employer virtually unlimited discretion to exclude Section 7 communications, so long as the employer couches its rule in facially neutral terms. Accordingly, we dissent.

PROBLEMS FOR DISCUSSION

1. The three-member majority of the Board in *Register Guard* used the analytical framework of cases in which employees seek to use employer property to aid in pro-union solicitation. This is strongly weighted toward the employer, with the employee solicitors prevailing only if they are "entirely deprived" of other communicational access. (This is indeed the way the majority reads the Supreme Court decision in *Republic Aviation*. Did you read that case that way?) The two dissenters in Register Guard used the analytical framework of its interpretation of *Republic Aviation*, which begins with a finding of interference with pro-union solicitation, and asks whether there is a significant business or property justification. This approach decidedly favors the employee(s), as compared with the majority's approach. Which is the more convincing approach?

2. How would you go about deciding the earlier Board cases involving bans upon employee pro-union solicitations on company bulletin boards, company videorecorders and televisions sets, company telephones, and company scrap paper? Do email solicitations fall, as the Board majority would have it, within the same principle, because involving "employer property" pure and simple? Does it matter that union solicitations by email are not likely to tie up the employer's server, and that such solicitations can be reserved by employees for reading on nonworking time?

3. All five Board members agreed in *Register Guard* that even a facially valid no-solicitation rule may be invalidated under section 8(a)(1) if it is applied "discriminatorily." Why is that? Because this shows anti-union motive (as the majority would have it), or because it undermines the employer claim of a legitimate business need to apply the rule to union solicitations (as the dissenters would have it)? What, if anything, is unconvincing about the view of the dissenting Board members that an employer business justification—necessary, in order to justify a ban on union email solicitations—is altogether undermined when the employer allows frequent email exchanges about babysitting, dog-walking, sporting event tickets, party invitations, and property sales?

4. The Board and the federal courts have for decades found, in the sorts of cases just mentioned, that there has been a "discriminatory" application of the facially uniform ban on solicitations, in violation of section 8(a)(1). But the *Register Guard* majority expressly declined to follow these decisions; stating that discrimination constitutes "the unequal treatment of equals," they found that babysitting, etc. and union activities are not "equal," so that the employer may lawfully ban the latter solicitations while allowing the former. Consider whether this makes sense, given that the NLRA exalts and protects employee engagement in union activities, and does not noticeably shelter babysitting and dog-walking. Consider too, that in St. Margaret Mercy Healthcare Centers v. NLRB, 519 F.3d 373 (7th Cir. 2008), the very same court of appeals that decided the *Fleming* and *Guardian* cases (the only cases that the *Register Guard* majority could apparently find to support their analysis of "discrimination"), sustained—without mentioning either of those cases—a Board finding of a section 8(a)(1) and (3) violation when a broad and facially valid no-solicitation ban was applied by the healthcare employer only to union solicitations but not to solicitations for charitable organizations, birthday and office parties, and product-sales.

Page 151. Insert new Problem for Discussion:

3. A group of researchers and their assistants, and shipboard workers, are employed onboard a university-owned ship that is not expected to return to port for three months. Shortly before the sailing period, a representation-election petition was filed on behalf of the Seafarers' Union, seeking to represent all 15 persons living and working on the ship. (Only two sailors made their way briefly back to shore and home.) When the time came for the university to provide the *Excelsior* List of employee names and addresses, it did so—but it provided the names and only the on-shore home addresses of the voting employees. A representative of the union asked that the employer provide instead the names and onboard email addresses of the voters so that there could be regular communication from the shore about the union. The university has outfitted the ship with an email system, to which all of the employees have regular access for personal and business use (provided they use the email only on nonworking time). The university insisted that it had complied with the *Excelsior* decision, which (it asserted) requires no more than the production of employee names and home addresses. It also insisted that the email system is the employer's property, which need not be made available at all for the union's use. The election was held, and a 6–to–6 tie resulted. Can the union have the election set aside because of noncompliance with the *Excelsior* requirement? *See* Trustees of Columbia University, 350 NLRB No. 54 (2007).

Page 161. Add to Problem 2:

In *W & M Properties of Conn., Inc. v. NLRB*, 514 F.3d 1341 (D.C. Cir. 2008), during the hiring process the employer expressed its intent to be non-union and questioned one applicant about his union membership. That evidence was relied upon to support the finding of a wrongful refusal to hire violative of §§ 8(a)(1) and (3). In *Local Joint Executive Board of Las Vegas v. NLRB*, 515 F.3d 942 (9th Cir. 2008), a manager's interrogating about employee solicitations of co-workers for union support, and informing the solicited employees in the presence of the union supporter that they would have to pay union dues and that there was no guarantee that the union would get them better benefits, was held not to be wrongful in light of § 8(c). Had there been no questioning of the employee in *W & M Properties*, would § 8(c) have precluded reliance on the employer's expression of desire to remain union-free? Was the manager's visual observation of the solicitation and her interrogation something more than an expression of opinion under § 8(c)?

Page 164. Add to Problems for Discussion:

8. The plumbers union has made a demand for recognition and adherence to the plumber's area-standards agreement, a copy of which was provided the employer. The employer rejected the demand, informing the union that, under the contract, it would have to assign work done by sheet-metal workers to plumbers. The union faxed the employer that it was not seeking any work done by sheet-metal workers. The sheet-metal workers were supporting the plumbers' demand and the employer asked a sheet-metal worker which of his co-workers he, the employer, should fire should he accept the plumber's contract. Is his statement insulated by § 8(c)? See Center Construction Co., Inc. v. NLRB, 482 F.3d 425 (6th Cir. 2007).

Page 178. Add to Problems for Discussion:

8. A union has secured the work-station e-mail addresses of the employees of Utopiks, Inc., whom it wishes to organize. It has sent a message to them headed **"Company to Abolish Medical Benefits!"** The text read in pertinent part:

> You already know that Utopiks has retained Lea & Perrin [a well known benefit consulting firm] to overhaul our benefits. What you don't know is that they will advise the company to double our individual and family medical co-payments. Those co-pays will exceed any possible pay and raise we might get out of the company's "good heart." A good deal for the company. A lousy deal for us. Only a Union can stave off this disaster.

The e-mail was identified as coming from the "Utopiks Organizing Committee." No return address was given nor mention made of how employees could decline to receive future messages from it. In fact, the consultant's report had not been drafted. Though the national trend on which such recommendations commonly rely is toward the assumption of greater medical costs by employees, the "organizing committee" had no factual basis for this claim. Does this message fail the "laboratory conditions" test?

Under the CAN–SPAM Act, 15 U.S.C. §§ 7701 *et. seq*, messages covered by the Act must be identified as an advertisement, must provide a valid physical postal address of the sender, and must provide the means, conspicuously, for recipients to opt out of receiving future messages. The Act makes it unlawful for a sender to transmit a commercial electronic mail message

> if such person has actual knowledge, or knowledge fairly implied on the basis of objective circumstances, that a subject heading of the message would be likely to mislead a recipient, acting reasonably under the circumstances, about a material fact regarding the contents or subject matter of the message.

15 U.S.C. § 7704 (2). A "commercial electronic mail message" is defined as "any electronic mail message the primary purpose of which is the commercial advertisement or promotion of commercial product or service...." Is the union a provider of a "commercial service"? Aitken v. Communications Workers of America, 496 F.Supp.2d 653, 665 (E.D. Va. 2007), held it is:

> While union organizing certainly implicates First Amendment associational interests, it is also true that CWA [the union whose message it was] performs economically valuable services for its members in exchange for a fee, namely union dues—an arrangement which has all the characteristics of a commercial transaction. Further, the statutory purposes of labor unions, namely "dealing with employers concerning grievances, labor disputes, wages, rates of pay, hours of employment, or conditions of work," are all services performed for a fee in the marketplace, both by competing unions and by other commercial enterprises (*e.g.* law firms, arbitrators, mediators, and the like), with whom the CWA effectively competes. Thus, it is apparent that a solicitation to join CWA may promote a "commercial service" within the meaning of the Act, and thus that emails promoting CWA representation may be regulated by the Act.

Cf. RICHARD LIPSKY & PETER STEINER, ECONOMICS 359 (6th ed. 1981):

> No one bothers to define unions any more, perhaps because everyone knows what they are, or perhaps because a union is so many things: a social club, an educational instrument, a political club, one more source of

withholding money from a worker's pay, a bargaining agent for an individual worker, and, to some, a way of life.

Does the union message violate the CAN–SPAM Act? If it does, is the Act's application consistent with the First Amendment standards that govern speech in the context of a union organizing campaign? See *Linn v. United Plant Guard Workers, Local 114*, discussed in the Main Volume at pp. 1016–1018 in connection with federal preemption, and *Old Dominion Branch No. 496, Nat'l Ass'n of Letter Carriers v. Austin*, discussed, *id.*, in Problem 6, page 1021.

Page 187.   Add at the end of Problem 4:

On remand the NLRB held, 3–2, that union videotaping of employees while soliciting their support was presumptively coercive. Randell Warehouse, 347 NLRB No. 56 (2006).

Page 263.   After *ABF Freight*:

The availability and calculation of back pay has occupied the Labor Board in 2007. On the former—availability—the Board took up the issue, remanded to it by the D.C. Circuit in *Teamster's Local 6 v. NLRB*, 414 F.3d 36 (D.C. Cir. 2005), of whether it could award reinstatement and back pay for unionized employees discharged for misconduct that was discovered by the use of hidden surveillance cameras that were installed without bargaining over that installation, *i.e.* where their misconduct was discovered by unlawful means. The Board held, 3–2, that an employer may discipline employees for misconduct detected through unlawful means, overruling *Taracorp Indus.*, 273 NLRB 221 (1984), and *Great Western Produce, Inc.*, 299 NLRB 1004 (1990), the cases cited by the D.C. Circuit as warranting remand. The majority reasoned that § 10(c) of the Act precludes the Board from granting make-whole relief and that the Board's remedial order for the § 8 (a)(5) violation—essentially to cease and desist—was an adequate deterrent to unlawful behavior. The dissenters argued that § 10(c) had no such legally preclusive effect; that misbehaving employees receive no windfall as, under antecedent law, the employer could still prove that it would have discharged these employees absent the unlawful change in working conditions; and that make-whole relief is "the most effective deterrent to future unilateral changes."

On the second issue—calculation of backpay when it *is* due—the Board took up the question of the victim's duty to mitigate his or her employer's liability. In *St. George Warehouse*, 351 NLRB No. 42 (2007), the Board reaffirmed that the employer has the "burden of persuasion" on whether the victim had made a reasonable search for work. But, 3–2, it took a different position on the "burden of going forward with the evidence" on that issue—reversing 45 years of Board precedent:

> The contention that a discriminatee has failed to make a reasonable search for work generally has two elements: (1) there were substantially equivalent jobs within the relevant geographic area, and (2) the discriminatee unreasonably failed to apply for these jobs. Current Board law places on the respondent-employer the burden of production or going forward with evidence as to both

elements of the defense. As to the first element, we reaffirm that the respondent-employer has the burden of going forward with the evidence. However, as to the second element, the burden of going forward with the evidence is properly on the discriminatee and the General Counsel who advocates on his behalf to show that the discriminatee took reasonable steps to seek those jobs. They are in the best position to know of the discriminatee's search or his reasons for not searching. Thus, following the principle that the burden of going forward should be placed on the party who is the more likely repository of the evidence, we place this burden on the discriminatee and the General Counsel.

The dissenters noted that the Board's longstanding practice was consistent with the rule that a party asserting an affirmative defense bears the burden of producing evidence to support it; and that there had been no evidence over the years that the prior apportionment of the evidentiary burden had proven unfair or difficult to administer. They also noted that in labor arbitration, where back pay for a wrongful discharge is the universal remedy and where it, too, is limited by a duty to mitigate, the burden of proving lack of mitigation is on management.

The Grosvenor Resort, 350 NLRB No. 86 (2007), concerned the back pay due ten housekeeping and maintenance employees who had been discharged for union activity in 1996, which discharges the Board held to be unlawful in 2001. Eleven years after their discharge and six years after the Board had held in their favor, the Board confronted the question of how to account for the time they'd taken to look for work, to mitigate their employer's back pay liability. The Board majority reiterated the Board's established doctrine that "the reasonableness of interim job searches depends on an assessment of the circumstances of the individual discriminatees." It went on to announce what appears to be a rule:

> We recognize that many of the discriminatees were elderly, with limited skills and education, a long history of employment with the Respondent, and, in some instances, limited transportation. All of these factors warrant consideration in determining whether an individual discriminatee exercised reasonable diligence when searching for interim work. None of these factors, however, justifies a discriminatee's failure to search for work *at all* for periods of time beyond the first 2 weeks. Furthermore, since virtually all discriminatees found some employment once they commenced a reasonable job search, we know that work was available in the relevant labor market to applicants of similar age with similar experience and skill levels. Under these circumstances, to award backpay to discriminatees who delayed their initial search for interim work beyond an initial 2–week period would be to reward idleness. [Italics in original.]

Member Walsh, dissenting, argued that although the majority acknowledged the well-established guiding principles, its decision here constitutes a radical departure from them. With-out taking account of the backpay period as a whole, the individual employees, or the surrounding circumstances the majority faults some of the employees for not seeking work quickly enough, others for not looking hard enough, and still others who found interim employment that did not commence right away. In so doing, the majority replaces the foregoing principles with mechanical rules of its own devise. The result is unfair to the employees, but it is also bad policy, for it produces an inadequate remedy for substantial violations of the law, and thus it will embolden others to commit violations that would otherwise result in more substantial backpay obligations. Indeed, today's decision is of a piece with other recent decisions of the majority limiting the backpay or (re)instatement rights of employees.

PROBLEM FOR DISCUSSION

1. On September 27, housekeeping and maintenance employees went on strike to protest their employer's refusal to bargain. Four days later they were discharged. (At the time of discharge, 17 of the 44 strikers had more than ten years of service with the employer; eight were in their fifties and nine were in their sixties.) The picketing continued, the picket signs now adding a demand to be returned to work. The latter was added on the advice of the union's business agent who told the employees that the employer's action was so patently unlawful that they would be returned to work "in the matter of a few days." Two weeks later the business agent told the employees that "it looked like things were not going to be as quick as we thought." On November 15, the union business agent advised them to make an unconditional offer to return to work, which they did even as the picketing continued. On December 27, the employer told the striking employees that they had all been permanently replaced, whereupon they started to search for alternative employment. The ALJ has found that the employer refused to bargain in violation of § 8(a)(5) and that the discharges were violative of § 8(a)(3). The employer has argued that any back pay due should be tolled from October 11, two weeks after the commencement of the strike, to December 27, when the strikers started to search for work; and that attributing those amounts to it would only "reward the employee's idleness." How should the ALJ rule?

Page 269.   Correction to Table I:

The third set of data on the processing of unfair labor practices is *not* to 1990 but to 2004.

III.   SECURING BARGAINING RIGHTS THROUGH UNFAIR PRACTICE PROCEEDINGS

Page 336.   Add to Question 3:

On the role "changed circumstances" play in the Board's consideration of whether to issue a *Gissel* bargaining order, *compare* Cogburn Health Center, Inc. v. NLRB,

437 F.3d 1266 (D.C. Cir. 2006), *with* California Gas Transport, Inc. v. NLRB, 507 F.3d 847 (5th Cir. 2007).

Page 350. After *Lee Lumber*:

In a 3–2 decision the Board glossed *Lee Lumber*'s allowance of a "reasonable period" of time for a union to enjoy unchallengeable bargaining status after it has secured an order to bargain to remedy an employer's violation of § 8(a)(5). The Board majority held the estimation of the "reasonable period" to include the amount of time spent in bargaining prior to the remedial bargaining order. Badlands Golf Course, 350 NLRB No. 28 (2007). The dissent argued that the practical result was to convert *Lee Lumber*'s minimum six-month period following renewed bargaining into a *per se* rule. The majority disagreed:

> Had the parties done little or no previous bargaining, the difficulties often encountered in bargaining for an initial contract might loom larger in the overall analysis. That might also be the case if there were unusually complex issues involved. Here, however, a substantial amount of bargaining had already occurred, and the issues were apparently not complex.

Page 353. Following the Problems for Discussion:

Dana Corporation

351 NLRB No. 28 (2007).

■ Chairman Battista, Members Schaumber and Kirsanow.

I. INTRODUCTION

Metaldyne Corporation and Dana Corporation (the Employers) independently entered into separate neutrality and card-check agreements with the International Union, United Automobile, Aerospace, and Agricultural Implement Workers of America, AFL–CIO. Subsequently, the Employers recognized the Union upon a showing of majority support of the respective unit employees. Shortly after the Employers' recognition of the Union (22 days for the Metaldyne unit and 34 days for the Dana unit), employees in each unit filed a petition seeking a decertification election. The Metaldyne petitions were supported by over 50 percent of the unit employees, while the Dana petition was supported by over 35 percent of the unit employees. The Regional Director for Region 6 and the Regional Director for Region 8 dismissed the Metaldyne and Dana petitions, respectively, based on an application of the Board's recognition-bar doctrine. According to this doctrine, an employer's voluntary recognition of a union, in good faith and based on a demonstrated majority status, immediately bars an election petition filed by an employee or a rival union for a reasonable period of time. A collective-bargaining agreement executed during this insulated period generally bars Board elections for up to 3 years of the new contract's term.

The Petitioners filed timely requests for review of the Regional Directors' dismissals. Through their petitions, the employees sought a change in Board law in order to permit them to express their views, either for or against unionization, in a decertification election. The Board granted review to re-examine its recognition-bar doctrine.[2]

Our inquiry here requires us to strike the proper balance between two important but often competing interests under the National Labor Relations Act: "protecting employee freedom of choice on the one hand, and promoting stability of bargaining relationships on the other."[3] It is a well-recognized judicial doctrine that "the Board should be left free to utilize its administrative expertise in striking the proper balance."[4] In striking that balance here, we find that the immediate post-recognition imposition of an election bar does not give sufficient weight to the protection of the statutory rights of affected employees to exercise their choice on collective-bargaining representation through the preferred method of a Board-conducted election.

In order to achieve a "finer balance"[5] of interests that better protects employees' free choice, we herein modify the Board's recognition-bar doctrine and hold that no election bar will be imposed after a card-based recognition unless (1) employees in the bargaining unit receive notice of the recognition and of their right, within 45 days of the notice, to file a decertification petition or to support the filing of a petition by a rival union, and (2) 45 days pass from the date of notice without the filing of a valid petition.[6] If a valid petition supported by 30 percent or more of the unit employees is filed within 45 days of the notice, the petition will be processed. The requisite showing of interest in support of a petition may include employee signatures obtained before as well as after the recognition. These principles will govern regardless of whether a card-check and/or neutrality agreement preceded the union's recognition.[7]

---

2. Dana Corp., 341 NLRB 1283 (2004) (Members Liebman and Walsh dissenting). The Board also granted the Petitioners' motions to consolidate the cases and to solicit amicus briefs on the issues raised. In response, the Board received 24 amicus briefs, in addition to briefs on review and reply briefs from the Petitioners, the Employers, and the Union, which filed jointly with amicus AFL–CIO. In reaching our Decision, we have carefully reviewed the briefs on review, reply briefs, and amicus briefs.

3. MV Transportation, 337 NLRB 770 (2002).

4. NLRB v. Montgomery Ward & Co., 399 F.2d 409, 412 (7th Cir. 1968).

5. Deluxe Metal Furniture Co., 121 NLRB 995, 997 (1958).

6. As set forth infra, the required notice will be an official NLRB notice that the employer shall post in conspicuous places at the workplace throughout the 45–day period. The 45–day period for filing a petition after a card-check recognition runs from the posting of the official NLRB notice.

7. As used herein, the phrase "card-check and/or neutrality agreement" refers to an agreement whereby the employer recognizes the union upon the showing of a card majority and/or the employer remains neutral during the union's organizational campaign. The term "recognition" refers to the actual grant of recognition to the union by the employer.

Modifications of the recognition bar cannot be fully effective without also addressing the election-bar status of contracts executed within the 45–day notice period, or contracts executed without employees having been given the newly-required notice of voluntary recognition. Consequently, we make parallel modifications to current contract-bar rules as well such that a collective-bargaining agreement executed on or after the date of voluntary recognition will not bar a decertification or rival union petition unless notice of recognition has been given and 45 days have passed without a valid petition being filed.

The Board's usual practice is to apply a change in law retroactively, including in the case in which the change is announced. However, we find that an exception is warranted here to avoid inequitable disruption of bargaining relationships established on the basis of the former voluntary recognition-bar doctrine. We therefore apply the recognition-bar modifications adopted herein prospectively only. Accordingly, we affirm the Regional Directors' administrative dismissals of the petitions before us under extant law.

II.   FACTS OF THE CASES

In September 2002, Metaldyne Corporation and the Union entered into a neutrality and card-check agreement. The Union then began an organizing drive and solicited authorization cards from employees in an agreed-upon bargaining unit. On November 26, 2003, the Union notified Metaldyne that it had the support of a majority of the unit employees. On December 1, 2003, after a card check by a neutral third party, Metaldyne voluntarily recognized the Union as the exclusive bargaining representative of the unit employees. Three weeks later, on December 23, 2003, Petitioners Alan P. Krug and Jeffrey A. Sample each filed a petition for a Board decertification election in the recognized unit. The petitions were supported by a showing of interest obtained after the grant of recognition. Metaldyne and the Union began contract negotiations in January 2004 and reached final agreement the following June.

On August 6, 2003, Dana Corporation and the Union entered into a neutrality and card-check agreement, and the Union began soliciting authorization cards. About November 26, 2003, the Union notified Dana that it had the support of a majority of employees in the agreed-upon unit. On December 4, 2003, after a card check by a neutral third party, Dana voluntarily recognized the Union as the exclusive bargaining representative of the unit employees. On January 7, 2004, Petitioner Clarice K. Atherholt filed a petition for a Board decertification election, supported by a showing of interest obtained after the grant of recognition. Contract negotiations had not begun when the petition was filed.

* * * *

IV.   ANALYSIS

It may be worthwhile at the outset to identify those issues we will not address in these cases. We do not question the legality of voluntary recognition agreements based on a union's showing of majority support. Voluntary recognition itself predates the National Labor Relations Act and is undisputedly lawful under it.[10] We also do not address the legality of card-check and/or neutrality agreements preceding recognition. While some allegations have been made that the agreements and subsequent recognitions were not arms-length, there is no 8(a)(2) challenge to the negotiations of the agreements or to the agreements themselves. Nor is there an 8(a)(2) challenge to the grant of recognition. Although the Petitioners have asserted that the authorization cards were coercively obtained or otherwise tainted, such evidence has not been developed nor specific findings in that regard made. We also do not address circumstances in which employers may file postrecognition petitions or unilaterally withdraw recognition from a union. Finally, we will not decide in these cases whether the "reasonable period" standard for determining the length of a voluntary recognition bar period should be modified or replaced by a time-specific standard.[11]

In sum, the issue before us is limited to deciding whether an employer's voluntary recognition of a union based on a presumably valid majority showing—usually consisting of signed authorization cards—should bar a decertification or rival union election petition for some period of time thereafter.... Having now taken [a] critical look, with the benefit of extensive and helpful argument from the parties and amici, we conclude that the current recognition-bar doctrine should be modified to provide

---

10. NLRB v. Gissel Packing Co., 395 U.S. 575, 595–600 (1969).

11. Under current Board law, a " 'reasonable time' is not measured only by the number of days or months spent in bargaining, but by what transpired and what was accomplished in the bargaining sessions." Royal Coach Lines, 282 NLRB 1037, 1038 (1987). In the present cases, the Regional Directors determined that a reasonable time had not elapsed when the decertification petitions were filed, and the Petitioners did not seek review of this determination. We note that in MGM Grand Hotel, 329 NLRB 464 (1999), a Board majority found that the insulated "reasonable period" for bargaining was more than 356 days, thereby conferring on the recognized union the benefit of an insulated period substantially the same as a certified union would enjoy. Chairman Battista and Members Schaumber and Kirsanow did not participate in the MGM decision and question whether it was correctly decided. Even under a flexible, open-ended "reasonable period" standard, Members Schaumber and Kirsanow agree that appropriate weight should be given the importance of the Section 7 right to select and oust a representative, the significant distinctions between voluntary recognition and certification, the absence of unfair labor practices that might warrant a longer insulated period for remedial bargaining, and the likelihood that in many instances first contract negotiations for parties who voluntarily enter bargaining relationships will be less contentious and time-consuming. While there may be some benefit in having a maximum insulated period for the voluntary recognition bar, no party has asked the Board to impose such cutoff or overrule MGM Grand Hotel. Since this issue has not been briefed and brought sufficiently into focus for the Board to reliably address it, Members Schaumber and Kirsanow do not resolve these matters.

Chairman Battista believes that an open-ended period fosters unnecessary litigation, gives rise to results like that reached in MGM, and does not create the desirable sharp distinction between certification and card-based recognition. Accordingly, consistent with the views articulated in the briefs of two amici, and noting the factors set forth above by his colleagues, Chairman Battista would impose a maximum of 6 months for the insulated period. The 6 months would run from the end of the 45–day notice period.

greater protection for employees' statutory right of free choice and to give proper effect to the court—and Board—recognized statutory preference for resolving questions concerning representation through a Board secret-ballot election.

A.   The Current Recognition–Bar Doctrine

The Board announced the recognition-bar doctrine in Keller Plastics Eastern, Inc., 157 NLRB 583 (1966). This was an unfair labor practice case in which the complaint alleged that the respondent employer unlawfully executed a collective-bargaining agreement with a minority union. It was stipulated that the employer had lawfully recognized the union based on its majority representative status, but the union no longer retained majority support when the parties executed their contract a month later. The Board, id. at 587, dismissed the complaint, reasoning that,

> like situations involving certifications, Board orders, and settlement agreements, the parties must be afforded a reasonable time to bargain and to execute the contracts resulting from such bargaining. Such negotiations can succeed, however, and the policies of the Act can thereby be effectuated, only if the parties can normally rely on the continuing representative status of the lawfully recognized union for a reasonable period of time.

Soon after *Keller Plastics*, the Board relied on the recognition-bar doctrine in holding that a respondent employer unlawfully withdrew its voluntary recognition of a union based on the filing of a decertification petition approximately two and a half months after the recognition agreement. Universal Gear Services Corp., 157 NLRB 1169 (1966), *enfd*. 394 F.2d 396 (6th Cir. 1968). Then, in Sound Contractors, 162 NLRB 364 (1966), the Board said that the recognition-bar doctrine would apply in representation cases to bar the filing of election petitions for a reasonable time after voluntary recognition. . . .

B.   The Rationale for Modification of the Recognition–Bar Doctrine

While Section 9 of the Act permits the exercise of employee free choice concerning union representation through the voluntary recognition process, this does not require that Board policy in representation case proceedings must treat the majority card showings the same as the choice expressed in Board elections. On the contrary, both the Board and courts have long recognized that the freedom of choice guaranteed employees by Section 7 is better realized by a secret election than a card check.[14] "[S]ecret elections are generally the most satisfactory—indeed the preferred—method of ascertaining whether a union has majority support."[15]

As further discussed below, the 1947 Taft–Hartley amendments to Section 9 of the Act reflect the preference for Board elections by limiting

---

14. See, e.g., NLRB v. Gissel Packing Co., supra at 602; Linden Lumber Division v. NLRB, 419 U.S. 301, 304 (1974); Transportation Maintenance Services v. NLRB, 275 F.3d 112, 114 (D.C. Cir. 2002); Levitz Furniture Co. of the Pacific, 333 NLRB 717, 727 (2001); Underground Service Alert, 315 NLRB 958, 960 (1994).

15. Gissel, supra at 602.

Board certification of exclusive collective-bargaining representatives, and the benefits that inure from certification, to unions that prevail in a Board election. Those benefits include immunity from certain prohibitions in Section 8(b)(4) of the Act as well as a full one-year period during which the certified union's majority status cannot be challenged. In recognition of the Congressionally-approved practice of according special value to certifications, the Board has long maintained an exception to both the recognition-bar and contract-bar doctrines that permits a recognized union to file a representation petition to secure the benefits of certification.

Our administration of the Act should similarly reflect that preference by encouraging the initial resort to Board elections to resolve questions concerning representation. There is sound reason to believe that the current recognition-bar policy does not do so. The current policy fails to give adequate weight to the substantial differences between Board elections and union authorization card solicitations as reliable indicators of employee free choice on union representation and fails to distinguish between the circumstances of voluntary recognition and those present in the other election-bar situations cited in *Keller Plastics*. In light of these factors, discussed below, we conclude that some modifications in the voluntary recognition bar are required.

The dissent repeatedly asserts that "voluntary recognition is a favored element of national labor policy" and suggests that we have lost sight of that proposition. We disagree. Our colleagues fail to recognize that there is no statutory mandate that there be any voluntary recognition bar at all. There was none prior to the 1966 *Keller Plastics* decision, even though, as our colleagues point out, voluntary recognition has been embedded in Section 9(a) from the Act's inception. Thus, for years, the policy basis of voluntary recognition apparently was not thought to be inconsistent with the lack of a recognition bar altogether. We are not returning the law to the pre-*Keller Plastics* era. We continue to support voluntary recognition, and thereby encourage the stability of collective-bargaining relationships established on that basis, by continuing to apply the recognition bar. We simply modify that bar to provide greater protection for employee free choice.

1.   The Greater Reliability of Board Elections

The preference for the exercise of employee free choice in Board elections has solid foundation in distinctions between the statutory process for resolving questions concerning representation and the private voluntary recognition process. For a number of reasons, authorization cards are "admittedly inferior to the election process."[18] First, unlike votes cast in privacy by secret Board election ballots, card signings are public actions, susceptible to group pressure exerted at the moment of choice. The election is held under the watchful eye of a neutral Board agent and observers from the parties. A card signing has none of these protections. There is good

---

18. Gissel, supra at 603. The Supreme Court in *Gissel* held that the Board could impose a remedial bargaining order based on a union's prior card showing of employee support in extraordinary cases where a respondent employer's unfair labor practices foreclose the possibility of conducting a fair Board election.

reason to question whether card signings in such circumstances accurately reflect employees' true choice concerning union representation. "Workers sometimes sign union authorization cards not because they intend to vote for the union in the election but to avoid offending the person who asks them to sign, often a fellow worker, or simply to get the person off their back, since signing commits the worker to nothing (except that if enough workers sign, the employer may decide to recognize the union without an election)."[20]

Second, union card-solicitation campaigns have been accompanied by misinformation or a lack of information about employees' representational options. As to the former, misrepresentations about the purpose for which the card will be used [i.e., for a free election rather than for immediate employer recognition] may go unchecked in the voluntary recognition process. Even if no misrepresentations are made, employees may not have the same degree of information about the pros and cons of unionization that they would in a contested Board election, particularly if an employer has pledged neutrality during the card-solicitation process.[21] Employees uninterested in, or opposed to, union representation may not even understand the consequences of voluntary recognition until after it has been extended. In circumstances where recognition is preceded by a card-check agreement that provides for union access to the employer's facility, employees may even reasonably conclude they have no real choice but to accede to representation by that union.

Third, like a political election, a Board election presents a clear picture of employee voter preference at a single moment. On the other hand, card signings take place over a protracted period of time. In the present *Metaldyne* cases, for instance, the Union took over a year to collect the cards supporting its claim of majority support. During such an extended period, employees can and do change their minds about union representation. On this point, several briefs filed in this proceeding refer to statistics from a 1962 presentation by former Board Chairman McCulloch as empirical evidence of the lesser reliability of cards to indicate actual employee preference for union representation. These statistics showed a significant disparity between union card showings of support and ensuing Board election results. In particular, unions with a 50–to 70–percent majority card showing won only 48 percent of elections. Even unions with more than a 70–percent card showing won only 74 percent of elections.[24]

Finally, although critics of the Board election process claim that an employer opposed to union representation has a one-sided advantage to

---

20. NLRB v. Village IX, Inc., 723 F.2d 1360, 1371 (7th Cir. 1983).

21. "Among the factors that undoubtedly tend to impede [employee free choice] is a lack of information with respect to one of the choices available. In other words, an employee who has had an effective opportunity to hear the arguments concerning representation is in a better position to make a more fully informed and reasonable choice." Excelsior Underwear, 156 NLRB 1236, 1240 (1966).

24. McCulloch, A Tale of Two Cities: Or Law in Action, Proceedings of ABA Section of Labor Relations Law 14, 17 (1962)....

exert pressure on its employees throughout each workday of an election campaign, the fact remains that the Board will invalidate elections affected by improper electioneering tactics, and an employee's expression of choice is exercised by casting a ballot in private. There are no guarantees of comparable safeguards in the voluntary recognition process. While the provision of an orderly process for determining whether a fair election has been conducted may result in substantial delay in a small minority of Board elections,[25] it remains preferable to determine employee free choice by a method that can assure greater regularity, fairness, and certainty in the final outcome.[26]

2. Differences Between Voluntary Recognition and Other Election–Bar Situations

The Board's reliance in *Keller Plastics* on other election-bar doctrines for certification, Board orders, and settlement agreements to justify the immediate imposition of a voluntary recognition bar failed to account for the different contexts in which those doctrines arose. Most notably, the certification-year bar holds that a certified union's majority status is irrebuttably presumed to continue for one year from the date of certification after a Board election. The 1947 Taft–Hartley Act amendments to Section 9 of the Act effectively codified this limitation and also barred petitions filed within one year of a valid Board election, thus precluding repeated petition filings after a union loses an election.[27] In other words, the immediate imposition of a one-year election bar after a union's certification or defeat results from the exercise of employee free choice by the preferred method of a Board election.

The Supreme Court affirmed the Board's certification-year rule and held that an employer violated Section 8(a)(5) by refusing to bargain with a certified union in *Brooks v. NLRB*, supra. It listed, with apparent approval, five reasons for imposing an immediate insulated bargaining period. 348 U.S. at 99–100. Proponents of the current recognition bar contend that some, although admittedly not all, of these reasons apply as well to collective-bargaining relationships newly established by voluntary recognition, particularly the observations that "a union should be given ample time for carrying out its mandate ... and should not be under exigent pressure to produce hot-house results or be turned out," and that "it is scarcely conducive to bargaining in good faith for an employer to know that, if he dillydallies, union strength may erode and thereby relieve him of his statutory duties at any time, while if he works conscientiously toward agreement, the rank and file may, at the last moment, repudiate their

---

25. A recent release of NLRB field and headquarters statistics for the Office of the General Counsel reveals that "[i]nitial elections in union representation cases were conducted in a median of 39 days from the filing of the petition, with 94.2% of all elections conducted within 56 days" during Fiscal Year 2006. General Counsel's Memorandum GC 07–03, Summary of Operations FY 2006 (January 3, 2007).

26. In Fiscal Year 2005, only 5 percent of all representation elections resulted in the filing of objections. See 70 NLRB Annual Report 130 (2005).

27. See Sec. 9(c)(3).

agent." Id. at 100. As an abstract matter, these considerations could support the current recognition-bar doctrine, but the Court did not speak in the abstract. It spoke in the specific context of why protections should be accorded a union whose majority status was certified after a Board election, "a solemn and costly occasion, conducted under safeguards to voluntary choice." Id. at 99. In this context, the consensus of the Board, the Congress, and the Court is that the greater assurance of an accurate expression of employees' free choice justifies the immediate imposition of an insulated period for bargaining free from the threat of challenge to the certified union's status.

In Franks Bros. Co. v. NLRB, 321 U.S. 702 (1944), the Supreme Court affirmed a Board order that an employer bargain for a "reasonable period" after the employer's unfair labor practices had dissipated a union's card majority.... Thus, the election bar accompanying Board orders in [such] cases serves a remedial purpose that is not implicated in the voluntary recognition-bar setting, and it is applied to situations where an employer's unlawful conduct raises doubt about whether a subsequent showing of employee interest in support of an election petition, as well as any ensuing election, would truly represent the exercise of free choice....

In sum, there is a reasonable rationale for imposing an immediate bar in circumstances involving a certification, a Board bargaining order, and a settlement agreement containing a promise to bargain. However, the rationale is far less persuasive where there is only voluntary recognition. Accordingly, we find it appropriate to alter the bar in the latter situation.

Several courts of appeals have endorsed the current recognition-bar doctrine.[31] However, none of those judicial decisions state or suggest that the recognition bar is required as a policy or as a statutory matter, and neither the courts of appeals nor past Board decisions have expressly dealt with the alternative (jointly proposed by the General Counsel, Petitioners, and some amici here) of creating an initial post-recognition window period for filing election petitions before insulating the recognized union's majority status from challenge for a reasonable period of time. We conclude that a better balance between the protection of free choice and the encouragement of labor relations stability can be achieved by modifying the recognition bar in this way.

3. Current Practices of Card Check Recognition

It is asserted that unions are increasingly and successfully turning to card checks as their preferred means of achieving recognition and that the Board should not interfere. Assuming *arguendo* that unions are increasingly turning to card checks in lieu of Board elections for recognition, and assuming further that employers are voluntarily acceding to card-check

---

31. See, e.g., Exxel/Atmos. Inc. v. NLRB, 28 F.3d 1243 (D.C. Cir. 1994); NLRB v. Cayuga Crushed Stone, 474 F.2d 1380, 1383–1384 (2d Cir. 1973); NLRB v. Frick Co., 423 F.2d 1327, 1332 (3d Cir. 1970); NLRB v. Universal Gear Service Corp., 394 F.2d 396, 397–398 (6th Cir. 1968); NLRB v. Montgomery Ward & Co., 399 F.2d 409, 411–413 (7th Cir. 1968); and NLRB v. San Clemente Publishing Corp., 408 F.2d 367, 368 (9th Cir. 1969).

recognition, the Board's action today does not interfere with that voluntarism. Today's action improves upon it by better assuring that employee free choice has not been impaired by that recognition. That free choice is, after all, the fundamental value protected by the Act.

We acknowledge that the more rigid recognition-bar doctrine has been in effect since it was announced in *Keller Plastics*. Even in the context of administrative law, the principle of *stare decisis* is entitled to considerable weight. "The rules governing representation elections are not, however, 'fixed and immutable.' They have been changed and refined, generally in the direction of higher standards." To that end, we conclude a higher standard of notice to employees that recognition has been extended, and a post-recognition opportunity for employees to petition the Board for an election, must be met before an election bar is imposed.

C.   The Modified Recognition–Bar Doctrine

For all these reasons, we herein modify two aspects of the current recognition-bar doctrine. There will be no bar to an election following a grant of voluntary recognition unless (a) affected unit employees receive adequate notice of the recognition and of their opportunity to file a Board election petition within 45 days, and (b) 45 days pass from the date of notice without the filing of a validly-supported petition. These rules apply notwithstanding the execution of a collective-bargaining agreement following voluntary recognition. In other words, if the notice and window-period requirements have not been met, any post-recognition contract will not bar an election.[33]

If both conditions are satisfied, the recognized union's majority status will be irrebuttably presumed for a reasonable period of time to enable the parties to engage in negotiations for a first collective-bargaining agreement. Under the contract-bar doctrine, any agreement reached during this 45–day window period will further bar an electoral challenge for up to 3 years of the contract term, once the window period elapses without the filing of a decertification or rival union petition.

We agree with the General Counsel that the notice and window-period requirements should apply irrespective of whether voluntary recognition is preceded by a card-check/neutrality agreement. The previously-discussed problems with the current recognition-bar doctrine may be increased in, but are not limited to, situations in which recognition follows such agreements. . . .

We . . . reject the dissent's contention that modification of the recognition-bar doctrine will disserve the policy of promoting labor relations stability and remove the incentive for parties to enter into voluntary recognition agreements. Employers and unions agree to voluntary recognition for any number of reasons, economic and otherwise, that will remain

---

33. Keller Plastics, supra, Smith's Food & Drug Centers, supra, Seattle Mariners, supra, and their progeny are hereby overruled to the extent they are inconsistent with the modified recognition-bar doctrine that we announce in this decision.

unaffected by our decision today.[34] Furthermore, the provision of a post-recognition window period for filing decertification or rival election petitions merely postpones the recognition bar; it does not abolish it or destroy its benefits. If no valid petition is filed within 45 days of notice of recognition, then a union's majority status will not be subject to challenge during the ensuing recognition-bar period.

It is true that, during the initial 45–day window period, the newly-established bargaining relationship will be subject to some degree of uncertainty about potential challenges to the union's representative status. However, the same uncertainty exists at other times during which an incumbent union's majority status is merely rebuttable and election petitions can be filed. Moreover, although our modification of the recognition bar delays the onset of an insulated period in order to assure protection of employee free choice, it does not otherwise deny the advantages of incumbency to the recognized union and those employees who support it. The employer's obligation to bargain with the union attaches immediately. For instance, during this 45–day period, the union can begin its representation of employees, its processing of their grievances, and its bargaining with the employer for a first contract.

Our dissenting colleagues predict that an employer will have "little incentive to recognize a union voluntarily if it knows that its decision is subject to second guessing through a decertification petition." Unions, they predict, will be trapped in a "Catch 22": they will have no reason to bargain hard promptly for fear that they will be ousted in a decertification election, and yet failure to produce prompt results will induce employees to file a decertification petition.

It is not the Board's province to provide incentives for parties to enter into voluntary recognition agreements, particularly if their reasons for doing so give short shrift to affected employees' statutory rights of free choice. In any event, we seriously question whether our modification of the voluntary recognition bar will have the dire consequences predicted by the dissent. This modification merely permits the filing of an election petition during the 45–day window period. It does not encourage, much less guarantee, the filing of a petition. That is a matter left to employees, and an employer and union are both free during the window period to express their non-coercive views about the perceived benefits of a collective-bargaining relationship. If an employer, based on a cost-benefit analysis, believes voluntary recognition is on balance advantageous, it would not necessarily decline to recognize a union simply because there is some risk that a petition will be filed. Similarly, if a union has obtained a solid card majority and has been voluntarily recognized on that basis, it should not be deterred from promptly engaging in meaningful bargaining simply because of the risk of losing that majority in an election. . . .

---

34. See Brudney, Neutrality Agreements and Card Check Recognition: Prospects for Changing Paradigms, 90 Iowa L. Rev. 819, 832–841 (2005) (setting forth various reasons for neutrality and card-check agreements).

1. The notice requirement

The Board requires employers to post official Board election notices, containing a summary of statutory rights and election details, for 3 working days prior to the election at conspicuous places in the workplace.... [H]ereafter, the employer and/or the union must promptly notify the Regional Office of the Board, in writing, of the grant of voluntary recognition.[38] Upon being so apprised, the Regional Office of the Board will send an official NLRB notice to be posted in conspicuous places at the workplace throughout the 45–day period alerting employees to the recognition and using uniform language.

We request that the General Counsel prepare and distribute such notice for use by the Regional Offices. The notice should clearly state that (1) the employer (on date) has recognized the union as the employees' exclusive bargaining representative based on evidence indicating that a majority of employees in a described bargaining unit desire its representation; (2) all employees, including those who previously signed cards in support of the recognized union, have the Section 7 right to be represented by a union of their choice or by no union at all; (3) within 45 days from the date of this notice, a decertification petition supported by 30 percent or more of the unit employees may be filed with the National Labor Relations Board for a secret-ballot election to determine whether or not the unit employees wish to be represented by the union, or 30 percent or more of the unit employees can support another union's filing of a petition to represent them; (4) any properly supported petition filed within the 45–day period will be processed according to the Board's normal procedures; and (5) if no petition is filed within 45 days from the date of this notice, then the recognized union's status as the unit employees' exclusive majority bargaining representative will not be subject to challenge for a reasonable period of time following the expiration of the 45–day window period, to permit the union and the employer an opportunity to negotiate a collective-bargaining agreement.

2. The 45–day window period

Although the General Counsel and some others favor a 30–day post-recognition window period for filing election petitions, we believe that the slightly longer period of 45 days from the notice-posting date is more appropriate. The period must be of sufficient length to permit affected employees, after receiving notice, to fully discuss their views concerning collective-bargaining representation and, if they desire, to solicit support for decertification of the recognized union or support for another union to represent them.... Particularly in a large bargaining unit, 30 days is not a very long time for such discourse and action....

---

38. For election-bar purposes, the recognition itself shall be in writing, shall describe the unit, and shall set forth the date of recognition. A copy of the written recognition must accompany the notice to the Regional Office. We reiterate that the 45–day window period will not begin to run until the requisite notice has been provided and the posting has occurred.

D. Prospective Application

The Board's general practice is to apply new policies and standards to "all pending cases in whatever stage." However, the Board will make an exception in cases where retroactive application could, on balance, produce " 'a result which is contrary to a statutory design or to legal and equitable principles.' " We find an exception warranted here on equitable grounds. Our decision today marks a significant departure from preexisting law. In reliance on that law, the parties in the present cases entered into voluntary recognition agreements with the understanding that the established recognition bar would immediately preclude the filing of Board petitions for a reasonable period of time. Other unions and employers have also entered into voluntary recognition agreements, and subsequently executed collective-bargaining agreements, that would not bar election petitions under our new policy because employees did not receive the notice of recognition that has not heretofore been required. Moreover, although retroactive application would further employee free choice, it would also destabilize established bargaining relationships. Thus, retroactivity would produce mixed results in accomplishing the purposes of the Act, while the reliance interests of the parties and those similarly situated would be unequivocally and substantially frustrated.

Under the above circumstances, we will apply the modified recognition-bar requirements prospectively only to voluntary recognition agreements that postdate our decision in this case.

ORDER

It is ordered that the petitions . . . are dismissed.

■ Members Liebman and Walsh, dissenting in part, but concurring in the result.

Sadly, today's decision will surely enhance already serious disenchantment with the Act's ability to protect the right of employees to engage in collective bargaining. As the majority recognizes, the Board's task in these cases is to balance the Act's twin interests in promoting stable bargaining relationships and employee free choice. But the appropriate balance was struck 40 years ago, in *Keller Plastics*,[1] and nothing in the majority's decision justifies its radical departure from that well-settled, judicially approved precedent. The voluntary recognition bar, as consistently applied for the past four decades, promotes both interests: it honors the free choice already exercised by a majority of unit employees, while promoting stable bargaining relationships. By contrast, the majority's decision subverts both interests: it subjects the will of the majority to that of a 30 percent minority, and destabilizes nascent bargaining relationships. In addition, the majority's view fails to give sufficient weight to the role of voluntary recognition in national labor policy and to the efficacy of existing unfair

---

1. Keller Plastics Eastern, Inc., 157 NLRB 583 (1966). Any student of labor law knows what a rarity a 40–year old Board doctrine is.

labor practice sanctions to remedy the problems the majority claims to see. Accordingly, we dissent.[2]

I.

The ultimate object of the National Labor Relations Act, as the Supreme Court has repeatedly stated, is "industrial peace ..." Auciello Iron Works, Inc. v. NLRB, 517 U.S. 781,785 (1996).... To that end, the Board seeks to maximize and balance two sometimes competing goals: "preserving a free employee choice of bargaining representatives, and encouraging the collective-bargaining process." NLRB v. Montgomery Ward & Co., 399 F.2d 409, 412 (7th Cir. 1968).

.... Today's decision, as we will explain, undercuts the process of voluntary recognition as a legitimate mechanism for implementing employee free choice and promoting the practice of collective bargaining. It does so at a critical time in the history of our Act, when labor unions have increasingly turned away from the Board's election process—frustrated with its delays and the opportunities it provides for employer coercion—and have instead sought alternative mechanisms for establishing the right to represent employees. See, e.g., Brudney, Neutrality Agreements and Card Check Recognition: Prospects for Changing Paradigms, 90 Iowa L. Rev. 819 (2005).[4] If disillusionment with the Board's election process continues, while new obstacles to voluntary recognition are created, the prospects for industrial peace seem cloudy, at best .....

II.

Under the Act, an election is not the exclusive means of determining majority status. "Almost from the inception of the Act ... it was recognized that a union did not have to be certified as the winner of a Board election to invoke a bargaining obligation ...." NLRB v. Gissel Packing Co., 395 U.S. 575, 596–597 (1969). An employer's duty to bargain under Section 8(a)(5) of the Act is subject, not to Section 9(c), which deals with elections, but to Section 9(a), which states that a representative "designat-

---

2. We concur in the dismissal of the instant petitions.

Without passing on the issue, the members of the majority debate among themselves whether the Board should place a finite limit on the recognition bar's "reasonable time" for bargaining. No party has asked for such a limit, and therefore we need not respond to our colleagues' positions here.

4. Professor Brudney observes that "[a]s a factual matter, Board elections have ceased to be the dominant mechanism for determining whether employees want union representation." Brudney, Neutrality Agreements, supra, 90 Iowa L. Rev. at 824. In his view:

The development of substantial alternative approaches signals a recognition that assumptions about the basic fairness of Board elections have turned out not to be realistic. Participants on both sides understand that Board-supervised election campaigns regularly feature employers' exercise of their lawful yet disproportionate authority to help shape election results, as well as employers' use of their power to affect outcomes unlawfully but with relative impunity. These patterns of conduct have helped generate alternative contractually based approaches to organizing that appear to be used at least as widely as Board elections to determine whether employees wish to join unions.

Id.

ed or selected" by the majority of employees in a unit shall be the exclusive bargaining representative. Neither Section 9(a) nor any other provision of the Act specifies the manner in which the union must be chosen.[5] In enacting the Taft–Hartley amendments, Congress considered and rejected an amendment to Section 8(a)(5) that would have permitted the Board to find a refusal to bargain only if the union had been certified through an election. See Gissel, supra at 598 (citing H.R. Conf. Rep. No. 510, 80th Cong., 1st Sess., 41 (1947)).

Thus, it is beyond dispute that an employer may voluntarily recognize a union that has demonstrated majority support by means other than an election, including—as in the present cases—authorization cards signed by a majority of the unit employees. See Retail Clerk Local 455 v. NLRB, 510 F.2d 802, 807 (D.C. Cir. 1975) (legislative history indicates that Congress intended to permit nonelection recognition procedures); Rockwell International Corp., 220 NLRB 1262, 1263 (1975) (employer's "choice of a card check was not only reasonable but one long accepted and sanctioned by the Board"). . . . The Board and courts have uniformly endorsed voluntary recognition and have deemed it "a favored element of national labor policy."

III.

To give substance to the policy favoring voluntary recognition, the Board held in *Keller Plastics* that, when an employer voluntarily recognizes a union in good faith based on a demonstrated showing of majority support, the parties are permitted a reasonable time to bargain without challenge to the union's majority status. Keller Plastics, 157 NLRB at 587. The Board stated:

> With respect to the present dispute which involves a bargaining status established as the result of voluntary recognition of a majority representative, we conclude that . . . the parties must be afforded a reasonable time to bargain and to execute the contracts resulting from such bargaining. Such negotiations can succeed, however, and the policies of the Act can thereby be effectuated, only if the parties can normally rely on the continuing representative status of the lawfully recognized union for a reasonable period of time.

Keller Plastics was an unfair labor practice case. On its facts, the Board held that a reasonable period of time had not elapsed between the time of recognition (when the union had majority support) and the execution of a collective-bargaining agreement the following month (by which time the union had lost majority support). Therefore, the employer did not violate Section 8(a)(2) by executing the agreement. Id.

Later that same year, the Board expressly extended the rule of *Keller Plastics* to representation cases. Sound Contractors, 162 NLRB 364 (1966).

---

5. Accordingly, the majority flatly errs in stating that there is a "statutory preference" for elections.

The Board determined that a recognition bar should apply in representation cases where the employer had voluntarily recognized a union based on a showing of majority support, so long as only that union had been organizing the employees. In such cases, then, a petition seeking to challenge the recognized union's status is barred for a reasonable period of time following lawful recognition. Id. at 365.

By protecting the voluntary bargaining relationship from attack in its formative stages, the recognition bar effectuates the Act's interest in stability of labor-management relations. It also protects employee free choice: the bar extends for a reasonable period only. See Keller Plastics, supra at 587. If a reasonable time elapses and the parties have not reached agreement, the presumption of the union's majority status becomes rebuttable, and a decertification petition is no longer barred. Notably, voluntary recognition is lawful and the recognition bar applies only when the recognized union has the support of a majority of employees in the unit (as opposed to certification after an election, which requires only a majority of votes cast). An employer that recognizes a minority union, and a minority union that accepts recognition—even in good faith—will violate Section 8(a)(2) and Section 8(b)(1)(A), respectively.

. . . . In Brooks v. NLRB, 348 U.S. 96 (1954), which upheld the Board's certification bar rule, the Supreme Court reasoned that "[a] union should be given ample time for carrying out its mandate on behalf of its members, and should not be under exigent pressure to produce hot-house results or be turned out." Rather, "a bargaining relationship once rightfully established must be permitted to exist and function for a reasonable period in which it can be given a fair chance to succeed." Franks Bros. Co. v. NLRB, 321 U.S. 702, 705 (1944) (discussing the justification for a remedial bargaining order).[9]

Since *Keller Plastics* and *Sound Contractors*, the Board has unreservedly reaffirmed the voluntary recognition bar in numerous cases, and the appellate courts have repeatedly endorsed it. Indeed, in the 40 years since *Keller Plastics*, although individual Board members have occasionally disagreed over the application of the recognition bar in particular cases, no Board Member—until now—and no court [has] challenged the bar itself or espoused the theory that it would be improved by the "fine tuning" perpetrated by the majority.

---

9. The majority's lengthy discussion of the certification bar, settlement bar, and remedial bargaining order cases cited in *Keller Plastics*, and its attempts to distinguish them, create a red herring. We do not dispute that those cases arose in different contexts. But it does not follow that their animating principles—that a bargaining relationship should be given time to succeed before being subject to challenge—are inapplicable here, and that voluntary recognition is not also deserving of a bar against election petitions for a "reasonable period." Indeed, with full awareness of the differences between certification and voluntary recognition, appellate courts have relied on the Supreme Court's decisions in *Franks* and *Brooks*, both certification cases, in endorsing the recognition bar . . . .

IV.

The majority concedes that voluntary recognition is lawful, that the recognition bar is longstanding precedent, and that it has been endorsed by the courts. Nevertheless, the majority concludes that the recognition bar and corresponding aspects of the contract bar need "modification." The majority contends that its newly created notice requirement and 45–day post-recognition "window period" for filing a decertification petition, together with the majority's corresponding changes to the contract bar, "improve upon" the recognition bar without "destroy[ing] its benefits." We disagree. The majority decision cuts voluntary recognition off at the knees.

An employer has the right to refuse to voluntarily recognize a union and demand an election. Linden Lumber Division v. NLRB, 419 U.S. 301 (1974). One important reason employers choose voluntary recognition is to avoid the time, expense, and disruption of an election. That rationale, however, is critically undermined by the majority's modifications. An employer has little incentive to recognize a union voluntarily if it knows that its decision is subject to second-guessing through a decertification petition. Furthermore, even if an employer does choose to recognize a union voluntarily, the majority's new window period leaves the parties' bargaining relationship open to attack by a minority of employees at the very outset of the relationship, when it is at its most vulnerable. At the very least, the relationship will be in limbo for 45 days, even if a petition is not filed. If a petition is filed and the union ultimately prevails in the election, the election campaign and any post-election proceedings "nevertheless would have the deleterious consequence of 'disrupt[ing] the nascent relationship' between the employer and union pending the outcome of the election and any subsequent proceedings." Seattle Mariners, supra at 565 (citing Smith's Food, supra at 845–846). In that event, the disruption will not be limited to the 45–day window period, but will extend until the election is actually held, and even longer if objections are filed.[15]

The window period is also a "Catch 22" for the union. Although the parties will technically have an obligation to bargain upon recognition, the knowledge that an election petition may be filed gives the employer little incentive to devote time and attention to bargaining during the first 45 days following recognition. Yet, if unit employees perceive that nothing is being accomplished in that initial bargaining, it stands to reason that they may be more likely to sign an election petition and even, ultimately, to vote against the union—even if they previously had supported it. That is precisely what the recognition bar is designed to avoid: putting the union in a position where it is "under exigent pressure to produce hot-house results or be turned out." Brooks, 348 U.S. at 100.[16]

---

15. According to statistics cited by the majority (see fn. 25 of majority decision), the median time for conducting an election during Fiscal Year 2006 was 39 days from the filing of the petition, with 94.2% of elections being conducted within 56 days. Assuming those time frames remain steady in the future, the union's status could remain unresolved for more than 3 months after recognition—or much longer, if objections are filed.

16. The majority contends that its "modification" of the recognition bar will not

Furthermore, as the Board has often recognized, support for a union is rarely unanimous. In any successful organizing campaign, there will likely be a minority of employees who opposed the union. See, e.g., Seattle Mariners, supra at 565. The majority's window period allows this minority to thwart, or at the very least work against, the majority, by creating a disincentive to meaningful collective bargaining at the same time it gives that minority the opportunity to marshal support for ousting the union. That is contrary to the principle of majority rule on which the Act is premised. . . .

The majority's new approach also guts the Board's contract-bar rules and their purpose to promote industrial stability. A contract between an employer and a voluntarily-recognized union will not bar a decertification petition or a petition by a rival union, unless the newly-imposed procedural requirements—notice to the Board's Regional Office and posting of a notice to employees for 45 days—are satisfied. Should an employer and a voluntarily-recognized union fail to comply with these requirements, even through ignorance or inadvertence, any contract they reach will be subject to collateral attack at any time, for years.

The majority claims that this sea change in the law is necessary in order to give appropriate weight to employee free choice. In support, the majority cites the general proposition that an election is the "preferred" method for determining majority status. And that statement is true so far as it goes.[18] It does not follow from that statement, however, that the existing voluntary recognition bar, applied since *Keller Plastics*, does not embody the appropriate balance of the policies at stake.

First, the majority appears to give no weight to the principle that voluntary recognition is "a favored element of national labor policy." See discussion above, at fn. 6 and accompanying text.

Second, although the majority attacks card-check procedures as risking minority recognition and coercive union conduct, card checks are "long accepted and sanctioned by the Board." Rockwell International Corp., 220 NLRB at 1263. . . . According to the majority, a "wait and see" period is needed because authorization cards are inherently unreliable. As the majority sees it, employees who sign authorization cards in support of a union are likely do so because they (1) want to avoid "offending the person who asks them to sign"; (2) are "susceptible to group pressure exerted at the moment of choice"; (3) were given "misinformation or a lack of information

be a disincentive to voluntary recognition, because the modification does not "encourage" or "guarantee" the filing of a petition— it simply "permits" it. As explained above, it is the uncertainty over whether a petition will be filed that itself interferes with initial bargaining.

18. We note, however, that none of the decisions cited by the majority for the proposition that an election is preferable to a card check hold that authorization cards were an inappropriate or inherently unreliable basis for recognizing a union or imposing a recognition bar. . . . [T]he Court in Gissel, 395 U.S. at 601, although recognizing that elections are "generally" preferred, rejected the employers' arguments that cards were too unreliable to reflect employee choice. The Court observed that, at the time of its 1969 decision, cards had already been in use under the Act for 30 years. Id. at 600 fn. 17.

about employees' representational options"; (4) "may not even understand the consequences of voluntary recognition until after it has been extended"; (5) are fooled by an employer's voluntary grant of union access and will "conclude they have no real choice but to accede to representation by that union"; and (6) "can and do change their minds about union representation" thereby calling into question any signature in support of the union. There is no genuine empirical support for these claims, and, indeed, the majority concedes that there is no evidence in the record that "the authorization cards were coercively obtained or otherwise tainted."[19]

Although the majority argues that card signings are "public actions" subject to "group pressures" at the time of signing, the same is true of employee antiunion petitions, on which the majority would rely to disrupt recognition and contract bar. In addition, as the Supreme Court stated in Gissel, "group pressures" may be "equally present in an election," and employees generally "should be bound by the clear language of what they sign...." Gissel, supra at 604, 606.

Third, the Act already provides recourse for employees who believe that their employer recognized a minority union or that they were coerced into signing authorization cards.... Union coercion in soliciting cards violates Section 8(b)(1)(A) ..... An employer's recognition of a minority union, even if in good faith, violates Section 8(a)(2), and the union's acceptance of recognition violates Section 8(b)(1)(A).... The standard remedy for those violations is to order the employer to cease and desist from recognizing and bargaining with the union, and the union to cease and desist from accepting recognition, until the union has been certified by

---

19. The majority cites as "empirical evidence of the lesser reliability of cards" a speech given by former Board Chairman McCulloch, illustrating a disparity between showings of union support based on cards and ensuing election results. McCulloch, A Tale of Two Cities: Or Law in Action, Proceedings of ABA Section of Labor Relations Law 14, 17 (1962). But the study proves nothing about the inherent reliability of cards as opposed to elections. The disparity could just as easily result from employer coercion during the election campaign as from union coercion during card solicitation. In that case, it would be the cards, not the election results, that truly reflected the employees' free choice. Indeed, the majority ignores the much more recent literature highlighting how employer antiunion conduct, and attendant delays, can undermine union support during lengthy election campaigns. See, e.g., Brudney, Neutrality Agreements, supra, 90 Iowa L. Rev. at 832–834 & fn. 58–63 (summarizing scholarly literature).

The majority also states that in Fiscal Year 2005, only 5 percent of elections resulted in the filing of objections. To the extent the majority is suggesting that employer coercion is rare in election campaigns, the majority's statistics do not account for situations in which employer conduct was not known to the union or in which the union, for whatever reason, chose not to file objections.

The majority also attacks neutrality agreements in which the union is allowed access to the employer's property. We fail to see, and the majority does not explain why an employer's agreement to allow access would lead employees to "reasonably conclude they have no real choice" but to support the union. In any event, the majority decision applies to any voluntary recognition based on a card check—not just recognition that follows a grant of access—and therefore sweeps far too broadly to be justified by purported concerns over union access.

the Board. See, e.g., Crest Containers Corp., 223 NLRB 739, 742 (1976)[20]
. . . .

Finally, the majority insists that employees need the 45–day window period to "debate among themselves," to "fully discuss their views," and "to solicit support for decertification." The majority thus implies that employees need an antiunion campaign in order to exercise free choice. Employees, however, have already had the entire period during which the union solicited authorization cards—which the majority agrees may be a substantial period of time—to discuss their views and to marshal support for or against the union. There is no need for a "window period" that provides an antiunion minority of employees a second chance to drum up enough support to oust the union. To the extent the majority is concerned about the absence of an employer-driven anti-union campaign, nothing in the Act prohibits the employer from remaining silent or requires the employer to actively oppose unionization.... Section 8(c) protects the employer's right to voice its opinion about unionization, but does not require the employer to do so. If the employer chooses to remain neutral during a card-solicitation campaign, employees themselves still have the right to campaign against the union. In short, "it is unclear how any limitation on [the employer's] behavior during a [union] organizational campaign could affect ... employees' Section 7 rights." Dana, supra at 559.[22]

V.

Voluntary recognition is "a favored element of national labor policy." Lyon & Ryan Ford, supra at 750. Yet, the majority decision relegates voluntary recognition to disfavored status by allowing a minority of employees to hijack the bargaining process just as it is getting started. Ultimately, the majority decision effectively discourages voluntary recognition altogether.

When an employer has voluntarily recognized a union based on a showing of majority support, the Board should honor the majority's choice and protect it for a reasonable period of time. In that manner, and with the accompanying safeguard of unfair labor practice sanctions, the Board has achieved the appropriate balance of effectuating employee free choice while reasonably protecting the stability of bargaining relationships. That balance was struck 40 years ago in *Keller Plastics* and has stood the test of

---

20. No unfair labor practice charges were filed in either of the present cases alleging either that the recognition itself or the neutrality and card-check agreements violated Sec. 8(a)(2). The majority concedes that, although the Petitioners claim that the cards were tainted, there has been no evidence developed or findings made on that issue.

22. The majority asserts, without any citation of authority, that "union card-solicitation campaigns have been accompanied by misinformation," and that misrepresentations "may go unchecked in the voluntary recognition process." But the same is true whether the campaign is pro-or anti-union, and whether it is a card solicitation or a prelude to an election. There is no perfect system. It is noteworthy that, in the election sphere, the Board has for the last 25 years chosen to leave misrepresentations largely unregulated. See Midland National Life Insurance Co., 263 NLRB 127 (1982).

time, both before the Board and in the courts of appeal. For all those reasons, we dissent from today's decision.

PROBLEMS FOR DISCUSSION

1. Review the reasons given by the Supreme Court in *Brooks v. NLRB* (in 1954), at pages 347–48 of the casebook, for holding that the selection of a union by representation election bars an election petition within a year and also bars an employer's withdrawal of recognition. Which of those reasons obtain as well when recognition follows the valid gathering of a majority of authorization cards? Do you agree with the majority or the dissenters in *Dana Corp.* concerning the force of the *Brooks* decision?

2. In the *Dana Corp.* case, the Board departed from what had for some 40 years been accepted as foundational principles of the "recognition bar" and the "contract bar" in cases of voluntary recognition. What explains the departure? Was it simply a change in the membership and preferred policies of the NLRB, without any change at all in the facts "on the ground"? Does the Board now believe that representation elections are uniformly to be preferred to authorization-card solicitations, even when the latter are altogether valid? Although the *Dana* guidelines are to be applied whether or not recognition of the union is based upon a neutrality agreement, does the Board's decision manifest a suspicion of such agreements?

3. If, as in *Dana Corp.*, an employer's recognition of a union based on authorization cards is not illegal favoritism in violation of section 8(a)(2), and if the union's solicitation of the cards was not accompanied by illegal coercion (by the union or the employer), what are the reasons for postponing effective bargaining (for at least two or three months) at the request of 30 percent of the unit? Are these reasons convincing? Is the Board majority correct in believing that effective bargaining will normally take place during the notification and election period, and how does it (or the dissenting members) know?

4. In light of the Board's solicitation of many *amicus curiae* briefs; its departure from its decades of adjudicatory precedent; its newly declared requirements (meant to apply to all employers, generically) for informing the Board and posting notices, and the precise content thereof; its selection of an "artificial" number of days within which to allow for the filing of an election petition; and the prospective application of its decision—did the Board in *Dana Corp.* actually and invalidly make a "rule" without properly utilizing statutory rulemaking proceedings? *Cf. NLRB v. Wyman–Gordon*, at casebook p. 149. If the *Dana Corp.* guidelines are meant to apply to all employers and to all unions, ought not the Board have held legislative-like rulemaking proceedings?

Page 373. Add to Problems for Discussion:

5. After the expiration of a collective agreement, a number of employees submitted a decertification petition to the NLRB, with a copy to the employer. The petition read, "We the employees of [the company] wish for a vote to remove the union." The employer has compared the signatures on the petition with those on the employees' most recent paycheck receipts and determined that the petition had been signed by more than 50 percent of the employees in the bargaining unit. May it withdraw recognition? See Wurtland Nursing & Rehab Center, 351 NLRB No. 50 (2007). Should it make a difference if the words "to remove the union" were not used?

PART THREE

Negotiation of the Collective Bargaining Agreement

II. Duty to Bargain in Good Faith

Page 412. In Problem 2:

The citation to *International Chemical Workers v. NLRB* (on reconsideration) is 467 F.3d 742 (9th Cir. 2006).

Page 420. Add to Problem 6:

Northern Indiana Pub. Serv. Co., 347 NLRB No. 17 (2006).

Page 440. Add at the end of the Problem for Discussion:

Cf. Mail Contractors of America v. NLRB, 514 F.3d 27 (D.C. Cir. 2008) (after bargaining to impasse, the employer unilaterally invoked its proffered management-rights provision and altered the "relay points" at which company truckers pass along their truck to another company driver, and so affect the wages of both; the NLRB, invoking *McClatchy Newspapers,* held this to violate § 8(a)(5)). The *McClatchy* court of appeals refused to enforce, finding the Board decision "arbitrary and capricious," and stated *inter alia*:

> ... [T]he Board held MCA ran afoul of *McClatchy* when it unilaterally imposed a provision reserving the right to change relay points. That decision was arbitrary and capricious for three reasons. First, the management rights provision at issue is utterly unlike the provision in *McClatchy* or the provision at issue in any subsequent case to which the Board has applied *McClatchy.* Second, it is inconceivable the provision will jeopardize collective bargaining in the affected unit—the stated concern underlying *McClatchy.* Finally, the Board's decision here would impinge upon the employer's ability to run its business more severely than did *McClatchy* itself or any of its sequellae....

In affirming the ALJ, the Board rather limply stated only that "here, as in *McClatchy*, the unilateral change had a direct effect on wages," *MCA,* 347 N.L.R.B. No. 88, at 1 n. 2, without any more particularized examination of the significance of that effect. The Board gave no reason to believe the relay point provision here at issue would impede collective bargaining. Therefore, we think it necessary to reiterate a point we made in *McClatchy IV*: The Board must proceed cautiously in applying the *McClatchy* doctrine, taking care to tether its applications to the pragmatic justification for that decision, namely, to facilitate the process of collective bargaining.

IV.   ROLE OF THE STRIKE & THIRD–PARTY IMPASSE RESOLUTION

Page 504.   Add at the end of Question 2:

United Steelworkers v. Cooper Tire & Rubber Co., 474 F.3d 271 (6th Cir. 2007) (union can represent retirees in an arbitration sought to enforce retiree medical benefits only with the consent of the retirees).

Page 505.   Add to Problem 5:

Would it be an unfair labor practice under § 8(a)(5) for an employer to repudiate a collective agreement's provision for a "card check" of employee union sentiment at future-acquired facilities? Supervalu, Inc., 351 NLRB No. 41 (2007).

PART FOUR

STRIKES, PICKETING AND BOYCOTTS

I. RIGHTS OF EMPLOYEE PROTESTERS UNDER THE NLRA

Page 545. Add to Problems for Discussion:

7. After the cited NLRB decision in *Guardsmark,* the Court of Appeals held, contrary to the Board, that a broad "no fraternization" rule violated § 8(a)(1). Guardsmark, LLC v. NLRB, 475 F.3d 369 (D.C. Cir. 2007).

* * *

9. May a union steward be dismissed for signing an employee's name to a grievance—the contract requiring all grievances to be signed by the person aggrieved—without the employee's knowledge in order to preserve the claim of contractual violation under the collective agreement's time limits? NLRB v. Allied Aviation Fueling of Dallas LP, 490 F.3d 374 (5th Cir. 2007). May an employee be dismissed for sending an anonymous letter of collective protest to management the return addressee for which (i.e., a fellow employee) was falsely identified? International Union, UAW v. NLRB, 514 F.3d 574 (6th Cir. 2008). Should it make a difference that the writer did so without any intent to injure that worker but only to assure that the letter would be opened as the writer was well known as an advocate for unionization?

10. Ventnor Trucking, a unionized company, has acquired Park Place Trucking, a non-unionized company. It intends to close one terminal and integrate the workforces. The union has been bargaining with Ventnor for months but neither party has revealed any information about their proposals or possible resolutions. Seven of Ventnor's drivers, upon reporting for work and learning that a bargaining session was scheduled at a local motel, decided to delay their deliveries to go to the motel and get "straight answers," as they put it, to whether they would retain their jobs, and, if so, at what rate of pay and with what seniority. They proceeded to do so, but received no information. They went back to the terminal; the excursion took a total of about three hours. As they prepared to make their runs they were informed by Ventnor that they were discharged. Do the discharges violate § 8(a)(3)? Northeast Beverage Corp., 349 NLRB No. 110 (2007).

Page 580.   After *Jefferson Standard*:

Five Star Transportation, Inc., 349 NLRB No. 8 (2007), *enf'd,* 522 F.3d 46 (1st Cir. 2008). A school district's contract with a unionized transportation contractor, First Student, expired and the district was considering a lower bid by a non-union company, Five Star. The union protested to the school board; it also called a meeting of the drivers in which it circulated news accounts of seven years' previous of Five Star having hired a sex offender and a driver with a record of drunk driving. A number of drivers wrote personal letters to the school board to protest the award of the contract to Five Star, but to no avail. Five Star was awarded the contract. It had learned of the letters of protest and secured them from the school board under the state's Freedom of Information Act. Seventeen drivers who had worked for First Student applied for jobs with Five Star. Five Star hired the six who had not written, and refused to hire the eleven who had. The ALJ held that two drivers—Candy Ocasio and Charles Kupras—did not engage in protected activity, but the remaining nine had. In a 2–1 decision the Board sustained the ALJ as to those two but held that an additional three had also engaged in unprotected activity.

Turning to the two, the Board addressed what they had written. Ocasio's letter said,

> The safety of the children in Belchertown are at stake. It has been know in the past that the company has hired not only unlicensed bus drivers, but there has been two incidents of them hiring a convicted child Molester, and a driver who was driving a school bus with a half dozen children under the influence. They have also been known to be unreliable with buses being unsafe. . . .
>
> Would you feel safe putting your children on these buses knowing what you know? I know I would not and will not be placing my children on these buses if indeed they will be the school busing transportation company for this town.

And Kupras had written much the same. These letters focused, said the Board majority,

> solely on general safety concerns and did not indicate that their concerns were related to the safety of the drivers as opposed to others. As the Board recently reiterated, consistent with long standing precedent, merely raising safety or quality of care concerns on behalf of non-employee third parties is not protected conduct under the Act. *See Waters of Orchard Park*, 341 NLRB 642 (2004). Further, we are not persuaded that these two letters should be interpreted as raising the drivers' common concerns *simply* because they were written as part of the drivers' letter-writing campaign. *Instead, we determine whether certain communications are protected by examining the communications themselves.* [Italics added.]

The remaining three had made much of these prior incidents as well, but they had gone on to call Five Star "sub-standard," "reckless," incompetent, careless, and negligent. These letters, held the NLRB majority, though they did refer to the labor dispute, "disparaged" Five Star and were disloyal within the meaning of *Jefferson Standard*. Member Liebman, dissenting, pointed out that the duty of loyalty is implied out of the contractual relationship of employer and employee; one has no duty of loyalty to a company not one's employer. The majority responded that "Just as an employer legitimately wants extant employees to be loyal, so a prospective employer legitimately wants prospective employees to be loyal. In both cases, the goal is the same—not to have disloyal employees on the payroll."

PROBLEMS FOR DISCUSSION

1. Is it true that school bus drivers have no statutory interest as employees in the safety of the children they transport?

2. Is it true that whether a letter or other form of protest is for statutory "mutual aid or protection" must be determined exclusively by examining the content of the communication? *Compare* Petrochem Insulation v. NLRB, 240 F.3d 26 (D.C. Cir. 2001) (construction union's scheme of filing objections, on environmental grounds, to the issuance of zoning and construction permits to non-unionized contractors was protected; the union's purpose, revealed only in an internal report, was to use the permit process to force the affected companies to meet union wage and benefit standards), *with* Orchard Park Health Care Center, cited above and in the casebook, Question 4 at p. 570 (call by nurse to hotline to get water for dehydrated patients was not statutorily protected).

3. *Jefferson Standard* was defended in a contemporaneous student note on the ground that public product disparagement is likely to impose a reputational cost on the employer that survives the termination of the labor dispute. *Recent cases*, 66 HARV. L. REV. 1321 (1953). Does that rationale apply to *Five Star Transp.*?

4. Might any other future employer lawfully refuse to hire any of these five on the ground of their having written these letters?

5. If, in response to criticism of the union on a website devoted to discussion of an organizing effort at the town's major employer, a union activist said that management "had no good ability" to run the company, could he be discharged for it? *See* Endicott Interconnect Technologies, Inc. v. NLRB, 453 F.3d 532 (D.C. Cir. 2006).

Page 583.   Question 3, following the discussion of *Trompler*:

The Fourth Circuit rejected the Board's—and Judge Easterbrook's—reasoning, arguing that, absent a requirement of reasonableness, "employees could control the hiring and firing of their managers by walking out over every managerial change." *Smithfield Packing Co., Inc. v. NLRB*, 510 F.3d 507, 519 (4th Cir. 2007). In that case, the workforce of a contractor walked off the job to protest the removal of supervisors who had defended them against efforts by management to discipline them for alleged safety violations. The Board found that Smithfield had violated § 8(a)(1) by having its security force—consisting of a private police force authorized under North Carolina law to bear weapons and to exercise public police authority within the plant—threaten, beat, and falsely arrest the protesters. The Fourth Circuit refused to enforce on the ground that the walk-out was unprotected: "walkouts and strikes are unreasonable means of protesting personnel decisions regarding management: such actions cause financial injury to the employer." *Id.* at 520.

Page 584. Add to Problem 7:

Assume that a majority of the employees of a medical clinic have joined a union, that it has made a demand for recognition, that that demand has been rejected, and that a group of employees—on their off-duty hours—picket at the patient and visitor entrance for 45 minutes demanding union recognition. No notice was given under § 8(g) of the Act. The picketing was peaceful; there was no blockage to the flow of traffic. May the employees be discharged? See Correctional Med. Services, Inc., 349 NLRB No. 111 (2007).

* * *

9. In 2002, a group of non-unionized truck drivers became increasingly dissatisfied and angry with their management. They agreed that one of their number, Emerson Young, would collect their grievances from them and assemble them in a letter to higher management, and also send that letter to their employer's largest local customer—one known to be sensitive to bad publicity. The list of grievances was long and it included the following:

> Some drivers are being asked to fix their log books to make extra runs. These drivers are being asked by dispatchers and management to do these runs and either fix their log books or turn their heads on it. Mr. John Cox once said he would not go to jail for fixing log books for anyone. Well Mr. Cox pack your suitcase, it has and is presently being done at 001.

After investigation the company learned that Young had sent the letter with input from two employees the company was able to identify out of the group, John Jolliff and Steven Daniels; the company fired all three. An unfair labor practice complaint was filed. In 2003 the ALJ found the three to have engaged in statutorily protected concert of action for mutual aid and protection, crediting the testimony of the three employees.

Three years later, in a 2–1 decision, the Board held the letter unprotected in that it had been uttered with malice:

> The evidence supports a finding that the employees made this statement with knowledge of its falsity or at least reckless disregard for its truth. The employees' letter affirmatively represents that management "asked" employees to "fix" logbooks, but employee Jolliff admitted that management never made such a request [of him], and there was no evidence whatsoever to contradict this explicit admission.

Mr. Jolliff did not write the letter, Mr. Young did. Young was given the task of listing the complaints given to him by a number of drivers only one of whom was Mr. Jolliff. Is the Board's decision based on substantial evidence? See Jolliff v. NLRB, 513 F.3d 600 (6th Cir. 2008); International Union, UAW v. NLRB, 514 F.3d 574 (6th Cir. 2008); see also Center Construction Co. v. NLRB, 482 F.3d 425 (6th Cir. 2007), on what constitutes substantial evidence when the Board disagrees with an ALJ's findings of fact.

Page 613. Add to Problems for Discussion:

4. May an employer decide to replace its entire striking workforce with permanent replacements and to keep the fact that it was doing so a secret from the union until that end was accomplished? *See* Church Homes, Inc., No. 128, 350 NLRB No. 21 (2007), *on remand from* New England Health Care Employees Union v. NLRB, 448 F.3d 189 (2d Cir. 2006).

Page 625. Add to Problems for Discussion:

7. In the face of an economic strike at Graduated Plastics, the company hired fifty strike replacements. Each signed the following:

> I [name of replacement] hereby accept employment with Graduated Plastics, Inc., as a permanent replacement for a striker who is presently on strike against Graduated Plastics. I understand that my employment with Graduated Plastics may be terminated by myself or by Graduated Plastics at any time, with or without cause. I further understand that my employment may be terminated as a result of a strike settlement agreement reached between Graduated Plastics and the union or by order of the National Labor Relations Board.

Fifty strikers have made an unconditional offer to return to their jobs currently held by these strike replacements. Must Graduated Plastics return them to their jobs? *See* Jones Plastic & Engineering Co. (Camden Div.), 351 NLRB No. 11 (2007) (overruling Target Rock Corp., 324 NLRB 373 (1997), *enf'd*, 172 F.3d 921 (D.C. Cir. 1998)).

8. During negotiations and after the union membership had voted to authorize a strike, the employer informed the union that it would impose a lockout at the expiration of the collective agreement. The union offered to extend the collective agreement pending agreement on a successor contract. The company refused. The company requested from the union a no-strike assurance. It refused. As employees reported for the shift prior to the contact's expiration, they were given and asked to sign the following by the company:

> I give [the company] my unconditional offer to return to work. This means that I will not strike or otherwise withhold services or fail to perform my work responsibilities to the fullest of my abilities in support of the union's demands in connection with the current negotiations for a new collective-bargaining agreement. I understand that if I violate this unconditional offer to return to work, I may be subject to discipline.

Has the company committed an unfair labor practice? *See* Boehringer Ingelheim Vetmedica, Inc., 350 NLRB No. 60 (2007).

II. CONSTITUTIONAL LIMITATIONS ON GOVERNMENT REGULATION

Page 662. After *Overstreet*:

Both *Kentov* (p. 653–654) and *Overstreet* were cases dealing with the issuance of preliminary § 10(*l*) injunctions. The ultimate disposition of "street theater" to protest the labor policies of a hospital's contractor—by conducting a mock funeral on a public sidewalk one hundred feet from a hospital entrance, distributing leaflets headed "Going to [the named] Hospital Should Not Be a Grave Decision," and playing funereal music as a prop coffin was carried by pallbearers accompanied by a "Grim Reaper"—was reached in *Sheet Metal Workers v. NLRB*, 491 F.3d 429 (D.C. Cir. 2007). The court determined that "the mock funeral lies somewhere between the lawful handbilling in *DeBartolo* and unlawful picketing or patrolling," and so had to reach the ultimate question of whether it was coercive or " 'intimidating'." Contrary to the Labor Board majority, the court of appeals held that it was not. The funeral was conducted well away from the entrance and was conducted with the decorum that befit a funeral.

> The Board would have us believe, in the words of the ALJ, the mock funeral "forced" patrons to "cross a death march" in order to get to the Hospital, as if the horrors of Bataan in 1942 were being reenacted in front of the Hospital. The procession was not only orderly, the protesters went out of their way to convey a law-abiding, and therefore nonthreatening, attitude.... Their message may have been unsettling or even offensive to someone visiting a dying relative, ... but unsettling and even offensive speech is not without the protection of the First Amendment.

III. NATIONAL LABOR RELATIONS ACT

Page 750. Add to Problem for Discussion:

In Problem 6(a), the Board adopted the ALJ's decision, 348 NLRB No. 72 (2006) (2–1).

PART FIVE

ADMINISTRATION OF THE COLLECTIVE AGREEMENT

III. JUDICIAL ENFORCEMENT OF COLLECTIVE AGREEMENTS

Page 826.   After *Warrior & Gulf*:

Arbitrability continues on occasion to prove vexing. In *International Brotherhood of Elect. Workers, Local 21 v. Illinois Bell Tel. Co.*, 491 F.3d 685 (7th Cir. 2007), the court ordered a dispute over a new system of performance evaluation to proceed to arbitration even though no provision of the collective agreement addressed the issue and, according to the dissenting judge, the parties had bargained about it. If that was so, what was there to arbitrate? And *per contra* in *Local 827, IBEW v. Verizon New Jersey, Inc.*, 458 F.3d 305 (3d Cir. 2006), a change in overtime assignment from the practice prevailing for over twenty-five years was held inarbitrable.

Page 839.   Add to Problems for Discussion:

Add to Problem 2.

Assume the dues check-off provision included the following:

The Check Off Agreement and system heretofore entered into and established by the Employer and the Union for the check-off of Union dues by voluntary authorization, as set forth in Exhibit 2, attached to and made part of this Agreement, shall be continued in effect for the term of this Agreement.

Would the employer's unilateral cessation of dues remission at the expiration of the collective agreement violate § 8(a)(5)? *See* Hacienda Hotel, Inc., 351 NLRB No. 32 (2007).

* * *

5. The collective bargaining agreement between Balrog Bearings, Inc., and its employees' union expired on September 30. It contained the following in its grievance arbitration provision:

[T]he Arbitrator shall determine the question of fact as to the occurrence or non-occurrence of the circumstances upon which the discipline was based. If it is determined that such circumstances were as found by the Employer, the Employer's decision as to the kind and degree of discipline shall not be disturbed unless there is an express finding that the kind and degree of discipline was unreasonable.

On September 25, mechanic Chris Norwood signed out for a set of tools. On October 5, he reported the tools lost. After investigation, the company learned that he was not authorized to sign out for those tools and suspected that he'd stolen them. He was discharged on October 15. The union has grieved the discharge, the company has rejected the grievance, the union has noticed the grievance for arbitration, and the company has refused to arbitrate. The union sues to secure an order to arbitrate. How should the court rule in view of the September 30 expiration of the labor contract? *See* Operating Engineers Local 3 v. Newmont Mining Corp., 476 F.3d 690 (9th Cir. 2007).

Page 844. After the discussion of *Michigan Family Resources*:

The Sixth Circuit *en banc* accepted Judge Sutton's analysis. Michigan Family Resources v. SEIU, 475 F.3d 746 (6th Cir. 2007) (en banc). Nevertheless, the courts are still, at times, at 6s and 7s on how much deference is due an arbitrator under *Enterprise Wheel*. *E.g.*, Cuna Mut. Ins. Soc. v. Office & Professional Employees Int'l Union, 443 F.3d 556 (7th Cir. 2006) (award will be enforced so long as arbitrator read the contract, despite arguably contrary reading by another arbitrator); Salem Hospital v. Massachusetts Nurses Ass'n, 449 F.3d 234 (1st Cir. 2006) (vacation of award affirmed where arbitrator's reading of the contract was not plausible).

IV. THE ROLE OF THE NATIONAL LABOR RELATIONS BOARD AND THE ARBITRATOR DURING THE TERM OF A COLLECTIVE AGREEMENT

Page 885. After *Olin*:

Kvaerner Philadelphia Shipyard, Inc., 347 NLRB No. 36 (2006), deferring to an arbitrator's sustaining a discharge, challenged under § 8(a)(3), even though the arbitrator indicated that he or she thought the conduct was statutorily protected. Member Liebman dissented on the ground that the arbitrator's decision was "palpably wrong".

Page 895. After the discussion of *Wright v. Universal Maritime Serv. Corp.*:

On February 19, 2008, the U.S. Supreme Court granted a writ of certiorari in *Pyett v. 14 Penn Plaza LLC,* 498 F.3d 88 (2d Cir. 2007), No. 07–581. A group of older employees, represented by the union under a multi-employer collective bargaining agreement, were transferred by their employer (a building service and cleaning contractor) to jobs with lesser overtime opportunities and complained *inter alia* of age discrimination in that decision. The transfer was the result of the company's decision to subcontract security work. The collective agreement provided that:

> There shall be no discrimination against any present or future employee by reason of race, creed, color, age, disability, national origin, sex, union membership, or any characteristic protected by law, including, but not limited to, claims made pursuant to Title VII of the Civil Rights Act, the Americans with Disabilities Act, the Age Discrimination in Employment Act, the New York State Human Rights Law, the New York City Human Rights Code, New Jersey Law Against Discrimination, New Jersey Conscientious Employee Protection Act, Connecticut Fair Employer Practices Act, or any other similar laws, rules or regulations. All such claims shall be subject to the grievance and arbitration procedure (Articles V and VI [of the CBA]) as the sole and exclusive remedy for violations. Arbitrators shall apply appropriate law in rendering decisions based upon claims of discrimination.

The union pursued these employees' grievances to arbitration, but not on the theory of age discrimination, and lost. Meanwhile, the employees sought to pursue their age discrimination claim in federal court in an action against their employer and the owners of the building in which they had worked. The defendants moved to dismiss or, in the alternative, to compel arbitration. The district court denied the motion on the strength of precedent in the Court of Appeals for the Second Circuit holding that the union-negotiated waiver of statutory rights was unenforceable, and the Court of Appeals affirmed. Thus the writ was granted on the following question:

> Is an arbitration clause contained in a collective bargaining agreement, freely negotiated by a union and an employer, which clearly and unmistakably waives the union members' right to a judicial forum for their statutory discrimination claims, enforceable?

One element of the case may, or may not, feature in the Court's disposition—*i.e.*, the decision to reassign the older workers was the consequence of the employer's decision to subcontract security work. The collective agreement prohibits all subcontracting. Thus the union had to agree to waive that prohibition.

Note that the collective agreement mandates arbitration as the exclusive remedy for employee claims of discrimination based upon, *inter alia*, union membership. This would bar employee recourse to the NLRB with charges of a violation of § 8(a)(3)—and indeed when such alleged employer discrimination is allegedly induced by the union in violation of § 8(b)(2). Should such a "waiver" of resort to the Board and the courts be enforceable? (Comparable issues are of course raised by mandatory arbitration of claims—discrimination and otherwise—based upon other federal and state laws.) How strong is the policy opposing exclusive mandatory arbitration, given the willingness of the Board to defer to the jurisdiction of labor arbitrators in advance (see *Olin Corp.*, at p. 880 of the casebook) and the awards of arbitrators after the fact (see *United Technologies*, at p. 896)?

Page 903. Following *United Technologies*:

In *United Cerebral Palsy*, 347 NLRB No. 60 (2006), the Board refused to defer to arbitration a § 8(a)(5) complaint concerning an employer's issuance of a policy handbook that was completely at odds with the terms of the existing collective bargaining agreement.

Page 926. After *Jacobs Mfg.*:

The Court of Appeals for the First Circuit approached the duty to bargain during a contract's term by applying a test of "contract coverage." *Bath Marine Draftsmen's Ass'n v. NLRB*, 475 F.3d 14 (1st Cir. 2007). This is in conflict with established Board doctrine. As Chairman Battista explained, dissenting in *Provena Hospitals*, 350 NLRB No. 64 (2007), under the Board's "waiver" test

> The employer's conduct is unlawful unless the contract clause "clearly and unmistakably" waives the union's right to bargain. Unless the clause explicitly covers the action and clearly takes away the union's right to bargain, a violation is found.... Under ... [the "contract coverage" test] where there is a contract clause that is relevant to the dispute, it can reasonably be said that the parties *have bargained* about the subject and have reached some accord. Thus, there has been no refusal to bargain. In sum, the issue is not whether the union has *waived* its right to bargain. The issue is whether the union and the employer *have bargained* concerning the relevant subject matter. If so, the Board and the courts should honor the fruit of that bargaining. [Italics in original.]

He argued for the adoption of the "contract coverage" approach expanding on it in this way:

> [I] am not saying that broad and general language in a management rights clause (e.g. "the right to operate the business") would show that a given subject matter is covered by the contract. On the other hand, if the language can reasonably be interpreted as dealing with the subject matter at issue, i.e. it can reasonably be said that the subject matter is covered, that can suffice. The test is not "clear and unmistakable."

The majority, consisting of the two Democratic Board members, maintained adherence to the "clear and unmistakable" waiver standard relying in part on the long-established character of the rule going back to *Tide Water Associated Oil Co.*, 85 NLRB 1096 (1949), and approved by the Supreme Court in *NLRB v. C & C Plywood*, 385 U.S. 421, 87 S.Ct. 559, 17 L.Ed.2d 486 (1967), and *Metropolitan Edison Co. v. NLRB*, 460 U.S. 693, 103 S.Ct. 1467, 75 L.Ed.2d 387 (1983). They explained it this way:

> The clear-and-unmistakable waiver standard, then, requires bargaining partners to unequivocally and specifically express their mutual intention to permit unilateral employer action with respect to a particular employment term, notwithstanding the statutory

duty to bargain that would otherwise apply. The standard reflects the Board's policy choice, grounded in the Act, in favor of collective bargaining concerning changes in working conditions that might precipitate labor disputes.

They opined that there had been no change in the nature of labor relations, "no new experience" to justify the abandonment of so long-settled a principle. On the contrary,

Changing to a "contract-coverage" standard would very likely complicate the collective-bargaining process and increase the likelihood of labor disputes. The waiver standard, on the other hand, effectively requires the parties to focus on particular subjects over which the employer seeks the right to act unilaterally. Such a narrow focus has two clear benefits. First, it encourages the parties to bargain only over subjects of importance at the time and to leave other subjects to future bargaining. Second, if a waiver is won—in clear and unmistakable language—the employer's right to take future unilateral action should be apparent to all concerned. A "contract-coverage" standard, in contrast, creates an incentive for employers to seek contractual language that might be construed as authorizing unilateral action on subjects of no present concern, requires unions to be wary of agreeing to such provisions, and invites future disputes about the scope of the contractual provision.

Chairman Battista also argued to the conflict with the Board's policy deferring to arbitration in section 8(a)(5) cases where the arbitrator's disposition might resolve the unfair labor practice claim:

The Board, viewing a case through the "waiver" prism, would find a 8(a)(5) violation. An arbitrator, viewing the same case through normal principles of contract interpretation, would find that the clause privileges the conduct, albeit not "clearly and unmistakably" so. Phrased differently, the Board would start with the proposition that the unilateral change is unlawful, unless the right to bargain has been "clearly" and "unmistakably" waived. An arbitrator would ask whether the union has met its burden of establishing a breach of contract. Thus, there is a danger of different results depending on the choice of forum.

The Board majority took note of the argument in a footnote:

Even if the Board's approach to management-rights clauses diverged from the approach of an individual arbitrator, or from the prevailing approach among arbitrators as a class, there is no compelling reason why the Board should follow the lead of arbitrators, rather than the other way around. It is the Board's duty to enforce the Act and effectuate its policies. See *Radioear Corp.*, 199 NLRB 1161, 1162–1163 (1972) (dissenting opinion of Members Fanning and Jenkins, disagreeing with majority's deferral to arbitration). See also Gorman & Finkin, supra, *Basic Text on Labor Law* Sec. 20.16 and 630 (There are those who charge that—by deferring to arbitration, where tenets of contract construction will quite commonly favor the employer more than with the "clear and unmistakable waiver" principle under the Labor Act—the NLRB is tacitly acquiescing in a modification of the substantive standard of "waiver" to a degree that constitutes an abdication of the Board's function as a congressionally created administrative agency with a public charge.).

PROBLEM FOR DISCUSSION

The current collective agreement between Whole Grain Bakeries and the Baker's Union for the period 2006–2009 contains the following Management Rights clause as had all predecessor agreements:

> The Company also retains the right to promulgate, enforce, and periodically modify or change written rules and regulations, not in conflict with the expressed provisions of this Agreement, as it may from time to time deem best for the purposes of maintaining order, discipline, safety, and/or effective operation of the Company and, after advance notice thereof to the Union and the Employees, to require compliance therewith by Employees. It is recognized that the Union reserves the right to question the reasonableness of these rules or regulations issued pursuant to this particular paragraph through the Grievance and Arbitration procedure herein within the time limits set forth in such procedure after receipt of a copy of such rules or regulations, and such rules or regulations shall not be stayed pending grievance or arbitration procedures.

In 2001, during the term of the predecessor collective agreement, 2000–2003, the company adopted an absenteeism policy governing *inter alia* employees who fail to notify the employer two hours before an assigned shift that they will be absent and who fail to report for work ("no call/no show" policy). The third "occurrence" of a no call/no show would result in automatic dismissal, referred to as "three strikes and you're out." There was no negotiation with the Union about the policy nor did the Union protest against it.

During the negotiation for the collective agreement 2003–2006, the Company raised the persistence of the absenteeism problem. The Union proposed that employees be allowed to cash out accumulated sick leave and the Company agreed. During the negotiation for the collective agreement 2006–2009, the Company again raised the absenteeism problem arguing that the accumulation of sick leave had had no effect and was costly. The agreement abrogated the accumulation of sick leave.

In neither the negotiations for the contract 2003–2006 nor 2006–2009 did either party mention a change in the "three-strikes and you're out" absenteeism policy announced unilaterally by the Company in 2001. In June 2008, the Company announced a change in its absenteeism policy: henceforth a *second* occurrence would result in automatic dismissal.

Were the General Counsel to issue a complaint of violation of section 8(a)(5), should the Board hear the case or refer it to arbitration? If the former, what should the result be? If the latter, how should the arbitrator rule? Were the arbitrator to hold that the contract covered the dispute and that the new rule was reasonable, should the Board defer to the award? *Local 15, IBEU v. Exelon Corp.*, 495 F.3d 779 (7th Cir. 2007).

PART SEVEN

LABOR AND THE ANTITRUST LAWS

Page 998. Add to Problems for Discussion:

5. Road construction is done by contractors who belong to the Construction Contractors' Association (CCA). The CCA has a collective agreement with the Construction Workers' Union (CWU). It provides that no member contractor may

> contract any work covered by this Agreement to be done at the site of construction, alterations, repairs, or any new construction or any other work to any person, firm or company that does not have an existing labor agreement or will not sign an agreement, with the Union covering such work within the scope of this Agreement.

Road Chandlers, Inc. is a company that maintains the safety conditions for workers and road construction units: it puts up barrels and other barriers, signs and road markers to direct traffic away from workers, supplies flagmen, and the like. It has been unable to contract for the provision of services to any road construction contractor as all the roadwork is done by CCA members and Road Chandlers' employees are represented by a union other than CWU. It has sued the CCA and CWU for violation of the Sherman Act. The defendants have moved to dismiss. How should the court rule? *See* United Rentals Highway Technologies, Inc. v. Indiana Contractors, Inc., 518 F.3d 526 (7th Cir. 2008).

PART EIGHT

FEDERALISM AND LABOR RELATIONS

I. PREEMPTION OF STATE LABOR LAW: AN OVERVIEW

Page 1021–22.   Add to Problems for Discussion:

8. Amy O'Leary is the assistant manager of the Dew Drop Inn & Convention Center. Upon a union's commencing an organizing drive the manager of the facility, Sneed Hearn, ordered her to discharge the five employees most prominent in the organizing effort. O'Leary refused and was discharged, for not being a "team player." She has sued in state court on two tort theories: violation of public policy and infliction of emotional distress. On the former, she notes that the state has enacted a "little Wagner Act" that tracks the NLRA as amended in 1947 and 1959 verbatim, including a statement of policy that commits the state to "encourage the practice and procedure of collective bargaining." Is the lawsuit preempted? *See Lontz v. Tharp*, 220 W.Va. 282, 647 S.E.2d 718 (2007).

9. Grosvenor State Bank is located on the corner of a busy intersection in the downtown area of Fisher City. The bank's employees are unionized and are engaged in an economic strike. The bank has employed permanent replacements. The union has positioned a large inflated balloon in the shape of a rat to protest the hiring of strike replacements: the rat is ten feet tall; it is placed on a grassy strip between the sidewalk and the street directly across from the bank's main entrance; and it bears in large letters the statement, "Rats in the Bank—Unfair." Fisher City has a Signage Ordinance that provides in part:

> *Prohibited Signs.* All signs not permitted by this Ordinance are hereby prohibited with the following signs specifically prohibited:
>
> . . .
>
> > 2.   Banners, pennants, streamers, pinwheels, or similar devices; vehicle signs; portable signs, balloon signs or other inflated signs (excepting grand opening signs); and searchlights (excepting grand opening signs), displayed for the purpose of attracting the attention of pedestrians and motorists; unless otherwise excepted.

The bank has filed a complaint with the police department demanding that the rat be removed, and the police have issued a summons against the union's president for violation of the ordinance. The union's president has moved to dismiss on grounds of federal preemption. How should the court rule? *See* State v. De Angelo, 396 N.J.Super. 23, 930 A.2d 1236 (App.Div.2007).

10.   North Dakota is a so-called "Right to Work" state. N.D. Cent. Code § 34–01–14 provides:

> The right of persons to work may not be denied or abridged on account of membership or nonmembership in any labor union or labor organization, and all contracts in negation or abrogation of such right are hereby declared to be invalid, void, and unenforceable.

However, the "free rider" problem this engenders is dealt with in § 34–01–14.1:

> As used in this section, "actual representation expenses" are only those actual expenses which are sustained by a labor union or labor organization in processing any grievance of a nonunion employee. For grievances arising from actions occurring while an employee was a member of a bargaining unit of a management entity with which a labor union or labor organization has a contract, but while that employee was not a member of that union or organization, that labor union or labor organization shall collect actual representation expenses from that nonunion employee. Actual representation expenses may be assessed only in instances in which a nonunion employee has specifically requested in writing to use representation by the labor union organization.

Is § 34–01–14.1 preempted? *See* NLRB v. North Dakota, 504 F.Supp.2d 750 (D.N.D. 2007).

Page 1023.   Add to Problem 2:

2.   A casino has summoned the police to remove labor protesters from a sidewalk adjacent to its property claiming the sidewalk to be private property. An unfair labor practice complaint has issued and the NLRB has found the casino's property interest in the sidewalk not such as to allow it to exclude a labor protest. The casino argues, however, that its summoning of the police was protected by the First Amendment—as preliminary to litigation, which is expressive activity protected by the First Amendment, as well as a means of influencing the city's law enforcement practices—which precludes that action from being an unfair labor practice. How should the Board rule? *See* Venetian Casino Resort, L.L.C. v. NLRB, 484 F.3d 601 (D.C. Cir. 2007).

Page 1030.   Insert before Problems for Discussion:

Chamber of Commerce v. Brown
___ U.S. ___, 128 S.Ct. 2408 (2008).

■ Justice STEVENS delivered the opinion of the Court.

A California statute known as "Assembly Bill 1889" (AB 1889) prohibits several classes of employers that receive state funds from using the funds "to assist, promote, or deter union organizing." *See* Cal. Govt. Code Ann. §§ 16645–16649 (West Supp.2008). The question presented to us is whether two of its provisions—§ 16645.2, applicable to grant recipients, and § 16645.7, applicable to private employers receiving more than $10,000 in program funds in any year—are pre-empted by federal law mandating that certain zones of labor activity be unregulated.

I

As set forth in the preamble, the State of California enacted AB 1889 for the following purpose:

> "It is the policy of the state not to interfere with an employee's choice about whether to join or to be represented by a labor union. For this reason, the state should not subsidize efforts by an employer to assist, promote, or deter union organizing. It is the intent of the Legislature in enacting this act to prohibit an employer from using state funds and facilities for the purpose of influencing employees to support or oppose unionization and to prohibit an employer from seeking to influence employees to support or oppose unionization while those employees are performing work on a state contract." 2000 Cal. Stats. ch. 872, § 1.

AB 1889 forbids certain employers that receive state funds—whether by reimbursement, grant, contract, use of state property, or pursuant to a state program—from using such funds to "assist, promote, or deter union organizing." See Cal. Govt.Code Ann. §§ 16645.1 to 16645.7. This prohibition encompasses "any attempt by an employer to influence the decision of its employees" regarding "[w]hether to support or oppose a labor organization" and "[w]hether to become a member of any labor organization." § 16645(a). The statute specifies that the spending restriction applies to "any expense, including legal and consulting fees and salaries of supervisors and employees, incurred for . . . an activity to assist, promote, or deter union organizing." § 16646(a).

Despite the neutral statement of policy quoted above, AB 1889 expressly exempts "activit[ies] performed" or "expense[s] incurred" in connection with certain undertakings that promote unionization, including "[a]llowing a labor organization or its representatives access to the employer's facilities or property," and "[n]egotiating, entering into, or carrying out a voluntary recognition agreement with a labor organization." §§ 16647(b), (d).

To ensure compliance with the grant and program restrictions at issue in this case, AB 1889 establishes a formidable enforcement scheme. Covered employers must certify that no state funds will be used for prohibited expenditures; the employer must also maintain and provide upon request "records sufficient to show that no state funds were used for those expenditures." §§ 16645.2(c), 16645.7(b)-(c). If an employer commingles state and other funds, the statute presumes that any expenditures to assist, promote, or deter union organizing derive in part from state funds on a pro rata basis. § 16646(b). Violators are liable to the State for the amount of funds used for prohibited purposes plus a civil penalty equal to twice the amount of those funds. §§ 16645.2(d), 16645.7(d). Suspected violators may be sued by the state attorney general or any private taxpayer, and prevailing plaintiffs are "entitled to recover reasonable attorney's fees and costs." § 16645.8(d).

II

In April 2002, several organizations whose members do business with the State of California (collectively, Chamber of Commerce) brought this action against the California Department of Health Services and appropriate state officials (collectively, the State) to enjoin enforcement of AB 1889. Two labor unions (collectively, AFL–CIO) intervened to defend the statute's validity.

The District Court granted partial summary judgment in favor of the Chamber of Commerce, holding that the National Labor Relations Act (NLRA), 49 Stat. 449, as amended, 29 U.S.C. § 151 et seq. pre-empts Cal. Govt. Code Ann. § 16645.2 (concerning grants) and § 16645.7 (concerning program funds) because those provisions "regulat[e] employer speech about union organizing under specified circumstances, even though Congress intended free debate." Chamber of Commerce v. Lockyer, 225 F.Supp.2d 1199, 1205 (C.D.Cal.2002). The Court of Appeals for the Ninth Circuit, after twice affirming the District Court's judgment, granted rehearing *en banc* and reversed. See Chamber of Commerce v. Lockyer, 463 F.3d 1076, 1082 (2006). While the *en banc* majority agreed that California enacted §§ 16645.2 and 16645.7 in its capacity as a regulator, and not as a mere proprietor or market participant, see id., at 1082–1085, it concluded that Congress did not intend to preclude States from imposing such restrictions on the use of their own funds, see id., at 1085–1096. We granted certiorari, 552 U.S. ___, 128 S.Ct. 645, 169 L.Ed.2d 417 (2007), and now reverse.

Although the NLRA itself contains no express pre-emption provision, we have held that Congress implicitly mandated two types of pre-emption as necessary to implement federal labor policy. The first, known as *Garmon* pre-emption, see San Diego Building Trades Council v. Garmon, 359 U.S. 236, 79 S.Ct. 773, 3 L.Ed.2d 775 (1959), "is intended to preclude state interference with the National Labor Relations Board's interpretation and active enforcement of the 'integrated scheme of regulation' established by the NLRA." Golden State Transit Corp. v. Los Angeles, 475 U.S. 608, 613, 106 S.Ct. 1395, 89 L.Ed.2d 616 (1986) (*Golden State I*). To this end, *Garmon* pre-emption forbids States to "regulate activity that the NLRA protects, prohibits, or arguably protects or prohibits." Wisconsin Dept. of Industry v. Gould Inc., 475 U.S. 282, 286, 106 S.Ct. 1057, 89 L.Ed.2d 223 (1986). The second, known as *Machinists* pre-emption, forbids both the National Labor Relations Board (NLRB) and States to regulate conduct that Congress intended "be unregulated because left 'to be controlled by the free play of economic forces.'" Machinists v. Wisconsin Employment Relations Comm'n, 427 U.S. 132, 140, 96 S.Ct. 2548, 49 L.Ed.2d 396 (1976) (quoting NLRB v. Nash–Finch Co., 404 U.S. 138, 144, 92 S.Ct. 373, 30 L.Ed.2d 328 (1971)). *Machinists* pre-emption is based on the premise that " 'Congress struck a balance of protection, prohibition, and laissez-faire in respect to union organization, collective bargaining, and labor disputes.'" 427 U.S., at 140, n. 4, 96 S.Ct. 2548 (quoting Cox, Labor Law Preemption Revisited, 85 Harv. L.Rev. 1337, 1352 (1972)).

Today we hold that §§ 16645.2 and 16645.7 are pre-empted under *Machinists* because they regulate within "a zone protected and reserved for market freedom." Building & Constr. Trades Council v. Associated Builders & Contractors of Mass./R. I., Inc., 507 U.S. 218, 227, 113 S.Ct. 1190, 122 L.Ed.2d 565 (1993) (*Boston Harbor*). We do not reach the question whether the provisions would also be pre-empted under *Garmon*.

III

As enacted in 1935, the NLRA, which was commonly known as the Wagner Act, did not include any provision that specifically addressed the intersection between employee organizational rights and employer speech rights. See 49 Stat. 449. Rather, it was left to the NLRB, subject to review in federal court, to reconcile these interests in its construction of §§ 7 and 8. Section 7, now codified at 29 U.S.C. § 157, provided that workers have the right to organize, to bargain collectively, and to engage in concerted activity for their mutual aid and protection. Section 8(1), now codified at 29 U.S.C. § 158(a)(1), made it an "unfair labor practice" for employers to "interfere with, restrain, or coerce employees in the exercise of the rights guaranteed by section 7."

Among the frequently litigated issues under the Wagner Act were charges that an employer's attempts to persuade employees not to join a union—or to join one favored by the employer rather than a rival— amounted to a form of coercion prohibited by § 8. The NLRB took the position that § 8 demanded complete employer neutrality during organizing campaigns, reasoning that any partisan employer speech about unions would interfere with the § 7 rights of employees. See 1 J. Higgins, The Developing Labor Law 94 (5th ed.2006). In 1941, this Court curtailed the NLRB's aggressive interpretation, clarifying that nothing in the NLRA prohibits an employer "from expressing its view on labor policies or problems" unless the employer's speech "in connection with other circumstances [amounts] to coercion within the meaning of the Act." NLRB v. Virginia Elec. & Power Co., 314 U.S. 469, 477, 62 S.Ct. 344, 86 L.Ed. 348 (1941). We subsequently characterized *Virginia Electric* as recognizing the First Amendment right of employers to engage in noncoercive speech about unionization. Thomas v. Collins, 323 U.S. 516, 537–538, 65 S.Ct. 315, 89 L.Ed. 430 (1945). Notwithstanding these decisions, the NLRB continued to regulate employer speech too restrictively in the eyes of Congress.

Concerned that the Wagner Act had pushed the labor relations balance too far in favor of unions, Congress passed the Labor Management Relations Act, 1947 (Taft–Hartley Act). 61 Stat. 136. The Taft–Hartley Act amended §§ 7 and 8 in several key respects. First, it emphasized that employees "have the right to refrain from any or all" § 7 activities. 29 U.S.C. § 157. Second, it added § 8(b), which prohibits unfair labor practices by unions. 29 U.S.C. § 158(b). Third, it added § 8(c), which protects speech by both unions and employers from regulation by the NLRB. 29 U.S.C. § 158(c). Specifically, § 8(c) provides:

"The expressing of any views, argument, or opinion, or the dissemination thereof, whether in written, printed, graphic, or visual form, shall not constitute or be evidence of an unfair labor practice under any of the provisions of this subchapter, if such expression contains no threat of reprisal or force or promise of benefit."

From one vantage, § 8(c) "merely implements the First Amendment," NLRB v. Gissel Packing Co., 395 U.S. 575, 617, 89 S.Ct. 1918, 23 L.Ed.2d 547 (1969), in that it responded to particular constitutional rulings of the NLRB. See S.Rep. No. 105, 80th Cong., 1st Sess., pt. 2, pp. 23–24 (1947). But its enactment also manifested a "congressional intent to encourage free debate on issues dividing labor and management." Linn v. Plant Guard Workers, 383 U.S. 53, 62, 86 S.Ct. 657, 15 L.Ed.2d 582 (1966). It is indicative of how important Congress deemed such "free debate" that Congress amended the NLRA rather than leaving to the courts the task of correcting the NLRB's decisions on a case-by-case basis. We have characterized this policy judgment, which suffuses the NLRA as a whole, as "favoring uninhibited, robust, and wide-open debate in labor disputes," stressing that "freewheeling use of the written and spoken word ... has been expressly fostered by Congress and approved by the NLRB." Letter Carriers v. Austin, 418 U.S. 264, 272–273, 94 S.Ct. 2770, 41 L.Ed.2d 745 (1974).

Congress' express protection of free debate forcefully buttresses the pre-emption analysis in this case. Under *Machinists*, congressional intent to shield a zone of activity from regulation is usually found only "implicit[ly] in the structure of the Act," Livadas v. Bradshaw, 512 U.S. 107, 117, n. 11, 114 S.Ct. 2068, 129 L.Ed.2d 93 (1994), drawing on the notion that " '[w]hat Congress left unregulated is as important as the regulations that it imposed,' " Golden State Transit Corp. v. Los Angeles, 493 U.S. 103, 110, 110 S.Ct. 444, 107 L.Ed.2d 420 (1989) *(Golden State II)* (quoting New York Telephone Co. v. New York State Dept. of Labor, 440 U.S. 519, 552, 99 S.Ct. 1328, 59 L.Ed.2d 553 (1979) (Powell, J., dissenting)). In the case of noncoercive speech, however, the protection is both implicit and explicit. Sections 8(a) and 8(b) demonstrate that when Congress has sought to put limits on advocacy for or against union organization, it has expressly set forth the mechanisms for doing so. Moreover, the amendment to § 7 calls attention to the right of employees to refuse to join unions, which implies an underlying right to receive information opposing unionization. Finally, the addition of § 8(c) expressly precludes regulation of speech about unionization "so long as the communications do not contain a 'threat of reprisal or force or promise of benefit.' " Gissel Packing, 395 U.S., at 618, 89 S.Ct. 1918.

The explicit direction from Congress to leave noncoercive speech unregulated makes this case easier, in at least one respect, than previous NLRA cases because it does not require us "to decipher the presumed intent of Congress in the face of that body's steadfast silence." Sears, Roebuck & Co. v. Carpenters, 436 U.S. 180, 188, n. 12, 98 S.Ct. 1745, 56 L.Ed.2d 209 (1978). California's policy judgment that partisan employer speech necessarily "interfere[s] with an employee's choice about whether to join or to be represented by a labor union," 2000 Cal. Stats. ch. 872, § 1, is the same policy judgment that the NLRB advanced under the Wagner Act, and that Congress renounced in the Taft–Hartley Act. To the extent §§ 16645.2 and 16645.7 actually further the express goal of AB 1889, the provisions are unequivocally pre-empted. . . .

IV

* * * * In NLRA pre-emption cases, " 'judicial concern has necessarily focused on the nature of the activities which the States have sought to regulate, rather than on the method of regulation adopted.' " *Golden State I*, 475 U.S., at 614, n. 5, 106 S.Ct. 1395 (quoting *Garmon*, 359 U.S., at 243, 79 S.Ct. 773; brackets omitted); see also *Livadas*, 512 U.S., at 119, 114 S.Ct. 2068 ("Pre-emption analysis . . . turns on the actual content of [the State's] policy and its real effect on federal rights"). California plainly could not directly regulate noncoercive speech about unionization by means of an express prohibition. It is equally clear that California may not indirectly regulate such conduct by imposing spending restrictions on the use of state funds.

In *Gould*, we held that Wisconsin's policy of refusing to purchase goods and services from three-time NLRA violators was pre-empted under *Garmon* because it imposed a "supplemental sanction" that conflicted with the NLRA's " 'integrated scheme of regulation.' " 475 U.S., at 288–289, 106 S.Ct. 1057. Wisconsin protested that its debarment statute was "an exercise of the State's spending power rather than its regulatory power," but we dismissed this as "a distinction without a difference." Id., at 287, 106 S.Ct. 1057. "[T]he point of the statute [was] to deter labor law violations," and "for all practical purposes" the spending restriction was "tantamount to regulation." Id., at 287–289, 106 S.Ct. 1057. Wisconsin's choice "to use its spending power rather than its police power d[id] not significantly lessen the inherent potential for conflict" between the state and federal schemes; hence the statute was pre-empted. Id., at 289, 106 S.Ct. 1057.

We distinguished *Gould* in *Boston Harbor*, holding that the NLRA did not preclude a state agency supervising a construction project from requiring that contractors abide by a labor agreement. We explained that when a State acts as a "market participant with no interest in setting policy," as opposed to a "regulator," it does not offend the pre-emption principles of the NLRA. 507 U.S., at 229, 113 S.Ct. 1190. In finding that the state agency had acted as a market participant, we stressed that the challenged action "was specifically tailored to one particular job," and aimed "to ensure an efficient project that would be completed as quickly and effectively as possible at the lowest cost." Id., at 232, 113 S.Ct. 1190.

It is beyond dispute that California enacted AB 1889 in its capacity as a regulator rather than a market participant. AB 1889 is neither "specifically tailored to one particular job" nor a "legitimate response to state procurement constraints or to local economic needs." *Gould*, 475 U.S., at 291, 106 S.Ct. 1057. As the statute's preamble candidly acknowledges, the legislative purpose is not the efficient procurement of goods and services, but the furtherance of a labor policy. See 2000 Cal. Stats. ch. 872, § 1. Although a State has a legitimate proprietary interest in ensuring that state funds are spent in accordance with the purposes for which they are appropriated, this is not the objective of AB 1889. In contrast to a neutral affirmative requirement that funds be spent solely for the purposes of the relevant grant or program, AB 1889 imposes a targeted negative restriction on employer speech about unionization. Furthermore, the statute does not even apply this constraint uniformly. Instead of forbidding the use of state funds for all employer advocacy regarding unionization, AB 1889 permits use of state funds for select employer advocacy activities that promote unions. Specifically, the statute exempts expenses incurred in connection with, *inter alia*, giving unions access to the workplace, and voluntarily recognizing unions without a secret ballot election. §§ 16647(b), (d).

* * * *

Finally, the Court of Appeals reasoned that Congress could not have intended to pre-empt AB 1889 because Congress itself has imposed similar restrictions. See 463 F.3d, at 1090–1091. Specifically, three federal statutes include provisions that forbid the use of particular grant and program funds "to assist, promote, or deter union organizing."[2] We are not persuaded that these few isolated restrictions, plucked from the multitude of federal spending programs, were either intended to alter or did in fact alter the " 'wider contours of federal labor policy.' " Metropolitan Life, 471 U.S., at 753, 105 S.Ct. 2380.

A federal statute will contract the pre-emptive scope of the NLRA if it demonstrates that "Congress has decided to tolerate a substantial measure of diversity" in the particular regulatory sphere. New York Telephone, 440 U.S., at 546, 99 S.Ct. 1328 (plurality opinion). In *New York Telephone*, an employer challenged a state unemployment system that provided benefits to employees absent from work during lengthy strikes. The employer argued that the state system conflicted with the federal labor policy "of allowing the free play of economic forces to operate during the bargaining process." Id., at 531, 99 S.Ct. 1328. We upheld the statute on the basis that the legislative histories of the NLRA and Social Security Act, which were enacted within six weeks of each other, confirmed that "Congress intended that the States be free to authorize, or to prohibit, such payments." Id., at 544, 99 S.Ct. 1328; see also id., at 547, 99 S.Ct. 1328 (Brennan, J., concurring in result); id., at 549, 99 S.Ct. 1328 (Blackmun, J., concurring in judgment). Indeed, the tension between the Social Security Act and the NLRA suggested that the case could "be viewed as presenting a potential

---

2. See 29 U.S.C. § 2931(b)(7) ("Each recipient of funds under [the Workforce Investment Act] shall provide to the Secretary assurances that none of such funds will be used to assist, promote, or deter union organizing"); 42 U.S.C. § 9839(e) ("Funds appropriated to carry out [the Head Start Programs Act] shall not be used to assist, promote, or deter union organizing"); § 12634(b)(1) ("Assistance provided under [the National Community Service Act] shall not be used by program participants and program staff to ... assist, promote, or deter union organizing").

conflict between two federal statutes ... rather than between federal and state regulatory statutes." Id., at 539–540, n. 32, 99 S.Ct. 1328.

The three federal statutes relied on by the Court of Appeals neither conflict with the NLRA nor otherwise establish that Congress "decided to tolerate a substantial measure of diversity" in the regulation of employer speech. Unlike the States, Congress has the authority to create tailored exceptions to otherwise applicable federal policies, and (also unlike the States) it can do so in a manner that preserves national uniformity without opening the door to a 50–state patchwork of inconsistent labor policies. Consequently, the mere fact that Congress has imposed targeted federal restrictions on union-related advocacy in certain limited contexts does not invite the States to override federal labor policy in other settings.

Had Congress enacted a federal version of AB 1889 that applied analogous spending restrictions to all federal grants or expenditures, the pre-emption question would be closer. Cf. Metropolitan Life, 471 U.S., at 755, 105 S.Ct. 2380 (citing federal minimum labor standards as evidence that Congress did not intend to pre-empt state minimum labor standards). But none of the cited statutes is Government-wide in scope, none contains comparable remedial provisions, and none contains express pro-union exemptions.

* * *

The Court of Appeals' judgment reversing the summary judgment entered for the Chamber of Commerce is reversed, and the case is remanded for further proceedings consistent with this opinion.

[The dissenting opinion of Justice Breyer, for himself and Justice Ginsburg, is omitted.]

PROBLEMS FOR DISCUSSION

1. Why is it apparently not within the power of a state to mandate that government contractors not divert public funds into expenditures that do not directly advance the provision of goods or services to the state? Why, in other words, may not a state declare that a contractor, if it wishes to invest efforts in making anti-union (or pro-union) statements to its employees, should do so only through the expenditure of its own private funds—just as would an altogether private company doing private business?

In his dissenting opinion, Justice Breyer made the following observation: "[T]he law normally gives legislatures broad authority to decide how to spend the People's money. A legislature, after all, generally has the right not to fund activities that it would prefer not to fund—even where the activities are otherwise protected.... See, e.g., Regan v. Taxation With Representation of Wash., 461 U.S. 540, 549, 103 S.Ct. 1997, 76 L.Ed.2d 129 (1983) ('We have held in several contexts that a legislature's decision not to subsidize the exercise of a fundamental right does not infringe the right'). This Court has made the same point in the context of labor law.... As far as I can tell, States that do wish to pay for employer speech are generally free to do so. They might make clear, for example, through grant-related rules and regulations that a grant recipient can use the funds to pay salaries and overhead, which salaries and overhead might include expenditures related to management's role in labor organizing contests. If so, why should States that do not wish to pay be deprived of a similar freedom? Why should they be conscripted into paying?'' Does the majority opinion in the *Chamber of Commerce* case suggest any answers?

2. The Court placed considerable emphasis, in finding preemption, upon the fact that California, particularly in its statutory preamble, explicitly declared it the policy of the state to restrain inappropriate ''interference'' and ''influence'' with employee choices relating to unionization. The Court also noted a number of seemingly ''pro-union'' exclusions from the general ban upon union-related employer expenditures. What lessons might be drawn for another state (or California in a year or two?) that would wish to impose similar expenditure restrictions on companies doing business with the state? Would such ''lessons'' and such restrictions likely prevail when confronted by preemption arguments?

Page 1032.   End of Problem 6:

This decision was reversed, 471 F.3d 87 (2d Cir. 2006), holding the New York law to be preempted.

II.   SPECIFIC APPLICATIONS: REPRESENTATION, BARGAINING AND CONCERTED ACTIVITIES

Page 1058.   Add to Problems for Discussion:

4. The State of Washington has recently legislated comprehensively to deal with patient safety, S.B. 5696 (2007) *amending* Wash. Rev. Code § 70.56.020. The statute starts with a legislative finding:

> **Sec. 1.** The legislature finds that research demonstrates the critical role that registered nurses play in improving patient safety and quality of care. Greater numbers of registered nurses available to care for hospitalized patients are key to reducing errors, complications, and adverse patient care events. Moreover, higher nurse staffing levels result in improved staff safety and satisfaction and reduced incidences of workplace injuries. In addition, health care professional, technical, and support staff comprise vital components of the patient care team, bringing their particular skills and services to ensuring quality patient care. Therefore, in order to protect patients and to support greater retention of registered nurses, to promote evidence-based nurse staffing, and to increase transparency of health care data and decision making, the legislature finds that ensuring sufficient nurse staffing to meet patient care needs is an urgent public policy priority.

Rather exacting treatment of nurse staffing is set out including the use of staffing plans. These must be ''developed by the hospital staffing committee,'' the establishment of which is set out in the law as follows:

> **Sec. 4.** (1) By January 1, 2008, each hospital shall establish a staffing committee, at least one-half of whose members are registered nurses currently providing direct patient care. However, the composition of the staffing committee must be consistent with any applicable provisions of the collective bargaining agreement, if any, between the hospital and its nursing staff. If registered nurses are represented by a collective bargaining representative, the committee's direct-care registered nurse members must be selected by that collective bargaining representative. Participation

in the committee by a hospital employee shall be considered a part of the employee's regularly scheduled work.

Is this provision preempted? *Cf.* Matthew Finkin, *Employee Representation Outside the Labor Act: Thoughts on Arbitration Representation, Group Arbitration, and Workplace Committees*, 5 U. Pa. J. Lab & Emp. L. 75 (2002).

Page 1079. Add to Problems for Discussion:

Add to Problem 5:

Spratt's lawsuit seeks not only tort damages for a discharge violative of public policy, but also reinstatement. On the latter he argues that reinstatement is necessary to provide a deterrent to the employer's wrongful conduct and to make him whole as it is unlikely that he can secure another job as a trucker, his chosen vocation. He argues that as reinstatement would be an available remedy for a discharge without just cause under the collective agreement it ought to be available as a matter of public policy. Winona Trucking argues that as the latter would require an interpretation of the collective bargaining agreement, Spratt's lawsuit should be preempted. How should the court rule? *Cf.* Conley v. Yellow Freight System, Inc., 521 F.Supp.2d 713 (E.D. Tenn. 2007).

Page 1082. After *B E & K Construction Co.*:

On remand from the Supreme Court, the Board in a 3–2 decision held that "the filing and maintenance of a reasonably based lawsuit does not violate the Act, regardless of whether the lawsuit is ongoing or is completed, and regardless of the motive for initiating the lawsuit." *BE & K Construction Company*, 351 NLRB No. 29 (2007). The majority rested on the "fundamental right to petition the government for redress of grievances," not on the technical aspects of the petition clause but on the First Amendment's application to litigation as expressive activity. The majority acknowledged that the Supreme Court in *BE & K* had reserved on the question of whether the Board could declare an unsuccessful but reasonably based lawsuit to be an unfair labor practice if the lawsuit had been filed to impose the cost of litigation on the union regardless of the outcome. But the Board majority took that reservation as merely prudential, and stressed the need for legal uniformity and predictability. The dissenting Board members saw the question as one left open by the Court and not foreordained by First Amendment doctrine, citing *California Motor Transport Co. v. Trucking Unlimited*, 404 U.S. 508, 514, 92 S.Ct. 609, 30 L.Ed.2d 642 (1972) ("It is well settled that First Amendment rights are not immunized from regulation when they are used as an integral part of conduct which violates a valid statute").

PROBLEM FOR DISCUSSION

Adam Liptak, *A Corporate Vein of Mafia Tactics: Protesting, Lobbying and Citing Upton Sinclair*, N.Y. Times (Feb. 5, 2008) at A–14, reports on a lawsuit brought under the Racketeer Influenced and Corrupt Organizations Act (RICO) by Smithfield Foods against the union for "speaking out about labor, environment and safety issues in order to pressure the company to unionize" by using press releases, contacting civil rights and environmental groups, organizing protests and calling for boycotts. Smithfield's complaint alleges *inter alia*

> that the union was engaged in racketeering when it urged local governments in New York, Boston and other cities to pass resolutions condemning the company. After meeting with the union in 2006, a dozen members of the New York City Council sponsored a resolution calling for the city to stop buying meat from Smithfield's Tar Heel factory "until the company ends all forms of abuse, intimidation and violence against its workers," citing a ruling by a federal appeals court in Washington that Smithfield had engaged in "intense and widespread coercion" in battling unionization at its Tar Heel plant.

* * *

> "It's economic warfare," explained G. Robert Blakey, one of Smithfield's lawyers [and one of the drafters of RICO]. "It's actually the same thing as what John Gotti used to do. What the union is saying in effect to Smithfield is, 'You've got to partner up with us to run your company.'"

The complaint has survived a motion to dismiss and so, presumably, it is "reasonably based," given the sweep and the vagueness of the RICO Act. Assume further that it is ultimately unsuccessful. And assume that it could be proved that the suit was brought irrespective of the likelihood of success solely to suppress the union's organizational effort. Would the initiation and maintenance of the lawsuit be an unfair labor practice?

PART NINE

RECONSIDERING THE LABOR ACT IN THE CONTEMPORARY CONTEXT

III. LABOR LAW REFORM

Page 1100. Add at the end of section A:

On March 1, 2007, the House of Representatives passed H.R. 800 (110th Cong., 1st Sess.)—the "Employee Free Choice Act"—requiring the NLRB to certify representatives on the basis of a demonstration of majority support without holding an election; the Senate lacked sufficient votes to close debate.

PART TEN

THE INDIVIDUAL AND THE UNION

I.   THE RIGHT TO FAIR REPRESENTATION

Page 1147.   After the discussion of *Rawson*:

The United States Court of Appeals for the Ninth Circuit has adopted a more nuanced analysis, most recently explained and applied in *Beck v. United Food & Commercial Workers Union*, 506 F.3d 874 (9th Cir. 2007). The employer had a policy prohibiting the use of "profane, abusive or threatening language toward fellow employees." Ms. Beck, whom the employer claimed to have a " 'history of a foul mouth,' " got into a heated exchange with another employee (with whom she had been romantically involved), in the employer's parking lot before reporting for work. A disciplinary investigation and suspension ensued resulting in Ms. Beck being issued a Final Written Warning—in effect a "last chance" notice that any future infraction would result in dismissal. Beck asked her union representative to file a grievance. The representative agreed, but failed to do so. A little over two months later Beck got into another argument, was discharged, and this time the union did file a grievance. The employer shared its complete disciplinary file with the union which in turn asked its lawyer whether it was required to pursue the grievance to arbitration.

> The attorney provided an opinion letter stating that, in his view, a single incident of alleged profanity would not constitute just cause for discharge. However, the attorney opined that an arbitrator would "almost certainly" conclude that termination for a second incident of profanity constituted just cause when the first incident resulted in an unchallenged written warning less than three months earlier.

The union declined to submit this grievance for arbitration. Beck sued the union for violation of Title VII, on a claim of sex discrimination, and for breach of the duty of fair representation in failing to file her grievance for the first occurrence—and prevailed on both before the trial court.

On the duty of fair representation issue, the Ninth Circuit characterized its caselaw describing the duty as moving along a continuum.

> On one end of the continuum is intentional conduct by a union exercising its judgment.... [A] union's conduct constitutes an exercise of judgment entitled to deference even when the union's "judgments are ultimately wrong." ... Under Supreme Court precedents, so long as a union exercises its judgment, no matter how mistakenly, it will not be deemed to be wholly irrational.

* * *

> On the other end of the continuum are actions or omissions that are unintentional, irrational or wholly inexplicable, such as an irrational failure to perform a ministerial or procedural act....

It affirmed the trial court: Ms. Beck would not have been terminated for the July incident but for the status of the April incident which allowed the employer to act as it did because it was uncontested. Allowing the earlier warning to stand "extinguished her right to challenge her ultimate termination."

> Because "the individual interest at stake is strong and the union's failure to perform a ministerial act completely extinguishes the employee's right to pursue [her] claim," ... the union's failure to file the original grievance was not mere negligence. Rather, the union here treated Beck's claim "so lightly as to suggest an egregious disregard of her rights."

Are you persuaded that there is a difference between "mere negligence" in failing to file a grievance and "egregious disregard" in failing to file a grievance?

II. Union Security and the Encouragement of Union Activity

Page 1187. After paragraph (5) *Litigation*:

The U.S. Supreme Court has granted certiorari to hear a public-sector case presenting a First Amendment claim that a union may not use agency fees to finance the union's litigation outside the employee's bargaining unit. *Locke v. Karass*, 498 F.3d 49 (1st Cir. 2007), *cert. granted*, ___ U.S. ___, 128 S.Ct. 1224, 170 L.Ed.2d 57 (2008), Case No. 07–610.

Page 1190–91. Add after paragraph (5):

In *Teamsters Local 75 (Schreiber Foods)*, 329 NLRB 28 (1999), the Board remanded to an ALJ for reconsideration whether objectors can be charged with the costs of union organizing in other bargaining units in the same or similar industries; *e.g.*, whether the organizing was necessary to preserve uniformity of labor standards in the organized workforce. Subsequently, in *Meijer, Inc.*, 329 NLRB 730 (1999), *enf't denied in part sub nom. Food and Commercial Workers v. NLRB*, 284 F.3d 1099 (9th Cir. 2002), *modified*, 307 F.3d 760 (9th Cir. 2002), the Board held with judicial approval that expenses incurred in organizing employees in the same competitive product market were chargeable. On remand in *Schreiber Foods*, the ALJ seemed to hold the term "competitive market" to mean the labor market not the product market. Based largely on the testimony of an academic economist, the ALJ concluded that the expenses were chargeable:

> It is very plausible to conclude that an increase in union density in an area would cause wages and working conditions to improve in the area or occupations involved. This is especially true in a small city such as Green Bay, Wisconsin, with a population of about 88,000. So, for example, if the Respondent organized production, maintenance or warehouse employees of a large to medium sized employer located within the City of Green Bay, and wages of these newly organized employees improved, it appears to me that this would have a dual effect upon the Respondent and its members who were employed by Schreiber. First, it would be known that the wage scale in the city had gone up, and, secondly, there would be fewer lower paid employees in the area who would be available to work for Schreiber if it had to hire additional employees or if it and the Respondent were unable to agree on a new contract. Although this might not be true in New York City, Chicago, or Los Angeles, I believe that it would be so in a city the size of Green Bay. Further, although this proposition might be more obvious in a unit of truck drivers or nurses . . . it would also be true of a production and maintenance unit as is present herein. . . . It appears to me that the higher the union density in a certain area such as Green Bay, the less elasticity there is in the labor market, and the fewer choices employers such as Schreiber would have. This would have a tendency to raise the wages of the Schreiber unit employees.

The Board rejected the ALJ's decision by vote of 2–1. *Teamsters Local 75 (Schreiber Foods)*, 349 NLRB No. 14 (2007). Chairman Battista expressed doubt about the soundness of *Meijer, Inc.*, but held that, in any event, it required exacting findings of fact which had not been adduced before the ALJ, *i.e.*, a showing of " 'a direct, positive relationship between the levels of union–represented employees and the level of organization of employees of employers in the same competitive market.' " Conclusions drawn from generalized academic research—general propositions of the kind the ALJ accepted—will not do, apparently no matter how widely accepted: specific evidence of the economic impact of unionization in the particular geographic competitive product market is required. Member Schaumber concurred in the result, but dissented on the ground that *Meijer, Inc.*, should be overruled. Member Leibmen dissented in part, on the ground that *Meijer, Inc.* had accepted and proceeded from just those generally accepted economic conclusions that the Board now rejects.

Is the ability of a union to charge objectors for organizing other employees in the geographic competitive market now contingent on its ability to find—and fund—economic research demonstrating the precise connection between union density and these specific wage levels? To the extent the reasoned application of the Labor Act depends on the collection of economic data and their analysis, should the NLRB bear some responsibility for seeing to it that its decisions are well informed in just that regard? Compare two provisions of section 4(c) of the Act: "Nothing in the Act shall be construed to authorize the Board to appoint individuals for the purpose of . . . economic analysis"—and, "The Board may . . . utilize such voluntary and uncompensated services, as may from time to time be needed."

*

SHERMAN ACT

26 Stat. 209 (1890), as amended, 15 U.S.C. §§ 1 et seq. (1988).

Sec. 1. Every contract, combination in the form of a trust or otherwise, or conspiracy, in restraint of trade or commerce among the several States, or with foreign nations, is hereby declared to be illegal. Every person who shall make any such contract or engage in any such combination or conspiracy, shall be deemed guilty of a misdemeanor, and, on conviction thereof, shall be punished by fine not exceeding five thousand dollars, or by imprisonment not exceeding one year, or by both said punishments, in the discretion of the court.

Sec. 2. Every person who shall monopolize, or attempt to monopolize, or combine or conspire with any other person or persons, to monopolize any part of the trade or commerce among the several States, or with foreign nations, shall be deemed guilty of a misdemeanor, and, on conviction thereof, shall be punished by fine not exceeding five thousand dollars, or by imprisonment not exceeding one year, or by both said punishments, in the discretion of the court.

Sec. 3. Every contract, combination in form of trust or otherwise, or conspiracy, in restraint of trade or commerce in any territory of the United States or of the District of Columbia, or in restraint of trade or commerce between any such territory and another, or between any such territory or territories and any State or States or the District of Columbia, or with foreign nations, or between the District of Columbia and any State or States or foreign nations, is hereby declared illegal. Every person who shall make any such contract or engage in any such combination or conspiracy, shall be deemed guilty of a misdemeanor, and, on conviction thereof, shall be punished by fine not exceeding five thousand dollars, or by imprisonment not exceeding one year, or by both said punishments, in the discretion of the court.

Sec. 4. The several circuit courts of the United States are hereby invested with jurisdiction to prevent and restrain violations of this act; and it shall be the duty of the several district attorneys of the United States, in their respective districts, under the direction of the Attorney General, to institute proceedings in equity to prevent and restrain such violations. Such proceedings may be by way of petition setting forth the case and praying that such violation shall be enjoined or otherwise prohibited. When the parties complained of shall have been duly notified of such petition the court shall proceed, as soon as may be, to the hearing and determination of the case; and pending such petition and before final decree, the court may at any time make such temporary restraining order or prohibition as shall be deemed just in the premises.

Sec. 5. Whenever it shall appear to the court before which any proceeding under section 4 of this act may be pending, that the ends of justice require that other parties should be brought before the court, the court may cause them to be summoned, whether they reside in the district in which the court is held or not; and subpoenas to that end may be served in any district by the marshal thereof.

Sec. 6.   Any property owned under any contract or by any combination, or pursuant to any conspiracy (and being the subject thereof) mentioned in section 1 of this act, and being in the course of transportation from one State to another, or to a foreign country, shall be forfeited to the United States, and may be seized and condemned by like proceedings as those provided by law for the forfeiture, seizure, and condemnation of property imported into the United States contrary to law.

Sec. 7.   Any person who shall be injured in his business or property by any other person or corporation by reason of anything forbidden or declared to be unlawful by this act, may sue therefor in any Circuit Court of the United States in the district in which the defendant resides or is found, without respect to the amount in controversy, and shall recover three-fold the damages sustained, and the costs of suit, including a reasonable attorney's fee.

Sec. 8.   That the word "person," or "persons" wherever used in this act shall be deemed to include corporations and associations existing under or authorized by the laws of either the United States, the laws of any State or the laws of any foreign country.

CLAYTON ACT

38 Stat. 730 (1914), as amended, 15 U.S.C. §§ 12 et seq. (1988).

Be it enacted by the Senate and House of Representatives of the United States of America in Congress assembled, That "anti-trust laws," as used herein, includes the Act entitled "An Act to protect trade and commerce against unlawful restraints and monopolies", approved July second, eighteen hundred and ninety [Sherman Act, supra.] * * *

* * *

Sec. 6. That the labor of a human being is not a commodity or article of commerce. Nothing contained in the anti-trust laws shall be construed to forbid the existence and operation of labor, agricultural, or horticultural organizations, instituted for the purposes of mutual help, and not having capital stock or conducted for profit, or to forbid or restrain individual members of such organizations from lawfully carrying out the legitimate objects thereof; nor shall such organizations, or the members thereof, be held or construed to be illegal combinations or conspiracies in restraint of trade, under the anti-trust laws.

* * *

Sec. 16. That any person, firm, corporation, or association shall be entitled to sue for and have injunctive relief, in any court of the United States having jurisdiction over the parties, against threatened loss or damage by a violation of the anti-trust laws, including sections two, three, seven and eight of this Act, when and under the same conditions and principles as injunctive relief against threatened conduct that will cause loss or damage is granted by courts of equity, under the rules governing such proceedings, and upon the execution of proper bond against damages for an injunction improvidently granted and a showing that the danger of irreparable loss or damage is immediate, a preliminary injunction may issue: *Provided,* That nothing herein contained shall be construed to entitle any person, firm, corporation, or association, except the United States, to bring suit in equity for injunctive relief against any common carrier subject to the provisions of the Act to regulate commerce, approved February fourth, eighteen hundred and eighty-seven, in respect of any matter subject to the regulation, supervision, or other jurisdiction of the Interstate Commerce Commission.

* * *

Sec. 20. That no restraining order or injunction shall be granted by any court of the United States, or a judge or the judges thereof, in any case between an employer and employees, or between employers and employees, or between employees, or between persons employed and persons seeking employment, involving, or growing out of, a dispute concerning terms or conditions of employment, unless necessary to prevent irreparable injury to property, or to a property right, of the party making the application, for which injury there is no adequate remedy at law, and such property or property right must be described with particularity in the application, which must be in writing and sworn to by the applicant or by his agent or attorney.

And no such restraining order or injunction shall prohibit any person or persons, whether singly or in concert, from terminating any relation of employment, or from ceasing to perform any work or labor, or from recommending, advising, or persuading others by peaceful means so to do; or from attending at any place where any such person or persons may lawfully be, for the purpose of peacefully obtaining or communicating information, or from peacefully persuading any person to work or to abstain from working; or from ceasing to patronize or to employ any party to such dispute, or from recommending, advising, or persuading others by peaceful and lawful means so to do; or from paying or giving to, or withholding from, any person engaged in such dispute, any strike benefits or other moneys or things of value; or from peaceably assembling in a lawful manner, and for lawful purposes; or from doing any act or thing which might lawfully be done in the absence of such dispute by any party thereto; nor shall any of the acts specified in this paragraph be considered or held to be violations of any law of the United States.

* * *

NORRIS–LAGUARDIA ACT

47 Stat. 70 (1932), 29 U.S.C. §§ 101–15 (1988).

Sec. 1. No court of the United States, as herein defined, shall have jurisdiction to issue any restraining order or temporary or permanent injunction in a case involving or growing out of a labor dispute, except in a strict conformity with the provisions of this Act; nor shall any such restraining order or temporary or permanent injunction be issued contrary to the public policy declared in this Act.

Sec. 2. In the interpretation of this Act and in determining the jurisdiction and authority of the courts of the United States, as such jurisdiction and authority are herein defined and limited, the public policy of the United States is hereby declared as follows:

Whereas under prevailing economic conditions, developed with the aid of governmental authority for owners of property to organize in the corporate and other forms of ownership association, the individual unorganized worker is commonly helpless to exercise actual liberty of contract and to protect his freedom of labor, and thereby to obtain acceptable terms and conditions of employment, wherefore, though he should be free to decline to associate with his fellows, it is necessary that he have full freedom of association, self-organization, and designation of representatives of his own choosing, to negotiate the terms and conditions of his employment, and that he shall be free from the interference, restraint, or coercion of employers of labor, or their agents, in the designation of such representatives or in self-organization or in other concerted activities for the purpose of collective bargaining or other mutual aid or protection; therefore, the following definitions of, and limitations upon, the jurisdiction and authority of the courts of the United States are hereby enacted.

Sec. 3. Any undertaking or promise, such as is described in this section, or any other undertaking or promise in conflict with the public policy declared in section 2 of this Act, is hereby declared to be contrary to the public policy of the United States, shall not be enforceable in any court of the United States and shall not afford any basis for the granting of legal or equitable relief by any such court, including specifically the following:

Every undertaking or promise hereafter made, whether written or oral, express or implied, constituting or contained in any contract or agreement of hiring or employment between any individual, firm, company, association, or corporation, and any employee or prospective employee of the same whereby

(a) Either party to such contract or agreement undertakes or promises not to join, become, or remain a member of any labor organization or of any employer organization; or

(b) Either party to such contract or agreement undertakes or promises that he will withdraw from an employment relation in the event that he joins, becomes, or remains a member of any labor organization or of any employer organization.

Sec. 4. No court of the United States shall have jurisdiction to issue any restraining order or temporary or permanent injunction in any case involving or growing out of any labor dispute to prohibit any person or persons participating or interested in such dispute (as these terms are herein defined) from doing, whether singly or in concert, any of the following acts:

(a) Ceasing or refusing to perform any work or to remain in any relation of employment;

(b) Becoming or remaining a member of any labor organization or of any employer organization, regardless of any such undertaking or promise as is described in section 3 of this Act;

(c) Paying or giving to, or withholding from, any person participating or interested in such labor dispute, any strike or unemployment benefits or insurance, or other moneys or things of value;

(d) By all lawful means aiding any person participating or interested in any labor dispute who is being proceeded against in, or is prosecuting, any action or suit in any court of the United States or of any State;

(e) Giving publicity to the existence of, or the facts involved in, any labor dispute, whether by advertising, speaking, patrolling, or by any other method not involving fraud or violence;

(f) Assembling peaceably to act or to organize to act in promotion of their interests in a labor dispute;

(g) Advising or notifying any person of an intention to do any of the Acts heretofore specified;

(h) Agreeing with other persons to do or not to do any of the acts heretofore specified; and

(i) Advising, urging, or otherwise causing or inducing without fraud or violence the acts heretofore specified, regardless of any such undertaking or promise as is described in section 3 of this Act.

Sec. 5. No court of the United States shall have jurisdiction to issue a restraining order or temporary or permanent injunction upon the ground that any of the persons participating or interested in a labor dispute constitute or are engaged in an unlawful combination or conspiracy because of the doing in concert of the acts enumerated in section 4 of this Act.

Sec. 6. No officer or member of any association or organization, and no association or organization participating or interested in a labor dispute, shall be held responsible or liable in any court of the United States for the unlawful acts of individual officers, members, or agents, except upon clear proof of actual participation in, or actual authorization of, such acts, or of ratification of such acts after actual knowledge thereof.

Sec. 7. No court of the United States shall have jurisdiction to issue a temporary or permanent injunction in any case involving or growing out of a labor dispute, as herein defined, except after hearing the testimony of witnesses in open court (with opportunity for cross-examination) in support of the allegations of a complaint made under oath, and testimony in opposition thereto, if offered, and except after findings of fact by the court, to the effect—

(a) That unlawful acts have been threatened and will be committed unless restrained or have been committed and will be continued unless restrained, but no injunction or temporary restraining order shall be issued on account of any threat or unlawful act excepting against the person or persons, association, or organization making the threat or committing the unlawful act or actually authorizing or ratifying the same after actual knowledge thereof;

(b) That substantial and irreparable injury to complainant's property will follow:

(c) That as to each item of relief granted greater injury will be inflicted upon complainant by the denial of relief than will be inflicted upon defendants by the granting of relief;

(d) That complainant has no adequate remedy at law; and

(e) That the public officers charged with the duty to protect complainant's property are unable or unwilling to furnish adequate protection.

Such hearing shall be held after due and personal notice thereof has been given, in such manner as the court shall direct, to all known persons against whom relief is sought, and also to the chief of those public officials of the county and city within which the unlawful acts have been threatened or committed charged with the duty to protect complainant's property: *Provided, however,* That if a complainant shall also allege that, unless a temporary restraining order shall be issued without notice, a substantial and irreparable injury to complainant's property will be unavoidable, such a temporary restraining order may be issued upon testimony under oath, sufficient, if sustained, to justify the court in issuing a temporary injunction upon a hearing after notice. Such a temporary restraining order shall be effective for no longer than five days and shall become void at the expiration of said five days. No temporary restraining order or temporary injunction shall be issued except on condition that complainant shall first file an undertaking with adequate security in an amount to be fixed by the court sufficient to recompense those enjoined for any loss, expense, or damage caused by the improvident or erroneous issuance of such order or injunction, including all reasonable costs (together with a reasonable attorney's fee) and expense of defense against the order or against the granting of any injunctive relief sought in the same proceeding and subsequently denied by the court.

The undertaking herein mentioned shall be understood to signify an agreement entered into by the complainant and the surety upon which a decree may be rendered in the same suit or proceeding against said complainant and surety, upon a hearing to assess damages of which hearing complainant and surety shall have reasonable notice, the said complainant and surety submitting themselves to the jurisdiction of the court for that purpose. But nothing herein contained shall deprive any party having a claim or cause of action under or upon such undertaking from electing to pursue his ordinary remedy by suit at law or in equity.

Sec. 8. No restraining order or injunctive relief shall be granted to any complainant who has failed to comply with any obligation imposed by law which is involved in the labor dispute in question, or who has failed to make every reasonable effort to settle such dispute either by negotiation or with the aid of any available governmental machinery of mediation or voluntary arbitration.

Sec. 9. No restraining order or temporary or permanent injunction shall be granted in a case involving or growing out of a labor dispute, except on the basis of findings of fact made and filed by the court in the record of the case prior to the issuance of such restraining order or injunction; and every restraining order or injunction granted in a case involving or growing out of a labor dispute shall include only a prohibition of such specific act or acts as may be expressly complained of in the bill of complaint or petition filed in such case and as shall be expressly included in said findings of fact made and filed by the court as provided herein.

Sec. 10. Whenever any court of the United States shall issue or deny any temporary injunction in a case involving or growing out of a labor dispute, the court shall, upon the request of any party to the proceedings and on his filing the usual bond for costs, forthwith certify as in ordinary cases the record of the case to the circuit court of appeals for its review. Upon the filing of such record in the circuit court of appeals, the appeal shall be heard and the temporary injunctive order affirmed, modified, or set aside with the greatest possible expedition, giving the proceedings precedence over all other matters except older matters of the same character.

Sec. 11.* In all cases arising under this Act in which a person shall be charged with contempt in a court of the United States (as herein defined), the accused shall enjoy the right to a speedy and public trial by an impartial jury of the State and district wherein the contempt shall have been committed: *Provided,* That this right shall not apply to contempts committed in the presence of the court or so near thereto as to interfere directly with the administration of justice or to apply to the misbehavior, misconduct, or disobedience of any officer of the court in respect to the writs, orders, or process of the court.

Sec. 12.* The defendant in any proceeding for contempt of court may file with the court a demand for the retirement of the judge sitting in the proceeding, if the contempt arises from an attack upon the character or conduct of such judge and if the attack occurred elsewhere than in the

* Sections 11 and 12 were repealed in 1948, 62 Stat. 862. The text of Section 11 is now in 18 U.S.C. § 3692 (1982); Rule 42 of the Federal Rules of Criminal Procedure now governs the matters formerly treated in Section 12.

* Sections 11 and 12 were repealed in 1948, 62 Stat. 862. The text of Section 11 is now in 18 U.S.C. § 3692 (1982); Rule 42 of the Federal Rules of Criminal Procedure now governs the matters formerly treated in Section 12.

presence of the court or so near thereto as to interfere directly with the administration of justice. Upon the filing of any such demand the judge shall thereupon proceed no further, but another judge shall be designated in the same manner as is provided by law. The demand shall be filed prior to the hearing in the contempt proceeding.

Sec. 13.   When used in this Act, and for the purposes of this Act—

(a) A case shall be held to involve or to grow out of a labor dispute when the case involves persons who are engaged in the same industry, trade, craft, or occupation; or have direct or indirect interests therein; or who are employees of the same employer; or who are members of the same or an affiliated organization of employers or employees; whether such dispute is (1) between one or more employers or associations of employers and one or more employees or associations of employees; (2) between one or more employers or associations of employers and one or more employers or associations of employers; or (3) between one or more employees or associations of employees and one or more employees or associations of employees; or when the case involves any conflicting or competing interests in a "labor dispute" (as hereinafter defined) of "persons participating or interested" therein (as hereinafter defined).

(b) A person or association shall be held to be a person participating or interested in a labor dispute if relief is sought against him or it, and if he or it is engaged in the same industry, trade, craft, or occupation in which such dispute occurs, or has a direct or indirect interest therein, or is a member, officer, or agent of any association composed in whole or in part of employers or employees engaged in such industry, trade, craft, or occupation.

(c) The term "labor dispute" includes any controversy concerning terms or conditions of employment, or concerning the association or representation of persons in negotiating, fixing, maintaining, changing, or seeking to arrange terms or conditions of employment, regardless of whether or not the disputants stand in the proximate relation of employer and employee.

(d) The term "court of the United States" means any court of the United States whose jurisdiction has been or may be conferred or defined or limited by Act of Congress, including the courts of the District of Columbia.

Sec. 14.   If any provision of this Act or the application thereof to any person or circumstance is held unconstitutional or otherwise invalid, the remaining provisions of the Act and the application of such provisions to other persons or circumstances shall not be affected thereby.

Sec. 15.   All Acts and parts of Acts in conflict with the provisions of this Act are hereby repealed.

RAILWAY LABOR ACT

44 Stat., Part II, 577 (1926), as amended; 45 U.S.C. §§ 151–88 (1988).

TITLE I

Sec. 1. When used in this Act and for the purposes of this Act—

First. The term "carrier" includes any express company, sleeping-car company, carrier by railroad, subject to the Interstate Commerce Act, and any company which is directly or indirectly owned or controlled by or under common control with any carrier by railroad and which operates any equipment or facilities or performs any service (other than trucking service) in connection with the transportation, receipt, delivery, elevation, transfer in transit, refrigeration or icing, storage, and handling of property transported by railroad, and any receiver, trustee, or other individual or body, judicial or otherwise, when in the possession of the business of any such "carrier": *Provided, however,* That the term "carrier" shall not include any street, interurban, or suburban electric railway, unless such railway is operating as a part of a general steam-railroad system of transportation, but shall not exclude any part of the general steam-railroad system of transportation now or hereafter operated by any other motive power. The Interstate Commerce Commission is authorized and directed upon request of the Mediation Board or upon complaint of any party interested to determine after hearing whether any line operated by electric power falls within the terms of this proviso. The term "carrier" shall not include any company by reason of its being engaged in the mining of coal, the supplying of coal to a carrier where delivery is not beyond the mine tipple, and the operation of equipment or facilities therefor, or in any of such activities.

Second. The term "Adjustment Board" means the National Railroad Adjustment Board created by this Act.

Third. The term "Mediation Board" means the National Mediation Board created by this Act.

Fourth. The term "commerce" means commerce among the several States or between any State, Territory, or the District of Columbia and any foreign nation, or between any Territory or the District of Columbia and any State, or between any Territory and any other Territory, or between any Territory and the District of Columbia, or within any Territory or the District of Columbia, or between points in the same State but through any other State or any Territory or the District of Columbia or any foreign nation.

Fifth. The term "employee" as used herein includes every person in the service of a carrier (subject to its continuing authority to supervise and direct the manner of rendition of his service) who performs any work defined as that of an employee or subordinate official in the orders of the Interstate Commerce Commission now in effect, and as the same may be amended or interpreted by orders hereafter entered by the Commission pursuant to the authority which is conferred upon it to enter orders amending or interpreting such existing orders: *Provided, however,* That no occupational classification made by order of the Interstate Commerce Commission shall be construed to define the crafts according to which railway employees may be organized by their voluntary action, nor shall the jurisdiction or powers of such employee organizations be regarded as in any way limited or defined by the provisions of this Act or by the orders of the Commission. The term "employee" shall not include any individual while such individual is engaged in the physical operations consisting of the mining of coal, the preparation of coal, the handling (other than movement by rail with standard railroad locomotives) of coal not beyond the mine tipple, or the loading of coal at the tipple.

Sixth. The term "representative" means any person or persons, labor union, organization, or corporation designated either by a carrier or group of carriers or by its or their employees, to act for it or them.

Seventh. The term "district court" includes the United States District Court for the District of Columbia; and the term "circuit court of appeals" includes the United States Court of Appeals for the District of Columbia.

This Act may be cited as the "Railway Labor Act."

Sec. 2. The purposes of the Act are:

(1) To avoid any interruption to commerce or to the operation of any carrier engaged therein; (2) to forbid any limitation upon freedom of association among employees or any denial, as a condition of employment or otherwise, of the right of employees to join a labor organization; (3) to provide for the complete independence of carriers and of employees in the matter of self-organization; (4) to provide for the prompt and orderly settlement of all disputes concerning rates of pay, rules, or working conditions; (5) to provide for the prompt and orderly settlement of all disputes growing out of grievances or out of the interpretation or application of agreements covering rates of pay, rules, or working conditions.

First. It shall be the duty of all carriers, their officers, agents, and employees to exert every reasonable effort to make and maintain agreements concerning rates of pay, rules, and working conditions, and to settle all disputes, whether arising out of the application of such agreements or otherwise, in order to avoid any interruption to commerce or to the operation of any carrier growing out of any dispute between the carrier and the employees thereof.

Second. All disputes between a carrier or carriers and its or their employees shall be considered, and, if possible, decided, with all expedition, in conference between representatives designated and authorized so to confer, respectively, by the carrier or carriers and by the employees thereof interested in the dispute.

Third. Representatives, for the purposes of this Act, shall be designated by the respective parties without interference, influence, or coercion by either party over the designation of representatives by the other; and neither party shall in any way interfere with, influence, or coerce the other in its choice of representatives. Representatives of employees for the purposes of this Act need not be persons in the employ of the carrier, and no carrier shall, by interference, influence, or coercion seek in any manner to prevent the designation by its employees as their representatives of those who or which are not employees of the carrier.

Fourth. Employees shall have the right to organize and bargain collectively through representatives of their own choosing. The majority of any craft or class of employees shall have the right to determine who shall be the representative of the craft or class for the purposes of this Act. No carrier, its officers or agents, shall deny or in any way question the right of its employees to join, organize, or assist in organizing the labor organization of their choice, and it shall be unlawful for any carrier to interfere in any way with the organization of its employees, or to use the funds of the carrier in maintaining or assisting or contributing to any labor organization, labor representative, or other agency of collective bargaining, or in performing any work therefor, or to influence or coerce employees in an effort to induce them to join or remain or not to join or remain members of any labor organization or to deduct from the wages of employees any dues, fees, assessments, or other contributions payable to labor organizations, or to collect or to assist in the collection of any such dues, fees, assessments, or other contributions: *Provided,* That nothing in this Act shall be construed to prohibit a carrier from permitting an employee, individually, or local representatives of employees from conferring with management during working hours without loss of time, or to prohibit a carrier from furnishing free transportation to its employees while engaged in the business of a labor organization.

Fifth. No carrier, its officers, or agents shall require any person seeking employment to sign any contract or agreement promising to join or not to join a labor organization; and if any such contract has been enforced prior to the effective date of this Act, then such carrier shall notify the employees by an appropriate order that such contract has been discarded and is no longer binding on them in any way.

Sixth. In case of a dispute between a carrier or carriers and its or their employees, arising out of grievances or out of the interpretation or application of agreements concerning rates of pay, rules, or working conditions, it shall be the duty of the designated representative or representatives of such carrier or carriers and of such employees, within ten days after the receipt of notice of a desire on the part of either party to confer in respect to such dispute, to specify a time and place at which such conference shall be held: *Provided,* (1) That the place so specified shall be situated upon the line of the carrier involved or as otherwise mutually agreed upon; and (2) that the time so specified shall allow the designated conferees reasonable opportunity to reach such place of conference, but shall not exceed twenty days from the receipt of such notice: *And provided further,* That nothing in this Act shall be construed to supersede the provisions of any agreement (as to conferences) then in effect between the parties.

Seventh. No carrier, its officers, or agents shall change the rates of pay, rules, or working conditions of its employees, as a class as embodied in agreements except in the manner prescribed in such agreements or in section 6 of this Act.

Eighth. Every carrier shall notify its employees by printed notices in such form and posted at such times and places as shall be specified by the Mediation Board that all disputes between the carrier and its employees will be handled in accordance with the requirements of this Act, and in such notices there shall be printed verbatim, in large type, the third, fourth, and fifth paragraphs of this section. The provisions of said paragraphs are hereby made a part of the contract of employment between the carrier and each employee, and shall be held binding upon the parties, regardless of any other express or implied agreements between them.

Ninth. If any dispute shall arise among a carrier's employees as to who are the representatives of such employees designated and authorized in accordance with the requirements of this Act, it shall be the duty of the Mediation Board, upon request of either party to the dispute, to investigate such dispute and to certify to both parties, in writing, within thirty days after the receipt of the invocation of its services, the name or names of the individuals or organizations that have been designated and authorized to represent the employees involved in the dispute, and certify the same to the carrier. Upon receipt of such certification the carrier shall treat with the representative so certified as the representative of the craft or class for the purposes of this Act. In such an investigation, the Mediation Board shall be authorized to take a secret ballot of the employees involved, or to utilize any other appropriate method of ascertaining the names of their duly designated and authorized representatives in such manner as shall insure the choice of representatives by the employees without interference, influence, or coercion exercised by the carrier. In the conduct of any election for the purposes herein indicated the Board shall designate who may participate in the election and establish the rules to govern the election, or may appoint a committee of three neutral persons who after hearing shall within ten days designate the employees who may participate in the election. The Board shall have access to and have power to make copies of the books and records of the carriers to obtain and utilize such information as may be deemed necessary by it to carry out the purposes and provisions of this paragraph.

Tenth. The willful failure or refusal of any carrier, its officers, or agents to comply with the terms of the third, fourth, fifth, seventh, or eighth paragraph of this section shall be a misdemeanor, and upon conviction thereof the carrier, officer, or agent offending shall be subject to a fine of not less than $1,000 nor more than $20,000 or imprisonment for not more than six months, or both fine and imprisonment, for each offense, and each day during which such carrier, officer, or agent shall willfully fail or refuse to comply with the terms of the said paragraphs of this section shall constitute a separate offense. It shall be the duty of any United States attorney to whom any duly designated representative of a carrier's employees may apply to institute in the proper court and to prosecute under the direction of the Attorney General of the United States, all necessary proceedings for the enforcement of the provisions of this section, and for the punishment of all violations thereof and the costs and expenses of such prosecution shall be paid out of the appropriation for the expenses of the courts of the United States: *Provided,* That nothing in this Act shall be construed to require an individual employee to render labor or service without his consent, nor shall anything in this Act be construed to make the quitting of his labor by an individual employee an illegal act; nor shall any court issue any process to compel the performance by an individual employee of such labor or service, without his consent.

Eleventh. Notwithstanding any other provisions of this chapter, or of any other statute or law of the United States, or Territory thereof, or of any State, any carrier or carriers as defined in this chapter and a labor organization or labor organizations duly designated and authorized to represent employees in accordance with the requirements of this chapter shall be permitted—

(a) to make agreements, requiring, as a condition of continued employment, that within sixty days following the beginning of such employment, or the effective date of such agreements, whichever is the later, all employees shall become members of the labor organization representing their craft or class: *Provided,* That no such agreement shall require such condition of employment with respect to employees to whom membership is not available upon the same terms and conditions as are generally applicable to any other member or with respect to employees to whom membership was denied or terminated for any reason other than the failure of the employee to tender the periodic dues, initiation fees, and assessments (not including fines and penalties) uniformly required as a condition of acquiring or retaining membership.

(b) to make agreements providing for the deduction by such carrier or carriers from the wages of its or their employees in a craft or class and payment to the labor organization representing the craft or class of such employees, of any periodic dues, initiation fees, and assessments (not including fines and penalties) uniformly required as a condition of acquiring or retaining membership: *Provided,* That no such agreement shall be effective with respect to any individual employee until he shall have furnished the employer with a written assignment to the labor organization of such membership dues, initiation fees, and assessments, which shall be revocable in writing after the expiration of one year or upon the termination date of the applicable collective agreement, whichever occurs sooner.

* * *

Sec. 3. First. There is hereby established a Board, to be known as the "National Railroad Adjustment Board", the members of which shall be selected within thirty days after June 21, 1934, and it is hereby provided—

(a) That the said Adjustment Board shall consist of thirty-four members, seventeen of whom shall be selected by the carriers and seventeen by such labor organizations of the employees, national in scope, as have been or may be organized in accordance with the provisions of section 2 of this Act.

(b) The carriers, acting each through its board of directors or its receiver or receivers, trustee or trustees, or through an officer or officers designated for that purpose by such board, trustee or trustees, or receiver or receivers, shall prescribe the rules under which its representatives shall be selected and shall select the representatives of the carriers on the Adjustment Board and designate the division on which each such representative shall serve, but no carrier or system of carriers shall have more than one voting representative on any division of the Board.

(c) Except as provided in the second paragraph of subsection (h) of this section, the national labor organizations as defined in paragraph (a) of this section, acting each through the chief executive or other medium designated by the organization or association thereof, shall prescribe the rules under which the labor members of the Adjustment Board shall be selected and shall select such members and designate the division on which each member shall serve; but no labor organization shall have more than one voting representative on any division of the Board.

* * *

(h) The said Adjustment Board shall be composed of four divisions, whose proceedings shall be independent of one another, and the said divisions as well as the number of their members shall be as follows:

First division: To have jurisdiction over disputes involving train-and yard-service employees of carriers; that is, engineers, firemen, hostlers, and outside hostler helpers, conductors, trainmen, and yard-service employees. This division shall consist of eight members, four of whom shall be selected and designated by the carriers and four of whom shall be selected and designated by the labor organizations * * *.

Second division: To have jurisdiction over disputes involving machinists, boilermakers, blacksmiths, sheet-metal workers, electrical workers, car men, the helpers and apprentices of all the foregoing, coach cleaners, power-house employees, and railroad-shop laborers. This division shall consist of ten members, five of whom shall be selected by the carriers and five by the national labor organizations of the employees.

Third division: To have jurisdiction over disputes involving station, tower, and telegraph employees, train dispatchers, maintenance-of-way men, clerical employees, freight handlers, express, station, and store employees, signal men, sleeping-car conductors, sleeping-car porters, and maids and dining-car employees. This division shall consist of ten members, five of whom shall be selected by the carriers and five by the national labor organizations of employees.

Fourth division: To have jurisdiction over disputes involving employees of carriers directly or indirectly engaged in transportation of passengers or property by water, and all other employees of carriers over which jurisdiction is not given to the first, second, and third divisions. This division shall consist of six members, three of whom shall be selected by the carriers and three by the national labor organizations of the employees.

(i) The disputes between an employee or group of employees and a carrier or carriers growing out of grievances or out of the interpretation or application of agreements concerning rates of pay, rules, or working conditions, including cases pending and unadjusted on the date of approval of this Act, shall be handled in the usual manner up to and including the chief operating officer of the carrier designated to handle such disputes; but, failing to reach an adjustment in this manner, the disputes may be referred by petition of the parties or by either party to the appropriate division of the Adjustment Board with a full statement of the facts and all supporting data bearing upon the disputes.

(j) Parties may be heard either in person, by counsel, or by other representatives, as they may respectively elect, and the several divisions of the Adjustment Board shall give due notice of all hearings to the employee or employees and the carrier or carriers involved in any disputes submitted to them.

(k) Any division of the Adjustment Board shall have authority to empower two or more of its members to conduct hearings and make findings upon disputes, when properly submitted, at any place designated by the division: *Provided, however,* That except as provided in paragraph (h) of this section, final awards as to any such dispute must be made by the entire division as hereinafter provided.

* * *

(m) The awards of the several divisions of the Adjustment Board shall be stated in writing. A copy of the awards shall be furnished to the respective parties to the controversy, and the awards shall be final and binding upon both parties to the dispute. In case a dispute arises involving an interpretation of the award the division of the Board upon request of either party shall interpret the award in the light of the dispute.

(n) A majority vote of all members of the division of the Adjustment Board eligible to vote shall be competent to make an award with respect to any dispute submitted to it.

(o) In case of an award by any division of the Adjustment Board in favor of petitioner, the division of the Board shall make an order, directed to the carrier, to make the award effective and, if the award includes a requirement for the payment of money, to pay the employee the sum to which he is entitled under the award on or before a day named. In the event any division determines that an award favorable to the petitioner should not be made in any dispute referred to it, the division shall make an order to the petitioner stating such determination.

(p) If a carrier does not comply with an order of a division of the Adjustment Board within the time limit in such order, the petitioner, or any person for whose benefit such order was made, may file in the District Court of the United States for the district in which he resides or in which is located the principal operating office of the carrier, or through which the carrier operates, a petition setting forth briefly the causes for which he claims relief, and the order of the division of the Adjustment Board in the premises. Such suit in the District Court of the United States shall proceed in all respects as other civil suits, except that on the trial of such suit the findings and order of the division of the Adjustment Board shall be conclusive on the parties, and except that the petitioner shall not be liable for costs in the district court nor for costs at any subsequent stage of the proceedings, unless they accrue upon his appeal, and such costs shall be paid out of the appropriation for the expenses of the courts of the United States. If the petitioner shall finally prevail he shall be allowed a reasonable attorney's fee, to be taxed and collected as a part of the costs of the suit. The district courts are empowered, under the rules of the court governing actions at law, to make such order and enter such judgment, by writ of mandamus or otherwise, as may be appropriate to enforce or set aside the order of the division of the Adjustment Board: *Provided, however,* That such order may not be set aside except for failure of the division to comply with the requirements of this chapter, for failure of the order to conform, or confine itself, to matters within the scope of the division's jurisdiction, or for fraud or corruption by a member of the division making the order.

(q) If any employee or group of employees, or any carrier, is aggrieved by the failure of any division of the Adjustment Board to make an award in a dispute referred to it, or is aggrieved by any of the terms of an award or by the failure of the division to include certain terms in such award, then such employee or group of employees or carrier may file in any United States district court in which a petition under paragraph (p) could be filed, a petition for review of the division's order. A copy of the petition shall be forthwith transmitted by the clerk of the court to the Adjustment Board. The Adjustment Board shall file in the court the record of the proceedings on which it based its action. The court shall have jurisdiction to affirm the order of the division, or to set it aside, in whole or in part, or it may remand the proceeding to the division for such further action as it may direct. On such review, the findings and order of the division shall be conclusive on the parties, except that the order of the division may be set aside, in whole or in part, or remanded to the division, for failure of the division to comply with the requirements of this chapter, for failure of the order to conform, or confine itself, to matters within the scope of the division's jurisdiction, or for fraud or corruption by a member of the division making the order. The judgment of the court shall be subject to review as provided in sections 1291 and 1254 of title 28, United States Code.

(r) All actions at law based upon the provisions of this section shall be begun within two years from the time the cause of action accrues under the award of the division of the Adjustment Board, and not after.

* * *

Second. Nothing in this section shall be construed to prevent any individual carrier, system, or group of carriers and any class or classes of its or their employees, all acting through their representatives, selected in accordance with the provisions of this Act, from mutually agreeing to the establishment of system, group, or regional boards of adjustment for the purpose of adjusting and deciding disputes of the character specified in this section. In the event that either party to such a system, group, or regional board of adjustment is dissatisfied with such arrangement, it may upon ninety days' notice to the other party elect to come under the jurisdiction of the Adjustment Board.

    * * *

Sec. 4. First. * * * There is hereby established, as an independent agency in the executive branch of the Government, a board to be known as the "National Mediation Board," to be composed of three members appointed by the President, by and with the advice and consent of the Senate, not more than two of whom shall be of the same political party. Each member of the Mediation Board in office on January 1, 1965, shall be deemed to have been appointed for a term of office which shall expire on July 1 of the year his term would have otherwise expired. The terms of office of all successors shall expire three years after the expiration of the terms for which their predecessors were appointed; but any member appointed to fill a vacancy occurring prior to the expiration of the term of which his predecessor was appointed shall be appointed only for the unexpired term of his predecessor. * * *

A member of the Board may be removed by the President for inefficiency, neglect of duty, malfeasance in office, or ineligibility, but for no other cause.

    * * *

Sec. 5. First. The parties, or either party, to a dispute between an employee or group of employees and a carrier may invoke the services of the Mediation Board in any of the following cases:

(a) A dispute concerning changes in rates of pay, rules, or working conditions not adjusted by the parties in conference.

(b) Any other dispute not referable to the National Railroad Adjustment Board and not adjusted in conference between the parties or where conferences are refused.

The Mediation Board may proffer its services in case any labor emergency is found by it to exist at any time.

In either event the said Board shall promptly put itself in communication with the parties to such controversy, and shall use its best efforts, by mediation, to bring them to agreement. If such efforts to bring about an amicable settlement through mediation shall be unsuccessful, the said Board shall at once endeavor as its final required action (except as provided in paragraph third of this section and in section 10 of this Act) to induce the parties to submit their controversy to arbitration, in accordance with the provisions of this Act.

If arbitration at the request of the Board shall be refused by one or both parties, the Board shall at once notify both parties in writing that its mediatory efforts have failed and for thirty days thereafter, unless in the intervening period the parties agree to arbitration, or an emergency board shall be created under section 10 of this Act, no change shall be made in the rates of pay, rules, or working conditions or establish practices in effect prior to the time the dispute arose.

* * *

Sec. 6. Carriers and representatives of the employees shall give at least thirty days' written notice of an intended change in agreements affecting rates of pay, rules, or working conditions, and the time and place for the beginning of conference between the representatives of the parties interested in such intended changes shall be agreed upon within ten days after the receipt of said notice, and said time shall be within the thirty days provided in the notice. In every case where such notice of intended change has been given, or conferences are being held with reference thereto, or the services of the Mediation Board have been requested by either party, or said Board has proffered its services, rates of pay, rules, or working conditions shall not be altered by the carrier until the controversy has been finally acted upon as required by section 5 of this Act, by the Mediation Board, unless a period of ten days has elapsed after termination of conferences without request for or proffer of the services of the Mediation Board.

Sec. 7.   First. Whenever a controversy shall arise between a carrier or carriers and its or their employees which is not settled either in conference between representatives of the parties or by the appropriate adjustment board or through mediation, in the manner provided in the preceding sections, such controversy may, by agreement of the parties to such controversy, be submitted to the arbitration of a board of three (or, if the parties to the controversy so stipulate, of six) persons: *Provided, however,* That the failure or refusal of either party to submit a controversy to arbitration shall not be construed as a violation of any legal obligation imposed upon such party by the terms of this Act or otherwise.

Second. Such board of arbitration shall be chosen in the following manner:

(a) In the case of a board of three, the carrier or carriers and the representatives of the employees, parties respectively to the agreement to arbitrate, shall each name one arbitrator; the two arbitrators thus chosen shall select a third arbitrator. If the arbitrators chosen by the parties shall fail to name the third arbitrator within five days after their first meeting, such third arbitrator shall be named by the Mediation Board.

(b) In the case of a board of six, the carrier or carriers and the representatives of the employees, parties respectively to the agreement to arbitrate, shall each name two arbitrators; the four arbitrators thus chosen shall, by a majority vote, select the remaining two arbitrators. If the arbitrators chosen by the parties shall fail to name the two arbitrators within fifteen days after their first meeting, the said two arbitrators, or as many of them as have not been named, shall be named by the Mediation Board.

Third. (a) When the arbitrators selected by the respective parties have agreed upon the remaining arbitrator or arbitrators, they shall notify the Mediation Board, and, in the event of their failure to agree upon any or upon all of the necessary arbitrators within the period fixed by this Act, they shall, at the expiration of such period, notify the Mediation Board of the arbitrators selected, if any, or of their failure to make or complete such selection.

(b) The board of arbitration shall organize and select its own chairman and make all necessary rules for conducting its hearings: *Provided, however,* That the board of arbitration shall be bound to give the parties to the controversy a full and fair hearing, which shall include an opportunity to present evidence in support of their claims, and an opportunity to present their case in person, by counsel, or by other representative as they may respectively elect.

* * *

Sec. 9. First. The award of a board of arbitration, having been acknowledged as herein provided, shall be filed in the clerk's office of the district court designated in the agreement to arbitrate.

Second. An award acknowledged and filed as herein provided shall be conclusive on the parties as to the merits and facts of the controversy submitted to arbitration, and unless, within ten days after the filing of the award, a petition to impeach the award, on the grounds hereinafter set forth, shall be filed in the clerk's office of the court in which the award has been filed, the court shall enter judgment on the award, which judgment shall be final and conclusive on the parties.

Third. Such petition for the impeachment or contesting of any award so filed shall be entertained by the court only on one or more of the following grounds:

(a) That the award plainly does not conform to the substantive requirements laid down by this Act for such awards, or that the proceedings were not substantially in conformity with this Act;

(b) That the award does not conform, nor confine itself, to the stipulations of the agreement to arbitrate; or

(c) That a member of the board of arbitration rendering the award was guilty of fraud or corruption; or that a party to the arbitration practiced fraud or corruption which fraud or corruption affected the result of the arbitration. *Provided, however,* That no court shall entertain any such petition on the ground that an award is invalid for uncertainty; in such case the proper remedy shall be a submission of such award to a reconvened board, or subcommittee thereof, for interpretation, as provided by this Act: *Provided further,* That an award contested as herein provided shall be construed liberally by the court, with a view to favoring its validity, and that no award shall be set aside for trivial irregularity or clerical error, going only to form and not to substance.

* * *

Sec. 10. If a dispute between a carrier and its employees be not adjusted under the foregoing provisions of this Act and should, in the judgment of the Mediation Board, threaten substantially to interrupt interstate commerce to a degree such as to deprive any section of the country of essential transportation service, the Mediation Board shall notify the President, who may thereupon, in his discretion, create a board to investigate and report respecting such dispute. Such board shall be composed of such number of persons as to the President may seem desirable: *Provided, however,* That no member appointed shall be pecuniarily or otherwise interested in any organization of employees or any carrier. The compensation of the members of any such board shall be fixed by the President. Such board shall be created separately in each instance and it shall investigate promptly the facts as to the dispute and make a report thereon to the President within thirty days from the date of its creation.

* * *

After the creation of such board, and for thirty days after such board has made its report to the President, no change, except by agreement, shall be made by the parties to the controversy in the conditions out of which the dispute arose.

* * *

TITLE II

Sec. 201. All of the provisions of title I of this Act, except the provisions of section 3 thereof, are extended to and shall cover every common carrier by air engaged in interstate or foreign commerce, and every carrier by air transporting mail for or under contract with the United States Government, and every air pilot or other person who performs any work as an employee or subordinate official of such carrier or carriers, subject to its or their continuing authority to supervise and direct the manner of rendition of his service.

Sec. 202. The duties, requirements, penalties, benefits, and privileges prescribed and established by the provisions of title I of this Act, except section 3 thereof, shall apply to said carriers by air and their employees in the same manner and to the same extent as though such carriers and their employees were specifically included within the definition of "carrier" and "employee", respectively, in section 1 thereof.

Sec. 203. The parties or either party to a dispute between an employee or a group of employees and a carrier or carriers by air may invoke the services of the National Mediation Board and the jurisdiction of said Mediation Board is extended to any of the following cases:

(a) A dispute concerning changes in rates of pay, rules, or working conditions not adjusted by the parties in conference.

(b) Any other dispute not referable to an adjustment board, as hereinafter provided, and not adjusted in conference between the parties, or where conferences are refused.

The National Mediation Board may proffer its services in case any labor emergency is found by it to exist at any time.

The services of the Mediation Board may be invoked in a case under this title in the same manner and to the same extent as are the disputes covered by section 5 of title I of this Act.

Sec. 204. The disputes between an employee or group of employees and a carrier or carriers by air growing out of grievances, or out of interpretation or application of agreements concerning rates of pay, rules, or working conditions, including cases pending and unadjusted on the date of approval of this Act before the National Labor Relations Board, shall be handled in the usual manner up to and including the chief operating officer of the carrier designated to handle such disputes; but, failing to reach an adjustment in this manner, the disputes may be referred by petition of the parties or by either party to an appropriate adjustment board, as hereinafter provided, with a full statement of the facts and supporting data bearing upon the disputes.

It shall be the duty of every carrier and of its employees, acting through their representatives, selected in accordance with the provisions of this title, to establish a board of adjustment of jurisdiction not exceeding the jurisdiction which may be lawfully exercised by system, group, or regional boards of adjustment, under the authority of section 3, Title I, of this Act.

Such boards of adjustment may be established by agreement between employees and carriers either on any individual carrier, or system, or group of carriers by air and any class or classes of its or their employees; or pending the establishment of a permanent National Board of Adjustment as hereinafter provided. Nothing in this Act shall prevent said carriers by air, or any class or classes of their employees, both acting through their representatives selected in accordance with provisions of this title, from mutually agreeing to the establishment of a National Board of Adjustment of temporary duration and of similarly limited jurisdiction.

* * *

NATIONAL LABOR RELATIONS ACT *

49 Stat. 449 (1935), as amended; 29 U.S.C. §§ 151–69 (1988).

FINDINGS AND POLICIES

Sec. 1. The denial by **some** employers of the right of employees to organize and the refusal by **some** employers to accept the procedure of collective bargaining lead to strikes and other forms of industrial strife or unrest, which have the intent or the necessary effect of burdening or obstructing commerce by (a) impairing the efficiency, safety, or operation of the instrumentalities of commerce; (b) occurring in the current of commerce; (c) materially affecting, restraining, or controlling the flow of raw materials or manufactured or processed goods from or into the channels of commerce, or the prices of such materials or goods in commerce; or (d) causing diminution of employment and wages in such volume as substantially to impair or disrupt the market for goods flowing from or into the channels of commerce.

The inequality of bargaining power between employees who do not possess full freedom of association or actual liberty of contract, and employers who are organized in the corporate or other forms of ownership association substantially burdens and affects the flow of commerce, and tends to aggravate recurrent business depressions, by depressing wage rates and the purchasing power of wage earners in industry and by preventing the stabilization of competitive wage rates and working conditions within and between industries.

Experience has proved that protection by law of the right of employees to organize and bargain collectively safeguards commerce from injury, impairment, or interruption, and promotes the flow of commerce by removing certain recognized sources of industrial strife and unrest, by encouraging practices fundamental to the friendly adjustment of industrial disputes arising out of differences as to wages, hours, or other working conditions, and by restoring equality of bargaining power between employers and employees.

---

* The text of the original Wagner Act of 1935 is printed in roman type; the Taft-Hartley amendments of 1947 are in boldface type; the Landrum-Griffin amendments of 1959 are in italics; the 1974 amendments are underscored. Deleted matter is in brackets; bracketed matter in regular roman type was deleted in 1947, and bracketed matter in boldface type was deleted in 1959. Other amendments and deletions are specifically noted.

Experience has further demonstrated that certain practices by some labor organizations, their officers, and members have the intent or the necessary effect of burdening or obstructing commerce by preventing the free flow of goods in such commerce through strikes and other forms of industrial unrest or through concerted activities which impair the interest of the public in the free flow of such commerce. The elimination of such practices is a necessary condition to the assurance of the rights herein guaranteed.

It is hereby declared to be the policy of the United States to eliminate the causes of certain substantial obstructions to the free flow of commerce and to mitigate and eliminate these obstructions when they have occurred by encouraging the practice and procedure of collective bargaining and by protecting the exercise by workers of full freedom of association, self-organization, and designation of representatives of their own choosing, for the purpose of negotiating the terms and conditions of their employment or other mutual aid or protection.

DEFINITIONS

Sec. 2. When used in this Act—

(1) The term "person" includes one or more individuals, labor organizations, partnerships, associations, corporations, legal representatives, trustees, trustees in bankruptcy, or receivers.

(2) The term "employer" includes any person acting [in the interest of] **as an agent** of an employer, directly or indirectly, but shall not include the United States **or any wholly owned Government corporation, or any Federal Reserve Bank,** or any State or political subdivision thereof, [**or any corporation or association operating a hospital, if no part of the net earnings inures to the benefit of any private shareholder or individual,**]* or any person subject to the Railway Labor Act, as amended from time to time, or any labor organization (other than when acting as an employer), or anyone acting in the capacity of officer or agent of such labor organization.

(3) The term "employee" shall include any employee, and shall not be limited to the employees of a particular employer, unless the Act explicitly states otherwise, and shall include any individual whose work has ceased as a consequence of, or in connection with, any current labor dispute or because of any unfair labor practice, and who has not obtained any other regular and substantially equivalent employment, but shall not include any individual employed as an agricultural laborer, or in the domestic service of any family or person at his home, or any individual employed by his parent or spouse, **or any individual having the status of an independent contractor, or any individual employed as a supervisor, or any individual employed by an employer subject to the Railway Labor**

---

* The bracketed matter was deleted in 1974, by 88 Stat. 395 (1974).

Act, as amended from time to time, or by any other person who is not an employer as herein defined.

(4) The term "representatives" includes any individual or labor organization.

(5) The term "labor organization" means any organization of any kind, or any agency or employee representation committee or plan, in which employees participate and which exists for the purpose, in whole or in part, of dealing with employers concerning grievances, labor disputes, wages, rates of pay, hours of employment, or conditions of work.

(6) The term "commerce" means trade, traffic, commerce, transportation, or communication among the several States, or between the District of Columbia or any Territory of the United States and any State or other Territory, or between any foreign country and any State, Territory, or the District of Columbia, or within the District of Columbia or any Territory, or between points in the same State but through any other State or any Territory or the District of Columbia or any foreign country.

(7) The term "affecting commerce" means in commerce, or burdening or obstructing commerce or the free flow of commerce, or having led or tending to lead to a labor dispute burdening or obstructing commerce or the free flow of commerce.

(8) The term "unfair labor practice" means any unfair labor practice listed in section 8.

(9) The term "labor dispute" includes any controversy concerning terms, tenure or conditions of employment, or concerning the association or representation of persons in negotiating, fixing, maintaining, changing, or seeking to arrange terms or conditions of employment, regardless of whether the disputants stand in the proximate relation of employer and employee.

(10) The term "National Labor Relations Board" means the National Labor Relations Board provided for in section 3 of this Act.

(11) The term "supervisor" means any individual having authority, in the interest of the employer, to hire, transfer, suspend, lay off, recall, promote, discharge, assign, reward, or discipline other employees, or responsibly to direct them, or to adjust their grievances, or effectively to recommend such action, if in connection with the foregoing the exercise of such authority is not of a merely routine or clerical nature, but requires the use of independent judgment.

(12) The term "professional employee" means—

(a) any employee engaged in work (i) predominantly intellectual and varied in character as opposed to routine mental, manual, mechanical, or physical work; (ii) involving the consistent exercise of discretion and judgment in its performance; (iii) of such a character that the output produced or the result accomplished cannot be standardized in relation to a given

period of time; (iv) requiring knowledge of an advanced type in a field of science or learning customarily acquired by a prolonged course of specialized intellectual instruction and study in an institution of higher learning or a hospital, as distinguished from a general academic education or from an apprenticeship or from training in the performance of routine mental, manual, or physical processes; or

(b) any employee, who (i) has completed the courses of specialized intellectual instruction and study described in clause (iv) of paragraph (a), and (ii) is performing related work under the supervision of a professional person to qualify himself to become a professional employee as defined in paragraph (a).

(13) In determining whether any person is acting as an "agent" of another person so as to make such other person responsible for his acts, the question of whether the specific acts performed were actually authorized or subsequently ratified shall not be controlling.

(14) The term "health care institution" shall include any hospital, convalescent hospital, health maintenance organization, health clinic, nursing home, extended care facility, or other institution devoted to the care of sick, infirm, or aged person.

NATIONAL LABOR RELATIONS BOARD

Sec. 3.* (a) The National Labor Relations Board (hereinafter called the "Board") created by this Act prior to its amendment by the Labor Management Relations Act, 1947, is continued as an agency of the United States, except that the Board shall consist of five instead of three members, appointed by the President by and with the advice and consent of the Senate. Of the two additional members so provided for, one shall be appointed for a term of five years and the other for a term of two years. Their successors, and the successors of the other members, shall be appointed for terms of five years each, excepting that any individual chosen to fill a vacancy shall be appointed only for the unexpired term of the member whom he shall succeed. The President shall designate one member to serve as Chairman of the Board. Any member of the Board may be removed by the President, upon notice and hearing, for neglect of duty or malfeasance in office, but for no other cause.

(b) **The Board is authorized to delegate to any group of three or more members any or all of the powers which it may itself exercise.** *The Board is also authorized to delegate to its regional directors its powers under section 9 to determine the unit appropriate for the purpose*

---

* The changes made in Sections 3 and 4 by the Taft-Hartley amendments were so extensive, that the typeface designations for these two sections show only the 1947 and 1959 amendments.

of collective bargaining, to investigate and provide for hearings, and determine whether a question of representation exists, and to direct an election or take a secret ballot under subsection (c) or (e) of section 9 and certify the results thereof, except that upon the filing of a request therefor with the Board by any interested person, the Board may review any action of a regional director delegated to him under this paragraph, but such a review shall not, unless specifically ordered by the Board, operate as a stay of any action taken by the regional director. **A vacancy in the Board shall not impair the right of the remaining members to exercise all of the powers of the Board, and three members of the Board shall, at all times, constitute a quorum of the Board, except that two members shall constitute a quorum of any group designated pursuant to the first sentence hereof. The Board shall have an official seal which shall be judicially noticed.**

(c) The Board shall at the close of each fiscal year make a report in writing to Congress and to the President [stating in detail the cases it has heard, the decisions it has rendered, the names, salaries, and duties of all employees and officers in the employ or under the supervision of the Board, and an account of all moneys it has disbursed.]* summarizing significant case activities and operations for that fiscal year.

(d) **There shall be a General Counsel of the Board who shall be appointed by the President, by and with the advice and consent of the Senate, for a term of four years. The General Counsel of the Board shall exercise general supervision over all attorneys employed by the Board (other than administrative law judges ** and legal assistants to Board members) and over the officers and employees in the regional offices. He shall have final authority, on behalf of the Board, in respect of the investigation of charges and issuance of complaints under section 10, and in respect of the prosecution of such complaints before the Board, and shall have such other duties as the Board may prescribe or as may be provided by law.** *In case of a vacancy in the office of the General Counsel the President is authorized to designate the officer or employee who shall act as General Counsel during such vacancy, but no person or persons so designated shall so act (1) for more than forty days when the Congress is in session unless a nomination to fill such vacancy shall have been submitted to the Senate, or (2) after the adjournment sine die of the session of the Senate in which such nomination was submitted.*

Sec. 4.   (a) Each member of the Board and the General Counsel of the Board [shall receive a salary of $12,000 per annum,] shall be eligible for reappointment, and shall not engage in any other business, vocation, or employment. The Board shall appoint an executive secretary, and such attorneys, examiners, and regional directors, and such other employees as it may from time to time

---

* The bracketed matter was deleted in part in 1975 and in part in 1982, and the matter following was added in 1982.

** The title "administrative law judge" was adopted in 5 U.S.C. § 3105, in 1972.

find necessary for the proper performance of its duties. The Board may not employ any attorneys for the purpose of reviewing transcripts of hearings or preparing drafts of opinions except that any attorney employed for assignment as a legal assistant to any Board member may for such Board member review such transcripts and prepare such drafts. No administrative law judge's report shall be reviewed, either before or after its publication, by any person other than a member of the Board or his legal assistant, and no administrative law judge shall advise or consult with the Board with respect to exceptions taken to his findings, rulings, or recommendations. The Board may establish or utilize such regional, local, or other agencies, and utilize such voluntary and uncompensated services, as may from time to time be needed. Attorneys appointed under this section may, at the direction of the Board, appear for and represent the Board in any case in court. Nothing in this Act shall be construed to authorize the Board to appoint individuals for the purpose of conciliation or mediation, or for economic analysis.

(b) All of the expenses of the Board, including all necessary traveling and subsistence expenses outside the District of Columbia incurred by the members or employees of the Board under its orders, shall be allowed and paid on the presentation of itemized vouchers therefor approved by the Board or by any individual it designates for that purpose.

Sec. 5. The principal office of the Board shall be in the District of Columbia, but it may meet and exercise any or all of its powers at any other place. The Board may, by one or more of its members or by such agents or agencies as it may designate, prosecute any inquiry necessary to its functions in any part of the United States. A member who participates in such an inquiry shall not be disqualified from subsequently participating in a decision of the Board in the same case.

Sec. 6. The Board shall have authority from time to time to make, amend, and rescind, **in the manner prescribed by the Administrative Procedure Act,** such rules and regulations as may be necessary to carry out the provisions of this Act. [Such rules and regulations shall be effective upon publication in the manner which the Board shall prescribe.]

RIGHTS OF EMPLOYEES

Sec. 7. Employees shall have the right to self-organization, to form, join, or assist labor organizations, to bargain collectively through representatives of their own choosing, and to engage in other concerted activities for the purpose of collective bargaining or other mutual aid or protection, **and shall also have the right to refrain from any or all of such activities except to the extent that such right may be affected by an agreement requiring membership in a labor organization as a condition of employment as authorized in section 8(a)(3).**

UNFAIR LABOR PRACTICES

Sec. 8.   (a) It shall be an unfair labor practice for an employer—

(1) to interfere with, restrain, or coerce employees in the exercise of the rights guaranteed in section 7;

(2) to dominate or interfere with the formation or administration of any labor organization or contribute financial or other support to it: *Provided,* That subject to rules and regulations made and published by the Board pursuant to section 6, an employer shall not be prohibited from permitting employees to confer with him during working hours without loss of time or pay;

(3) by discrimination in regard to hire or tenure of employment or any term or condition of employment to encourage or discourage membership in any labor organization: *Provided,* That nothing in this Act, or in any other statute of the United States, shall preclude an employer from making an agreement with a labor organization (not established, maintained, or assisted by any action defined in **section 8(a) of** this Act as an unfair labor practice) to require as a condition of employment membership therein **on or after the thirtieth day following the beginning of such employment or the effective date of such agreement, whichever is the later, (i)** if such labor organization is the representative of the employees as provided in section 9(a), in the appropriate collective-bargaining unit covered by such agreement when made, **[and has at the time the agreement was made or within the preceding twelve months received from the Board a notice of compliance with Section 9(f), (g), (h)], and (ii) unless following an election held as provided in section 9(e) within one year preceding the effective date of such agreement, the Board shall have certified that at least a majority of the employees eligible to vote in such election have voted to rescind the authority of such labor organization to make such an agreement:*** *Provided further,* **That no employer shall justify any discrimination against an employee for non-membership in a labor organization (A) if he has reasonable grounds for believing that such membership was not available to the employee on the same terms and conditions generally applicable to other members, or (B) if he has reasonable grounds for believing that membership was denied or terminated for reasons other than the failure of the employee to tender the periodic dues and the initiation fees uniformly required as a condition of acquiring or retaining membership;**

(4) to discharge or otherwise discriminate against an employee because he has filed charges or given testimony under this Act;

(5) to refuse to bargain collectively with the representatives of his employees, subject to the provisions of section 9(a).

---

* The (ii) provision was added in 1951 by 65 Stat. 601.

(b) **It shall be an unfair labor practice for a labor organization or its agents—**

(1) to restrain or coerce (A) employees in the exercise of the rights guaranteed in section 7: *Provided,* **That this paragraph shall not impair the right of a labor organization to prescribe its own rules with respect to the acquisition or retention of membership therein; or (B) an employer in the selection of his representatives for the purposes of collective bargaining or the adjustment of grievances;**

(2) to cause or attempt to cause an employer to discriminate against an employee in violation of subsection (a)(3) or to discriminate against an employee with respect to whom membership in such organization has been denied or terminated on some ground other than his failure to tender the periodic dues and the initiation fees uniformly required as a condition of acquiring or retaining membership;

(3) to refuse to bargain collectively with an employer, provided it is the representative of his employees subject to the provisions of section 9(a);

(4) *(i)*to engage in, or to induce or encourage [**the employees of any employer**] *any individual employed by any person engaged in commerce or in an industry affecting commerce* **to engage in, a strike or a [concerted] refusal in the course of [their]** *his* **employment to use, manufacture, process, transport, or otherwise handle or work on any goods, articles, materials, or commodities or to perform any services**[,]; *or (ii) to threaten, coerce, or restrain any person engaged in commerce or in an industry affecting commerce,* **where** *in either case* **an object thereof is—**

(A) forcing or requiring any employer or self-employed person to join any labor or employer organization [or any employer or other person to cease using, selling, handling, transporting, or otherwise dealing in the products of any other producer, processor, or manufacturer, or to cease doing business with any other person;] *or to enter into any agreement which is prohibited by section 8(e);*

(B) *forcing or requiring any* [**any employer or other**] *person to cease using, selling, handling, transporting, or otherwise dealing in the products of any other producer, processor, or manufacturer, or to cease doing business with any other person, or* **forcing or requiring any other employer to recognize or bargain with a labor organization as the representative of his employees unless such labor organization has been certified as the representative of such employees under the provisions of section 9**[;]; *Provided, That nothing contained in this clause (B) shall be construed to make unlawful, where not otherwise unlawful, any primary strike or primary picketing;*

(C) forcing or requiring any employer to recognize or bargain with a particular labor organization as the representative of his employees if another labor organization has been certified as the representative of such employees under the provisions of section 9;

(D) forcing or requiring any employer to assign particular work to employees in a particular labor organization or in a particular trade, craft, or class rather than to employees in another labor organization or in another trade, craft, or class, unless such employer is failing to conform to an order or certification of the Board determining the bargaining representative for employees performing such work:

Provided, That nothing contained in this subsection (b) shall be construed to make unlawful a refusal by any person to enter upon the premises of any employer (other than his own employer), if the employees of such employer are engaged in a strike ratified or approved by a representative of such employees whom such employer is required to recognize under this Act: *Provided further, That for the purposes of this paragraph (4) only, nothing contained in such paragraph shall be construed to prohibit publicity, other than picketing, for the purpose of truthfully advising the public, including consumers and members of a labor organization, that a product or products are produced by an employer with whom the labor organization has a primary dispute and are distributed by another employer, as long as such publicity does not have an effect of inducing any individual employed by any person other than the primary employer in the course of his employment to refuse to pick up, deliver, or transport any goods, or not to perform any services, at the establishment of the employer engaged in such distribution:*

(5) to require of employees covered by an agreement authorized under subsection (a)(3) the payment, as a condition precedent to becoming a member of such organization, of a fee in an amount which the Board finds excessive or discriminatory under all the circumstances. In making such a finding, the Board shall consider, among other relevant factors, the practices and customs of labor organizations in the particular industry, and the wages currently paid to the employees affected; [and]

(6) to cause or attempt to cause an employer to pay or deliver or agree to pay or deliver any money or other thing of value, in the nature of an exaction, for services which are not performed or not to be performed[.]; *and*

(7) to picket or cause to be picketed, or threaten to picket or cause to be picketed, any employer where an object thereof is forcing or requiring an employer to recognize or bargain with a labor organization as the representatives of his employees, or forcing or requiring the employees of an employer to accept or select such labor organization as their collec-

tive bargaining representative, unless such labor organization is currently certified as the representative of such employees:

(A) where the employer has lawfully recognized in accordance with this Act any other labor organization and a question concerning representation may not appropriately be raised under section 9(c) of this Act.

(B) where within the preceding twelve months a valid election under section 9(c) of this Act has been conducted, or

(C) where such picketing has been conducted without a petition under section 9(c) being filed within a reasonable period of time not to exceed thirty days from the commencement of such picketing: Provided, That when such a petition has been filed the Board shall forthwith, without regard to the provisions of section 9(c)(1) or the absence of a showing of a substantial interest on the part of the labor organization, direct an election in such unit as the Board finds to be appropriate and shall certify the results thereof: Provided further, That nothing in this subparagraph (C) shall be construed to prohibit any picketing or other publicity for the purpose of truthfully advising the public (including consumers) that an employer does not employ members of, or have a contract with, a labor organization, unless an effect of such picketing is to induce any individual employed by any other person in the course of his employment, not to pick up, deliver or transport any goods or not to perform any services.

Nothing in this paragraph (7) shall be construed to permit any act which would otherwise be an unfair labor practice under this section 8(b).

(c) The expressing of any views, argument, or opinion, or the dissemination thereof, whether in written, printed, graphic, or visual form, shall not constitute or be evidence of an unfair labor practice under any of the provisions of this Act, if such expression contains no threat of reprisal or force or promise of benefit.

(d) For the purposes of this section, to bargain collectively is the performance of the mutual obligation of the employer and the representative of the employees to meet at reasonable times and confer in good faith with respect to wages, hours, and other terms and conditions of employment, or the negotiation of an agreement, or any question arising thereunder, and the execution of a written contract incorporating any agreement reached if requested by either party, but such obligation does not compel either party to agree to a proposal or require the making of a concession: *Provided,* That where there is in effect a collective-bargaining contract covering employees in an industry affecting commerce, the duty to bargain collectively shall also mean that no party to such contract shall terminate or modify such contract, unless the party desiring such termination or modification—

(1) serves a written notice upon the other party to the contract of the proposed termination or modification sixty days prior to the expiration date thereof, or in the event such contract contains no expiration date, sixty days prior to the time it is proposed to make such termination or modification;

(2) offers to meet and confer with the other party for the purpose of negotiating a new contract or a contract containing the proposed modifications;

(3) notifies the Federal Mediation and Conciliation Service within thirty days after such notice of the existence of a dispute, and simultaneously therewith notifies any State or Territorial agency established to mediate and conciliate disputes within the State or Territory where the dispute occurred, provided no agreement has been reached by that time; and

(4) continues in full force and effect, without resorting to strike or lock-out, all the terms and conditions of the existing contract for a period of sixty days after such notice is given or until the expiration date of such contract, whichever occurs later:

The duties imposed upon employers, employees, and labor organizations by paragraphs (2), (3), and (4) shall become inapplicable upon an intervening certification of the Board, under which the labor organization or individual, which is a party to the contract, has been superseded as or ceased to be the representative of the employees subject to the provisions of section 9(a), and the duties so imposed shall not be construed as requiring either party to discuss or agree to any modification of the terms and conditions contained in a contract for a fixed period, if such modification is to become effective before such terms and conditions can be reopened under the provisions of the contract. Any employee who engages in a strike within [the sixty-day] any notice period specified in this subsection, or who engages in any strike within the appropriate period specified in subsection (g) of this section, shall lose his status as an employee of the employer engaged in the particular labor dispute, for the purposes of sections 8, 9, and 10 of this Act, but such loss of status for such employee shall terminate if and when he is reemployed by such employer. Whenever the collective bargaining involves employees of a health care institution, the provisions of this section 8(d) shall be modified as follows:

(A) The notice of section 8(d)(1) shall be ninety days; the notice of section 8(d)(3) shall be sixty days; and the contract period of section 8(d)(4) shall be ninety days.

(B) Where the bargaining is for an initial agreement following certification or recognition, at least thirty days' notice of the existence of a dispute shall be given by the labor organization to the agencies set forth in section 8(d)(3).

(C) After notice is given to the Federal Mediation and Conciliation Service under either clause (A) or (B) of this sentence, the Service shall promptly communicate with the parties and use its best efforts, by mediation and conciliation, to bring them to agreement. The parties shall participate fully and promptly in such meetings as may be undertaken by the Service for the purpose of aiding in a settlement of the dispute.

(e) It shall be an unfair labor practice for any labor organization and any employer to enter into any contract or agreement, express or implied, whereby such employer ceases or refrains or agrees to cease or refrain from handling, using, selling, transporting or otherwise dealing in any of the products of any other employer, or to cease doing business with any other person, and any contract or agreement entered into heretofore or hereafter containing such an agreement shall be to such extent unenforcible and void: Provided, That nothing in this subsection (e) shall apply to an agreement between a labor organization and an employer in the construction industry relating to the contracting or subcontracting of work to be done at the site of the construction, alteration, painting, or repair of a building, structure, or other work: Provided further, That for the purposes of this subsection (e) and section 8(b)(4)(B) the terms "any employer", "any person engaged in commerce or an industry affecting commerce", and "any person" when used in relation to the terms "any other producer, processor, or manufacturer", "any other employer", or "any other person" shall not include persons in the relation of a jobber, manufacturer, contractor, or subcontractor working on the goods or premises of the jobber or manufacturer or performing parts of an integrated process of production in the apparel and clothing industry: Provided further, That nothing in this Act shall prohibit the enforcement of any agreement which is within the foregoing exception.

(f)* It shall not be an unfair labor practice under subsections (a) and (b) of this section for an employer engaged primarily in the building and construction industry to make an agreement covering employees engaged (or who, upon their employment, will be engaged) in the building and construction industry with a labor organization of which building and construction employees are members (not established, maintained, or assisted by any action defined in section 8(a) of this Act as an unfair labor practice) because (1) the majority status of such labor organization has not been established under the provisions of section 9 of this Act prior to the making of such agreement, or (2) such agreement requires as a condition of employment, membership in such labor organization after the seventh day following the beginning of such employment or the effective date of the agreement,

---

* Sec. 8(f) was inserted in the Act by subsec. (a) of Sec. 705 of Public Law 86–257. Sec. 705(b) provides:

Nothing contained in the amendment made by subsection (a) shall be construed as authorizing the execution or application of agreements requiring membership in a labor organization as a condition of employment in any State or Territory in which such execution or application is prohibited by State or Territorial law.

whichever is later, or (3) such agreement requires the employer to notify such labor organization of opportunities for employment with such employer, or gives such labor organization an opportunity to refer qualified applicants for such employment, or (4) such agreement specifies minimum training or experience qualifications for employment or provides for priority in opportunities for employment based upon length of service with such employer, in the industry or in the particular geographical area: Provided, That nothing in this subsection shall set aside the final proviso to section 8(a)(3) of this Act: Provided further, That any agreement which would be invalid, but for clause (1) of this subsection, shall not be a bar to a petition filed pursuant to section 9(c) or 9(e).

(g) A labor organization before engaging in any strike, picketing, or other concerted refusal to work at any health care institution shall, not less than ten days prior to such action, notify the institution in writing and the Federal Mediation and Conciliation Service of that intention, except that in the case of bargaining for an initial agreement following certification or recognition the notice required by this subsection shall not be given until the expiration of the period specified in clause (B) of the last sentence of section 8(d) of this Act. The notice shall state the date and time that such action will commence. The notice, once given, may be extended by the written agreement of both parties.

REPRESENTATIVES AND ELECTIONS

Sec. 9.   (a) Representatives designated or selected for the purposes of collective bargaining by the majority of the employees in a unit appropriate for such purposes, shall be the exclusive representatives of all the employees in such unit for the purposes of collective bargaining in respect to rates of pay, wages, hours of employment, or other conditions of employment: *Provided,* That any individual employee or a group of employees shall have the right at any time to present grievances to their employer **and to have such grievances adjusted, without the intervention of the bargaining representative, as long as the adjustment is not inconsistent with the terms of a collective-bargaining contract or agreement then in effect:** *Provided further,* **That the bargaining representative has been given opportunity to be present at such adjustment.**

(b) The Board shall decide in each case whether, in order to assure to employees the fullest freedom in exercising the rights guaranteed by this Act, the unit appropriate for the purposes of collective bargaining shall be the employer unit, craft unit, plant unit, or subdivision thereof: ***Provided,*** **That the Board shall not (1) decide that any unit is appropriate for such purposes if such unit includes both professional employees and employees who are not professional employees unless a majority of such professional employees vote for inclusion in such unit; or (2) decide that any craft unit is inappropriate for such purposes on the ground that a different unit has been established by a prior Board determination, unless a majority of the employees in the proposed craft unit vote against separate representation or (3)** decide that any unit is appropriate for such purposes if it includes, together with other employees, any individual employed as a guard to enforce against employees and other persons rules to protect property of the employer or to protect the safety of persons on the employer's premises; but no labor organization shall be certified as the representative of employees in a bargaining unit of guards if such organization admits to membership, or is affiliated directly or indirectly with an organization which admits to membership, employees other than guards.

|(c) Whenever a question affecting commerce arises concerning the representation of employees, the Board may investigate such controversy and certify to the parties, in writing, the name or names of the representatives that have been designated or selected. In any such investigation, the Board shall provide for an appropriate hearing upon due notice, either in conjunction with a proceeding under section 10 or otherwise, and may take a secret ballot of employees, or utilize any other suitable method to ascertain such representatives.Œ

(c)(1) **Whenever a petition shall have been filed, in accordance with such regulations as may be prescribed by the Board—**

(A) **by an employee or group of employees or any individual or labor organization acting in their behalf alleging that a substantial number of employees (i) wish to be represented for collective bargaining and that their employer declines to recognize their representative as the representative defined in section 9(a), or (ii) assert that the individual or labor organization, which has been certified or is being currently recognized by their employer as the bargaining representative, is no longer a representative as defined in section 9(a); or**

(B) **by an employer, alleging that one or more individuals or labor organizations have presented to him a claim to be recognized as the representative defined in section 9(a);**

the Board shall investigate such petition and if it has reasonable cause to believe that a question of representation affecting commerce exists shall provide for an appropriate hearing upon due notice. Such hearing may be conducted by an officer or employee of the regional office, who shall not make any recommendations with respect thereto. If the Board finds upon the record of such hearing that such a question of representation exists, it shall direct an election by secret ballot and shall certify the results thereof.

(2) In determining whether or not a question of representation affecting commerce exists, the same regulations and rules of decision shall apply irrespective of the identity of the persons filing the petition or the kind of relief sought and in no case shall the Board deny a labor organization a place on the ballot by reason of

an order with respect to such labor organization or its predecessor not issued in conformity with section 10(c).

(3) No election shall be directed in any bargaining unit or any subdivision within which, in the preceding twelve-month period, a valid election shall have been held. Employees [on strike] *engaged in an economic strike* **who are not entitled to reinstatement shall [not] be eligible to vote** *under such regulations as the Board shall find are consistent with the purposes and provisions of this Act in any election conducted within twelve months after the commencement of the strike.* **In any election where none of the choices on the ballot receives a majority, a run-off shall be conducted, the ballot providing for a selection between the two choices receiving the largest and second largest number of valid votes cast in the election.**

(4) Nothing in this section shall be construed to prohibit the waiving of hearings by stipulation for the purpose of a consent election in conformity with regulations and rules of decision of the Board.

(5) In determining whether a unit is appropriate for the purposes specified in subsection (b) the extent to which the employees have organized shall not be controlling.

(d) Whenever an order of the Board made pursuant to section 10(c) is based in whole or in part upon facts certified following an investigation pursuant to subsection (c) of this section and there is a petition for the enforcement or review of such order, such certification and the record of such investigation shall be included in the transcript of the entire record required to be filed under section 10(e) or 10(f), and thereupon the decree of the court enforcing, modifying, or setting aside in whole or in part the order of the Board shall be made and entered upon the pleadings, testimony, and proceedings set forth in such transcript.

(e) *(1) Upon the filing with the Board, by 30 per centum or more of the employees in a bargaining unit covered by an agreement between their employer and a labor organization made pursuant to section 8(a)(3), of a petition alleging they desire that such authority be rescinded, the Board shall take a secret ballot of the employees in such unit, and shall certify the results thereof to such labor organization and to the employer.

(2) No election shall be conducted pursuant to this subsection in any bargaining unit or any subdivision within which, in the preceding twelve-month period, a valid election shall have been held.

---

* As enacted in 1947, Section 9(e) had three subsections. In 1951, the first subsection was deleted and the two remaining subsections were renumbered (1) and (2). 65 Stat. 601. The deleted subsection required, as a condition to the inclusion of a union-shop provision in a collective agreement, that a majority of employees authorize such inclusion in a Board-conducted election.

[Subsections (f), (g) and (h) were deleted by the Labor-Management Reporting and Disclosure Act.]

PREVENTION OF UNFAIR LABOR PRACTICES

Sec. 10. (a) The Board is empowered, as hereinafter provided, to prevent any person from engaging in any unfair labor practice (listed in section 8) affecting commerce. This power shall not be affected by any other means of adjustment or prevention that has been or may be established by agreement, law, or otherwise: *Provided,* **That the Board is empowered by agreement with any agency of any State or Territory to cede to such agency jurisdiction over any cases in any industry (other than mining, manufacturing, communications, and transportation except where predominantly local in character) even though such cases may involve labor disputes affecting commerce, unless the provision of the State of Territorial statute applicable to the determination of such cases by such agency is inconsistent with the corresponding provision of this Act or has received a construction inconsistent therewith.**

(b) Whenever it is charged that any person has engaged in or is engaging in any such unfair labor practice, the Board, or any agent or agency designated by the Board for such purposes, shall have power to issue and cause to be served upon such person a complaint stating the charges in that respect, and containing a notice of hearing before the Board or a member thereof, or before a designated agent or agency, at a place therein fixed, not less than five days after the serving of said complaint: *Provided,* **That no complaint shall issue based upon any unfair labor practice occurring more than six months prior to the filing of the charge with the Board and the service of a copy thereof upon the person against whom such charge is made, unless the person aggrieved thereby was prevented from filing such charge by reason of service in the armed forces, in which event the six-month period shall be computed from the day of his discharge.** Any such complaint may be amended by the member, agent, or agency conducting the hearing or the Board in its discretion at any time prior to the issuance of an order based thereon. The person so complained of shall have the right to file an answer to the original or amended complaint and to appear in person or otherwise and give testimony at the place and time fixed in the complaint. In the discretion of the member, agent, or agency conducting the hearing or the Board, any other person may be allowed to intervene in the said proceeding and to present testimony. [In any such proceeding the rules of evidence prevailing in courts of law or equity shall not be controlling.] **Any such proceeding shall, so far as practicable, be conducted in accordance with the rules of evidence applicable in the district courts of the United States under the rules of civil procedure for the district courts of the United States, adopted by the Supreme Court of the United States pursuant to section 2072 of Title 28.**

(c) The testimony taken by such member, agent, or agency or the Board shall be reduced to writing and filed with the Board. Thereafter, in its discretion, the Board upon notice may take further testimony or hear argument. If upon [all] **the preponderance of** the testimony taken the Board shall be of the opinion that any person named in the complaint has engaged in or is engaging in any such unfair labor practice, then the Board shall state its findings of fact and shall issue and cause to be served on such person an order requiring such person to cease and desist from such unfair labor practice, and to take such affirmative action including reinstatement of employees with or without back pay, as will effectuate the policies of this Act: *Provided,* **That where an order directs reinstatement of an employee, back pay may be required of the employer or labor organization, as the case may be, responsible for the discrimination suffered by him:** *And provided further,* **That in determining whether a complaint shall issue alleging a violation of section 8(a)(1) or section 8(a)(2), and in deciding such cases, the same regulations and rules of decision shall apply irrespective of whether or not the labor organization affected is affiliated with a labor organization national or international in scope.** Such order may further require such person to make reports from time to time showing the extent to which it has complied with the order. If upon [all] **the preponderance of** the testimony taken the Board shall not be of the opinion that the person named in the complaint has engaged in or is engaging in any such unfair labor practice, then the Board shall state its findings of fact and shall issue an order dismissing the said complaint. **No order of the Board shall require the reinstatement of any individual as an employee who has been suspended or discharged, or the payment to him of any back pay, if such individual was suspended or discharged for cause. In case the evidence is presented before a member of the Board, or before an administrative law judge or judges * thereof, such member, or such judge or judges, as the case may be, shall issue and cause to be served on the parties to the proceeding a proposed report, together with a recommended order, which shall be filed with the Board, and if no exceptions are filed within twenty days after service thereof upon such parties, or within such further period as the Board may authorize, such recommended order shall become the order of the Board and become effective as therein prescribed.**

(d) Until [**a transcript of**] the record in a case shall have been filed in a court, as hereinafter provided, the Board may at any time, upon reasonable notice and in such manner as it shall deem proper, modify or set aside, in whole or in part, any finding or order made or issued by it.

(e) The Board shall have power to petition any [United States] court of appeals of the United States [(including the United States court of appeals for the District of Columbia)] or if all the courts of appeals to which application may be made are in vacation, any [United States] district court

---

* The title "administrative law judge" was adopted in 5 U.S.C. § 3105, in 1972.

of the United States, within any circuit or district, respectively, wherein the unfair labor practice in question occurred or wherein such person resides or transacts business, for the enforcement of such order and for appropriate temporary relief or restraining order, and shall [certify and] file in the court [a transcript of] the [entire] record in the proceedings, [including the pleadings and testimony upon which such order was entered and the findings and order of the Board.] *as printed in section 2112 of Title 28.* Upon [such filing] *the filing of such petition,* the court shall cause notice thereof to be served upon such person, and thereupon shall have jurisdiction of the proceeding and of the question determined therein, and shall have power to grant such temporary relief or restraining order as it deems just and proper, and to make and enter [upon the pleadings, testimony, and proceedings set forth in such transcript] a decree enforcing, modifying, and enforcing as so modified, or setting aside in whole or in part the order of the Board. No objection that has not been urged before the Board, its member, agent, or agency, shall be considered by the court, unless the failure or neglect to urge such objection shall be excused because of extraordinary circumstances. The findings of the Board with respect to questions of fact if supported by **substantial** evidence **on the record considered as a whole** shall be conclusive. If either party shall apply to the court for leave to adduce additional evidence and shall show to the satisfaction of the court that such additional evidence is material and that there were reasonable grounds for the failure to adduce such evidence in the hearing before the Board, its member, agent, or agency, the court may order such additional evidence to be taken before the Board, its member, agent, or agency, and to be made a part of [the transcript] *record.* The Board may modify its findings as to the facts, or make new findings, by reason of additional evidence so taken and filed, and it shall file such modified or new findings, which findings with respect to questions of fact if supported by **substantial** evidence **on the record considered as a whole** shall be conclusive, and shall file its recommendations, if any, for the modification or setting aside of its original order. *Upon the filing of the record with it* the jurisdiction of the court shall be exclusive and its judgment and decree shall be final, except that the same shall be subject to review by the appropriate circuit court of appeals if application was made to the district court as hereinabove provided, and by the Supreme Court of the United States upon writ of certiorari or certification as provided in section 1254 of Title 28.

(f) Any person aggrieved by a final order of the Board granting or denying in whole or in part the relief sought may obtain a review of such order in any United States court of appeals in the circuit wherein the unfair labor practice in question was alleged to have been engaged in or wherein such person resides or transacts business, or in the United States Court of Appeals for the District of Columbia, by filing in such court a written petition praying that the order of the Board be modified or set aside. A copy of such petition shall be forthwith [served upon the Board] *transmitted by the clerk of the court to the Board* and thereupon the aggrieved party shall file in the court [a transcript of] the [entire] record in the proceeding, certified by the Board, [including the pleading and testimony upon which the order complained of was entered, and the findings and order of the Board.] *as provided in section 2112 of Title 28.* Upon [such filing,] *the filing of such petition,* the court shall proceed in the same manner as in the case of an application by the Board under subsection (e) *of this section,* and shall have the same exclusive jurisdiction to grant to the Board such temporary relief or restraining order as it deems just and proper, and in like manner to make and enter a decree enforcing, modifying, and enforcing as so modified, or setting aside in whole or in part the order of the Board; the findings of the Board with respect to questions of fact if supported by **substantial** evidence **on the record considered as a whole** shall in like manner be conclusive.

(g) The commencement of proceedings under subsection (e) or (f) of this section shall not, unless specifically ordered by the court, operate as a stay of the Board's order.

(h) When granting appropriate temporary relief or a restraining order, or making and entering a decree enforcing, modifying, and enforcing as so modified, or setting aside in whole or in part an order of the Board, as provided in this section, the jurisdiction of courts sitting in equity shall not be limited by sections 101 to 115 of title 29, United States Code.*

(i) [Repealed.]

(j) The Board shall have power, upon issuance of a complaint as provided in subsection (b) charging that any person has engaged in or is engaging in an unfair labor practice, to petition any United States district court within any district wherein the unfair labor practice in question is alleged to have occurred or wherein such person resides or transacts business, for appropriate temporary relief or restraining order. Upon the filing of any such petition the court shall cause notice thereof to be served upon such person, and thereupon shall have jurisdiction to grant to the Board such temporary relief or restraining order as it deems just and proper.

(k) Whenever it is charged that any person has engaged in an unfair labor practice within the meaning of paragraph (4)(D) of section 8(b), the Board is empowered and directed to hear and determine the dispute out of which such unfair labor practice shall have arisen, unless, within ten days after notice that such charge has been filed, the parties to such dispute submit to the Board satisfactory evidence that they have adjusted, or agreed upon methods for the voluntary adjustment of, the dispute. Upon compliance by the parties to the dispute with the decision of the Board or upon such voluntary adjustment of the dispute, such charge shall be dismissed.

* The Norris–LaGuardia Act of 1932.

(*l*) Whenever it is charged that any person has engaged in an unfair labor practice within the meaning of paragraph (4)(A), (B), or (C) of section 8(b), *or section 8(e) or section 8(b)(7)* the preliminary investigation of such charge shall be made forthwith and given priority over all other cases except cases of like character in the office where it is filed or to which it is referred. If, after such investigation, the officer or regional attorney to whom the matter may be referred has reasonable cause to believe such charge is true and that a complaint should issue, he shall, on behalf of the Board, petition any United States district court within any district where the unfair labor practice in question has occurred, is alleged to have occurred, or wherein such person resides or transacts business, for appropriate injunctive relief pending the final adjudication of the Board with respect to such matter. Upon the filing of any such petition the district court shall have jurisdiction to grant such injunctive relief or temporary restraining order as it deems just and proper, notwithstanding any other provision of law: *Provided further,* That no temporary restraining order shall be issued without notice unless a petition alleges that substantial and irreparable injury to the charging party will be unavoidable and such temporary restraining order shall be effective for no longer than five days and will become void at the expiration of such period[.]: *Provided further, That such officer or regional attorney shall not apply for any restraining order under section 8(b)(7) if a charge against the employer under section 8(a)(2) has been filed and after the preliminary investigation, he has reasonable cause to believe that such charge is true and that a complaint should issue.* Upon filing of any such petition the courts shall cause notice thereof to be served upon any person involved in the charge and such person, including the charging party, shall be given an opportunity to appear by counsel and present any relevant testimony: *Provided further,* That for the purposes of this subsection district courts shall be deemed to have jurisdiction of a labor organization (1) in the district in which such organization maintains its principal office, or (2) in any district in which its duly authorized officers or agents are engaged in promoting or protecting the interests of employee members. The service of legal process upon such officer or agent shall constitute service upon the labor organization and make such organization a party to the suit. In situations where such relief is appropriate the procedure specified herein shall apply to charges with respect to sections 8(b)(4)(D).

(*m*) *Whenever it is charged that any person has engaged in an unfair labor practice within the meaning of subsection (a)(3) or (b)(2) of section 8, such charge shall be given priority over all other cases except cases of like character in the office where it is filed or to which it is referred and cases given priority under subsection (l) of this section.*

INVESTIGATORY POWERS

Sec. 11. For the purpose of all hearings and investigations, which, in the opinion of the Board, are necessary and proper for the exercise of the powers vested in it by section 9 and section 10—

(1) The Board, or its duly authorized agents or agencies, shall at all reasonable times have access to, for the purpose of examination, and the right to copy any evidence of any person being investigated or proceeded against that relates to any matter under investigation or in question. The Board, or any member thereof, shall upon application of any party to such proceedings, forthwith issue to such party subpenas requiring the attendance and testimony of witnesses or the production of any evidence in such proceeding or investigation requested in such application. **Within five days after the service of a subpena on any person requiring the production of any evidence in his possession or under his control, such person may petition the Board to revoke, and the Board shall revoke, such subpena if in its opinion the evidence whose production is required does not relate to any matter under investigation, or any matter in question in such proceedings, or if in its opinion such subpena does not describe with sufficient particularity the evidence whose production is required.** Any member of the Board, or any agent or agency designated by the Board for such purposes, may administer oaths and affirmations, examine witnesses, and receive evidence. Such attendance of witnesses and the production of such evidence may be required from any place in the United States or any Territory or possession thereof, at any designated place of hearing.

(2) In case of contumacy or refusal to obey a subpena issued to any person, any district court of the United States or the United States courts of any Territory or possession, or the District Court of the United States for the District of Columbia, within the jurisdiction of which the inquiry is carried on or within the jurisdiction of which said person guilty of contumacy or refusal to obey is found or resides or transacts business, upon application by the Board shall have jurisdiction to issue to such person an order requiring such person to appear before the Board, its member, agent, or agency, there to produce evidence if so ordered, or there to give testimony touching the matter under investigation or in question; and any failure to obey such order of the court may be punished by said court as a contempt thereof.

[(3) No person shall be excused from attending and testifying or from producing books, records, correspondence, documents, or other evidence in obedience to the subpena of the Board, on the ground that the testimony or evidence required of him may tend to incriminate him or subject him to a penalty or forfeiture; but no individual shall be prosecuted or subjected to any penalty or forfeiture for or on account of any transaction, matter, or thing concerning which he is compelled, after having claimed his privilege against self-incrimination, to testify or produce evidence, except that such individual so testifying shall not be exempt from prosecution and punishment for perjury committed in so testifying.]*

(4) Complaints, orders, and other process and papers of the Board, its member, agent, or agency, may be served either personally or by registered mail or by telegraph or by leaving a copy thereof at the principal office or place of business of the person required to be served. The verified return by the individual so serving the same setting forth the manner of such service shall be proof of the same, and the return post office receipt or telegraph receipt therefor when registered and mailed or telegraphed as aforesaid shall be proof of service of the same. Witnesses summoned before the Board, its member, agent, or agency, shall be paid the same fees and mileage that are paid witnesses in the courts of the United States, and witnesses whose depositions are taken and the persons taking the same shall severally be entitled to the same fees as are paid for like services in the courts of the United States.

(5) All process of any court to which application may be made under this Act may be served in the judicial district wherein the defendant or other person required to be served resides or may be found.

(6) The several departments and agencies of the Government, when directed by the President, shall furnish the Board, upon its request, all records, papers, and information in their possession relating to any matter before the Board.

Sec. 12. Any person who shall willfully resist, prevent, impede, or interfere with any member of the Board or any of its agents or agencies in the performance of duties pursuant to this Act shall be punished by a fine of not more than $5,000 or by imprisonment for not more than one year, or both.

LIMITATIONS

Sec. 13. Nothing in this Act, **except as specifically provided for herein,** shall be construed so as either to interfere with or impede or diminish in any way the right to strike, **or to affect the limitations or qualifications on that right.**

Sec. 14. (a) Nothing herein shall prohibit any individual employed as a supervisor from becoming or remaining a member of a labor organization, but no employer subject to this Act shall be compelled to deem individuals defined herein as supervisors as employees for the purpose of any law, either national or local, relating to collective bargaining.

(b) Nothing in this Act shall be construed as authorizing the execution or application of agreements requiring membership in a labor organization as a condition of employment in any State or

---

* Section 11(3) was repealed in 1970, by 84 Stat. 930. Similar immunity provisions were substituted; see 18 U.S.C. §§ 6001, 6002, 6004 (1970).

Territory in which such execution or application is prohibited by State or Territorial law.

(c)(1) The Board, in its discretion, may, by rule of decision or by published rules adopted pursuant to the Administrative Procedure Act, decline to assert jurisdiction over any labor dispute involving any class or category of employers, where, in the opinion of the Board, the effect of such labor dispute on commerce is not sufficiently substantial to warrant the exercise of its jurisdiction: Provided, That the Board shall not decline to assert jurisdiction over any labor dispute over which it would assert jurisdiction under the standards prevailing upon August 1, 1959.

(2) Nothing in this Act shall be deemed to prevent or bar any agency or the courts of any State or Territory (including the Commonwealth of Puerto Rico, Guam, and the Virgin Islands), from assuming and asserting jurisdiction over labor disputes over which the Board declines, pursuant to paragraph (1) of this subsection, to assert jurisdiction.

Sec. 15. [Reference to repealed provisions of the Bankruptcy Act.]

Sec. 16. If any provision of this Act, or the application of such provision to any person or circumstances, shall be held invalid, the remainder of this Act, or the application of such provision to persons or circumstances other than those as to which it is held invalid, shall not be affected thereby.

Sec. 17. This Act may be cited as the "National Labor Relations Act."

Sec. 18. [This section, which refers to the now-repealed Sections 9(f), (g), (h), is omitted.]

INDIVIDUALS WITH RELIGIOUS CONVICTIONS

Sec. 19. Any employee who is a member of and adheres to established and traditional tenets or teachings of a bona fide religion, body, or sect which has historically held conscientious objections to joining or financially supporting labor organizations shall not be required to join or financially support any labor organization as a condition of employment; except that such employee may be required in a contract between such employee's employer and a labor organization in lieu of periodic dues and initiation fees, to pay sums equal to such dues and initiation fees to a nonreligious, nonlabor organization charitable fund exempt from taxation under section 501(c)(3) of title 26 of the Internal Revenue Code [section 501(c)(3) of title 26], chosen by such employee from a list of at least three such funds, designated in such contract or if the contract fails to designate such funds, then to any such fund chosen by the employee. If such employee who holds conscientious objections pursuant to this section requests the labor organization to use the grievance-arbitration procedure on the employee's behalf, the labor organization is authorized to charge the employee for the reasonable cost of using such procedure.*

* This section was added by Pub.L. 93–360, July 26, 1974, 88 Stat. 397, and amended, Pub.L. 96–593, Dec. 24, 1980, 94 Stat. 3452.

LABOR MANAGEMENT RELATIONS ACT

61 Stat. 136 (1947), as amended; 29 U.S.C. §§ 141–97 (1988).

SHORT TITLE AND DECLARATION OF POLICY

Sec. 1. (a) This Act may be cited as the "Labor Management Relations Act, 1947."

(b) Industrial strife which interferes with the normal flow of commerce and with the full production of articles and commodities for commerce, can be avoided or substantially minimized if employers, employees, and labor organizations each recognize under law one another's legitimate rights in their relations with each other, and above all recognize under law that neither party has any right in its relations with any other to engage in acts or practices which jeopardize the public health, safety, or interest.

It is the purpose and policy of this Act, in order to promote the full flow of commerce, to prescribe the legitimate rights of both employees and employers in their relations affecting commerce, to provide orderly and peaceful procedures for preventing the interference by either with the legitimate rights of the other, to protect the rights of individual employees in their relations with labor organizations whose activities affect commerce, to define and proscribe practices on the part of labor and management which affect commerce and are inimical to the general welfare, and to protect the rights of the public in connection with labor disputes affecting commerce.

TITLE I

AMENDMENT OF NATIONAL LABOR RELATIONS ACT

Sec. 101. The National Labor Relations Act is hereby amended to read as follows: [The text of the National Labor Relations Act as amended is set forth supra.]

TITLE II

CONCILIATION OF LABOR DISPUTES IN INDUSTRIES AFFECTING COMMERCE; NATIONAL EMERGENCIES

Sec. 201. That it is the policy of the United States that—

(a) sound and stable industrial peace and the advancement of the general welfare, health, and safety of the Nation and of the best interests of employers and employees can most satisfactorily be secured by the settlement of issues between employers and employees through the processes of conference and collective bargaining between employers and the representatives of their employees;

(b) the settlement of issues between employers and employees through collective bargaining may be advanced by making available full and adequate governmental facilities for conciliation, mediation, and voluntary arbitration to aid and encourage employers and the representatives of their employees to reach and maintain agreements concerning rates of pay, hours, and working conditions, and to make all reasonable efforts to settle their differences by mutual agreement reached through conferences and collective bargaining or by such methods as may be provided for in any applicable agreement for the settlement of disputes; and

(c) certain controversies which arise between parties to collective-bargaining agreements may be avoided or minimized by making available full and adequate governmental facilities for furnishing assistance to employers and the representatives of their employees in formulating for inclusion within such agreements provision for adequate notice of any proposed changes in the terms of such agreements, for the final adjustment of grievances or questions regarding the application or interpretation of such agreements, and other provisions designed to prevent the subsequent arising of such controversies.

Sec. 202. (a) There is hereby created an independent agency to be known as the Federal Mediation and Conciliation Service (herein referred to as the "Service," except that for sixty days after the date of the enactment of this Act such term shall refer to the Conciliation Service of the Department of Labor). The Service shall be under the direction of a Federal Mediation and Conciliation Director (hereinafter referred to as the "Director"), who shall be appointed by the President by and with the advice and consent of the Senate. The Director shall not engage in any other business, vocation, or employment.

(b) The Director is authorized, subject to the civil-service laws, to appoint such clerical and other personnel as may be necessary for the execution of the functions of the Service, and shall fix their compensation in accordance with chapter 51 and subchapter III of chapter 53 of title 5, and may, without regard to the provisions of the civil-service laws, appoint such conciliators and mediators as may be necessary to carry out the functions of the Service. The Director is authorized to make such expenditures for supplies, facilities, and services as he deems necessary. Such expenditures shall be allowed and paid upon presentation of itemized vouchers therefor approved by the Director or by any employee designated by him for that purpose.

(c) The principal office of the Service shall be in the District of Columbia, but the Director may establish regional offices convenient to localities in which labor controversies are likely to arise. The Director may by order, subject to revocation at any time, delegate any authority and discretion conferred upon him by this Act to any regional director, or other officer or employee of the Service. The Director may establish suitable procedures for cooperation with State and local mediation agencies. The Director shall make an annual report in writing to Congress at the end of the fiscal year.

(d) All mediation and conciliation functions of the Secretary of Labor or the United States Conciliation Service under section 8 of the Act entitled

"An Act to create a Department of Labor," approved March 4, 1913 (U.S.C., title 29, sec. 51), and all functions of the United States Conciliation Service under any other law are transferred to the Federal Mediation and Conciliation Service, together with the personnel and records of the United States Conciliation Service. Such transfer shall take effect upon the sixtieth day after June 23, 1947. Such transfer shall not affect any proceedings pending before the United States Conciliation Service or any certification, order, rule, or regulation theretofore made by it or by the Secretary of Labor. The Director and the Service shall not be subject in any way to the jurisdiction or authority of the Secretary of Labor or any official or division of the Department of Labor.

FUNCTIONS OF THE SERVICE

Sec. 203.   (a) It shall be the duty of the Service, in order to prevent or minimize interruptions of the free flow of commerce growing out of labor disputes, to assist parties to labor disputes in industries affecting commerce to settle such disputes through conciliation and mediation.

(b) The Service may proffer its services in any labor dispute in any industry affecting commerce, either upon its own motion or upon the request of one or more of the parties to the dispute, whenever in its judgment such dispute threatens to cause a substantial interruption of commerce. The Director and the Service are directed to avoid attempting to mediate disputes which would have only a minor effect on interstate commerce if State or other conciliation services are available to the parties. Whenever the Service does proffer its services in any dispute, it shall be the duty of the Service promptly to put itself in communication with the parties and to use its best efforts, by mediation and conciliation, to bring them to agreement.

(c) If the Director is not able to bring the parties to agreement by conciliation within a reasonable time, he shall seek to induce the parties voluntarily to seek other means of settling the dispute without resort to strike, lock-out, or other coercion, including submission to the employees in the bargaining unit of the employer's last offer of settlement for approval or rejection in a secret ballot. The failure or refusal of either party to agree to any procedure suggested by the Director shall not be deemed a violation of any duty or obligation imposed by this Act.

(d) Final adjustment by a method agreed upon by the parties is hereby declared to be the desirable method for settlement of grievance disputes arising over the application or interpretation of an existing collective-bargaining agreement. The Service is directed to make its conciliation and mediation services available in the settlement of such grievance disputes only as a last resort and in exceptional cases.

(e)* The Service is authorized and directed to encourage and support the establishment and operation of joint labor management activities conducted by plant, area, and industrywide committees designed to improve

---

* Subsection (e) was added in 1978, by
Pub.L. 95–524, § 6(c)(1), 92 Stat. 2020.

labor management relationships, job security and organizational effectiveness, in accordance with the provisions of section 205A.

Sec. 204. (a) In order to prevent or minimize interruptions of the free flow of commerce growing out of labor disputes, employers and employees and their representatives, in any industry affecting commerce, shall—

(1) exert every reasonable effort to make and maintain agreements concerning rates of pay, hours, and working conditions, including provision for adequate notice of any proposed change in the terms of such agreements;

(2) whenever a dispute arises over the terms or application of a collective-bargaining agreement and a conference is requested by a party or prospective party thereto, arrange promptly for such a conference to be held and endeavor in such conference to settle such dispute expeditiously; and

(3) in case such dispute is not settled by conference, participate fully and promptly in such meetings as may be undertaken by the Service under this Act for the purpose of aiding in a settlement of the dispute.

Sec. 205. (a) There is created a National Labor-Management Panel which shall be composed of twelve members appointed by the President, six of whom shall be selected from among persons outstanding in the field of management and six of whom shall be selected from among persons outstanding in the field of labor. Each member shall hold office for a term of three years, except that any member appointed to fill a vacancy occurring prior to the expiration of the term for which his predecessor was appointed shall be appointed for the remainder of such term, and the terms of office of the members first taking office shall expire, as designated by the President at the time of appointment, four at the end of the first year, four at the end of the second year, and four at the end of the third year after the date of appointment. Members of the panel, when serving on business of the panel, shall be paid compensation at the rate of $25 per day, and shall also be entitled to receive an allowance for actual and necessary travel and subsistence expenses while so serving away from their places of residence.

(b) It shall be the duty of the panel, at the request of the Director, to advise in the avoidance of industrial controversies and the manner in which mediation and voluntary adjustment shall be administered, particularly with reference to controversies affecting the general welfare of the country.

Sec. 205A.* **(a)**(1) The Service is authorized and directed to provide assistance in the establishment and operation of plant, area and industry-wide labor management committees which—

(A) have been organized jointly by employers and labor organizations representing employees in that plant, area, or industry; and

---

* This section was added in 1978, by
Pub.L. 95–524, § 6(c)(2), 92 Stat. 2020.

(B) are established for the purpose of improving labor management relationships, job security, organizational effectiveness, enhancing economic development or involving workers in decisions affecting their jobs including improving communication with respect to subjects of mutual interest and concern.

(2) The Service is authorized and directed to enter into contracts and to make grants, where necessary or appropriate, to fulfill its responsibilities under this section.

(b)(1) No grant may be made, no contract may be entered into and no other assistance may be provided under the provisions of this section to a plant labor management committee unless the employees in that plant are represented by a labor organization and there is in effect at that plant a collective bargaining agreement.

(2) No grant may be made, no contract may be entered into and no other assistance may be provided under the provisions of this section to an area or industrywide labor management committee unless its participants include any labor organizations certified or recognized as the representative of the employees of an employer participating in such committee. Nothing in this clause shall prohibit participation in an area or industrywide committee by an employer whose employees are not represented by a labor organization.

(3) No grant may be made under the provisions of this section to any labor management committee which the Service finds to have as one of its purposes the discouragement of the exercise of rights contained in section 7 of the National Labor Relations Act (29 U.S.C. § 157) [section 157 of this title], or the interference with collective bargaining in any plant, or industry.

(c) The Service shall carry out the provisions of this section through an office established for that purpose.

(d) There are authorized to be appropriated to carry out the provisions of this section $10,000,000 for the fiscal year 1979, and such sums as may be necessary thereafter.

NATIONAL EMERGENCIES

Sec. 206. Whenever in the opinion of the President of the United States, a threatened or actual strike or lock-out affecting an entire industry or a substantial part thereof engaged in trade, commerce, transportation, transmission, or communication among the several States or with foreign nations, or engaged in the production of goods for commerce, will, if permitted to occur or to continue, imperil the national health or safety, he may appoint a board of inquiry to inquire into the issues involved in the dispute and to make a written report to him within such time as he shall prescribe. Such report shall include a statement of the facts with respect to the dispute, including each party's statement of its position but shall not contain any recommendations. The President shall file a copy of such report with the Service and shall make its contents available to the public.

Sec. 207. (a) A board of inquiry shall be composed of a chairman and such other members as the President shall determine, and shall have power to sit and act in any place within the United States and to conduct such hearings either in public or in private, as it may deem necessary or proper, to ascertain the facts with respect to the causes and circumstances of the dispute.

(b) Members of a board of inquiry shall receive compensation at the rate of $50 for each day actually spent by them in the work of the board, together with necessary travel and subsistence expenses.

(c) For the purpose of any hearing or inquiry conducted by any board appointed under this title, the provisions of sections 9 and 10 (relating to the attendance of witnesses and the production of books, papers, and documents) of the Federal Trade Commission Act of September 16, 1914, as amended (U.S.C. 19, title 15, secs. 49 and 50, as amended), are made applicable to the powers and duties of such board.

Sec. 208. (a) Upon receiving a report from a board of inquiry the President may direct the Attorney General to petition any district court of the United States having jurisdiction of the parties to enjoin such strike or lock-out or the continuing thereof, and if the court finds that such threatened or actual strike or lock-out—

(i) affects an entire industry or a substantial part thereof engaged in trade, commerce, transportation, transmission, or communication among the several States or with foreign nations, or engaged in the production of goods for commerce; and

(ii) if permitted to occur or to continue, will imperil the national health or safety, it shall have jurisdiction to enjoin any such strike or lock-out, or the continuing thereof, and to make such other orders as may be appropriate.

(b) In any case, the provisions of the Act of March 23, 1932, entitled "An Act to amend the Judicial Code and to define and limit the jurisdiction of courts sitting in equity, and for other purposes," shall not be applicable.

(c) The order or orders of the court shall be subject to review by the appropriate United States court of appeals and by the Supreme Court upon writ of certiorari or certification as provided in sections 239 and 240 of the Judicial Code, as amended (U.S.C., title 29, secs. 346 and 347).

Sec. 209. (a) Whenever a district court has issued an order under section 208 enjoining acts or practices which imperil or threaten to imperil the national health or safety, it shall be the duty of the parties to the labor dispute giving rise to such order to make every effort to adjust and settle their differences, with the assistance of the Service created by this Act. Neither party shall be under any duty to accept, in whole or in part, any proposal of settlement made by the Service.

(b) Upon the issuance of such order, the President shall reconvene the board of inquiry which has previously reported with respect to the dispute. At the end of a sixty-day period (unless the dispute has been settled by that time), the board of inquiry shall report to the President the current position of the parties and the efforts which have been made for settlement, and shall include a statement by each party of its position and a statement of the employer's last offer of settlement. The President shall make such report available to the public. The National Labor Relations Board, within the succeeding fifteen days, shall take a secret ballot of the employees of each employer involved in the dispute on the question of whether they wish to accept the final offer of settlement made by their employer as stated by him and shall certify the results thereof to the Attorney General within five days thereafter.

Sec. 210. Upon the certification of the results of such ballot or upon a settlement being reached, whichever happens sooner, the Attorney General shall move the court to discharge the injunction, which motion shall then be granted and the injunction discharged. When such motion is granted, the President shall submit to the Congress a full and comprehensive report of the proceedings, including the findings of the board of inquiry and the ballot taken by the National Labor Relations Board, together with such recommendations as he may see fit to make for consideration and appropriate action.

COMPILATION OF COLLECTIVE BARGAINING AGREEMENTS, ETC.

Sec. 211. (a) For the guidance and information of interested representatives of employers, employees, and the general public, the Bureau of Labor Statistics of the Department of Labor shall maintain a file of copies of all available collective-bargaining agreements and other available agreements and actions thereunder settling or adjusting labor disputes. Such file shall be open to inspection under appropriate conditions prescribed by the Secretary of Labor, except that no specific information submitted in confidence shall be disclosed.

(b) The Bureau of Labor Statistics in the Department of Labor is authorized to furnish upon request of the Service, or employers, employees, or their representatives, all available data and factual information which may aid in the settlement of any labor dispute, except that no specific information submitted in confidence shall be disclosed.

EXEMPTION OF RAILWAY LABOR ACT

Sec. 212. The provisions of this title shall not be applicable with respect to any matter which is subject to the provisions of the Railway Labor Act, as amended from time to time.

CONCILIATION OF LABOR DISPUTES IN THE HEALTH CARE INDUSTRY

Sec. 213. (a) If, in the opinion of the Director of the Federal Mediation and Conciliation Service a threatened or actual strike or lockout affecting a health care institution will, if permitted to occur or to continue, substantially interrupt the delivery of health care in the locality concerned, the Director may further assist in the resolution of the impasse by establishing within 30 days after the notice to the Federal Mediation and Conciliation Service under clause (A) of the last sentence of section 8(d) (which is required by clause (3) of such section 8(d)), or within 10 days after the notice under clause (B), an impartial Board of Inquiry to investigate the issues involved in the dispute and to make a written report thereon to the parties within fifteen (15) days after the establishment of such a Board. The written report shall contain the findings of fact together with the Board's recommendations for settling the dispute, with the objective of achieving a prompt, peaceful and just settlement of the dispute. Each such Board shall be composed of such number of individuals as the Director may deem desirable. No member appointed under this section shall have any interest or involvement in the health care institutions or the employee organizations involved in the dispute.

(b)(1) Members of any board established under this section who are otherwise employed by the Federal Government shall serve without compensation but shall be reimbursed for travel, subsistence, and other necessary expenses incurred by them in carrying out its duties under this section.

(2) Members of any board established under this section who are not subject to paragraph (1) shall receive compensation at a rate prescribed by the Director but not to exceed the daily rate prescribed for GS-18 of the General Schedule under section 5332 of title 5, United States Code, including travel for each day they are engaged in the performance of their duties under this section and shall be entitled to reimbursement for travel, subsistence, and other necessary expenses incurred by them in carrying out their duties under this section.

(c) After the establishment of a board under subsection (a) of this section and for 15 days after any such board has issued its report, no change in the status quo in effect prior to the expiration of the contract in the case of negotiations for a contract renewal, or in effect prior to the time of the impasse in the case of an initial bargaining negotiation, except by agreement, shall be made by the parties to the controversy.

(d) There are authorized to be appropriated such sums as may be necessary to carry out the provisions of this section.

TITLE III

SUITS BY AND AGAINST LABOR ORGANIZATIONS

Sec. 301. (a) Suits for violation of contracts between an employer and a labor organization representing employees in an industry affecting commerce as defined in this Act, or between any such labor organizations, may be brought in any district court of the United States having jurisdiction of the parties, without respect to the amount in controversy or without regard to the citizenship of the parties.

(b) Any labor organization which represents employees in an industry affecting commerce as defined in this Act and any employer whose activities affect commerce as defined in this Act shall be bound by the acts of its agents. Any such labor organization may sue or be sued as an entity and in behalf of the employees whom it represents in the courts of the United States. Any money judgment against a labor organization in a district court of the United States shall be enforceable only against the organization as an entity and against its assets, and shall not be enforceable against any individual member or his assets.

(c) For the purposes of actions and proceedings by or against labor organizations in the district courts of the United States, district courts shall be deemed to have jurisdiction of a labor organization (1) in the district in which such organization maintains its principal office, or (2) in any district in which its duly authorized officers or agents are engaged in representing or acting for employee members.

(d) The service of summons, subpena, or other legal process of any court of the United States upon an officer or agent of a labor organization, in his capacity as such, shall constitute service upon the labor organization.

(e) For the purposes of this section, in determining whether any person is acting as an "agent" of another person so as to make such other person responsible for his acts, the question of whether the specific acts performed were actually authorized or subsequently ratified shall not be controlling.

RESTRICTIONS ON PAYMENTS TO EMPLOYEE REPRESENTATIVES

Sec. 302.   (a) It shall be unlawful for any employer or association of employers or any person who acts as a labor relations expert, adviser, or consultant to an employer or who acts in the interest of an employer to pay, lend, or deliver, or agree to pay, lend, or deliver, any money or other thing of value—

(1) to any representative of any of his employees who are employed in an industry affecting commerce; or

(2) to any labor organization, or any officer or employee thereof, which represents, seeks to represent, or would admit to membership, any of the employees of such employer who are employed in an industry affecting commerce; or

(3) to any employee or group or committee of employees of such employer employed in an industry affecting commerce in excess of their normal compensation for the purpose of causing such employee or group or committee directly or indirectly to influence any other employees in the exercise of the right to organize and bargain collectively through representatives of their own choosing; or

(4) to any officer or employee of a labor organization engaged in an industry affecting commerce with intent to influence him in respect to any of his actions, decisions, or duties as a representative of employees or as such officer or employee of such labor organization.

(b)(1) It shall be unlawful for any person to request, demand, receive, or accept, or agree to receive or accept, any payment, loan or delivery of any money or other thing of value prohibited by subsection (a).

(2) It shall be unlawful for any labor organization, or for any person acting as an officer, agent, representative, or employee of such labor organization, to demand or accept from the operator of any motor vehicle (as defined in part II of the Interstate Commerce Act) employed in the transportation of property in commerce, or the employer of any such operator, any money or other thing of value payable to such organization or to an officer, agent, representative or employee thereof as a fee or charge for the unloading, or in connection with the unloading, of the cargo of such vehicle: *Provided,* That nothing in this paragraph shall be construed to make unlawful any payment by an employer to any of his employees as compensation for their services as employees.

(c) The provisions of this section shall not be applicable (1) in respect to any money or other thing of value payable by an employer to any of his employees whose established duties include acting openly for such employer in matters of labor relations or personnel administration or to any representative of his employees, or to any officer or employee of a labor organization, who is also an employee or former employee of such employer, as compensation for, or by reason of, his service as an employee of such employer; (2) with respect to the payment or delivery of any money or other thing of value in satisfaction of a judgment of any court or a decision or award of an arbitrator or impartial chairman or in compromise, adjustment, settlement, or release of any claim, complaint, grievance, or dispute in the absence of fraud or duress; (3) with respect to the sale or purchase of an article or commodity at the prevailing market price in the regular course of business; (4) with respect to money deducted from the wages of employees in payment of membership dues in a labor organization: *Provided,* That the employer has received from each employee, on whose account such deductions are made, a written assignment which shall not be irrevocable for a period of more than one year, or beyond the termination date of the applicable collective agreement, whichever occurs sooner; (5) with respect to money or other thing of value paid to a trust fund established by such representative, for the sole and exclusive benefit of the employees of such employer, and their families and dependents (or of such employees, families, and dependents jointly with the employees of other employers making similar payments, and their families and dependents): *Provided,* That (A) such payments are held in trust for the purpose of paying, either from principal or income or both, for the benefit of employees, their families and dependents, for medical or hospital care, pensions on retirement or death of employees, compensation for injuries or illness resulting from occupational activity or insurance to provide any of the foregoing, or unemployment benefits or life insurance, disability and sickness insurance, or accident insurance; (B) the detailed basis on which such payments are to be made is specified in a written agreement with the employer, and employees and employers are equally represented in the administration of such fund, together with such neutral persons as the representatives of the employers and the representatives of employees may agree upon and in the event the employer and employee groups deadlock on the administration of such fund and there are no neutral persons empowered to break such deadlock, such agreement provides that the two groups shall agree on an impartial umpire to decide such dispute, or in event of their failure to agree within a reasonable length of time, an impartial umpire to decide such dispute shall, on petition of either group, be appointed by the district court of the United States for the district where the trust fund has its principal office, and shall also contain provisions for an annual audit of the trust fund, a statement of the results of which shall be available for inspection by interested persons at the principal office of the trust fund and at such other places as may be designated in such written agreement; and (C) such payments as are intended to be used for the purpose of providing pensions or annuities for employees are made to a separate trust which provides that the funds held therein cannot be used for any purpose other than paying such pensions or annuities; (6) with respect to money or other thing of value paid by any employer to a trust fund established by such representative for the purpose of pooled vacation, holiday, severance or similar benefits, or defraying costs of apprenticeship or other training programs: *Provided,* That the requirements of clause (B) of the proviso to clause (5) of this subsection, shall apply to such trust funds; (7) with respect to money or other thing of value paid by any employer to a pooled or individual trust fund established by such representative for the purpose of (A) scholarships for the benefit of employees, their families, and dependents for study at educational institutions, (B) child care centers for pre-school and school age dependents of employees, or (C) financial assistance for employee housing: *Provided,* That no labor organization or employer shall be required to bargain on the establishment of any such trust fund, and refusal to do so shall not constitute an unfair labor practice: *Provided further,* That the requirements of clause (B) of the proviso to clause (5) of this subsection shall apply to such trust funds; (8) with respect to money or any other thing of value paid by any employer to a trust fund established by such representative for the purpose of defraying the costs of legal services for employees, their families, and dependents for counsel or plan of their choice: *Provided,* That the requirements of clause (B) of the proviso to clause (5) of this subsection shall apply to such trust funds: *Provided further,* That no such legal services shall be furnished: (A) to initiate any proceeding directed (i) against any such employer or its officers or agents except in workman's compensation cases, or (ii) against such labor organization, or its parent or subordinate bodies, or their officers or agents, or (iii) against any other employer or labor organization, or their officers or agents, in any matter arising under the National Labor Relations Act, as amended, or this Act; and (B) in any proceeding where a labor organization would be prohibited from defraying the costs of legal services by the provisions of the Labor-Management Reporting and Disclosure Act of 1959; or (9) with respect to money or other things of value paid by an employer to a plant, area or industry-wide labor management committee established for one or more of the purposes set forth in section 5(b) of the Labor Management Cooperation Act of 1978.*

(d)(1) Any person who participates in a transaction involving a payment, loan, or delivery of money or other thing of value to a labor organization in payment of membership dues or to a joint labor-management trust fund as defined by clause (B) of the proviso to clause (5) of subsection (c) of this section or to a plant, area, or industry-wide labor-management committee that is received and used by such labor organization, trust fund, or committee, which transaction does not satisfy all the applicable requirements of subsections (c)(4) through (c)(9) of this section, and willfully and with intent to benefit himself or to benefit other persons he knows are not permitted to receive a payment, loan, money, or other thing of value under subsections (c)(4) through (c)(9) violates this subsection, shall, upon conviction thereof, be guilty of a felony and be subject to a fine of not more than $15,000, or imprisoned for not more than five years, or both; but if the value of the amount of money or thing of value involved in any violation of the provisions of this section does not exceed $1,000, such person shall be guilty of a misdemeanor and be subject to a fine of not more than $10,000, or imprisoned for not more than one year, or both.

(2) Except for violations involving transactions covered by subsection (d)(1) of this section, any person who willfully violates this section shall, upon conviction thereof, be guilty of a felony and be subject to a fine of not more than $15,000 or imprisoned for not more than five years, or both; but if the value of the amount of money or thing of value involved in any violation of the provisions of this section does not exceed $1,000, such person shall be guilty of a misdemeanor and be subject to a fine of not more than $10,000, or imprisoned for not more than one year, or both.**

(e) The district courts of the United States and the United States courts of the Territories and possessions shall have jurisdiction, for cause shown, and subject to the provisions of section 17 (relating to notice to opposite party) of the Act entitled "An Act to supplement existing laws against unlawful restraints and monopolies, and for other purposes," approved October 15, 1914, as amended (U.S.C., title 28, section 381), to restrain violations of this section, without regard to the provisions of sections 6 and 20 of such Act of October 15, 1914, as amended (U.S.C., title 15, section 17, and title 29, section 52), and the provisions of the Act entitled "An Act to amend the Judicial Code and to define and limit the jurisdiction of courts sitting in equity, and for other purposes," approved March 23, 1932 (U.S.C., title 29, sections 101–115).

(f) This section shall not apply to any contract in force on the date of enactment of this Act, until the expiration of such contract, or until July 1, 1948, whichever first occurs.

* Sec. 302(c)(7) was added by Pub.L. 91–86, Oct. 14, 1969, 83 Stat. 133; Sec. 302(c)(8) by Pub.L. 93–95, Aug. 15, 1973, 87 Stat. 314; and Sec. 302(c)(9) by Pub.L. 95–524, Oct. 27, 1978, 92 Stat. 2021.

** Section 302(d) was amended by Pub.L. 98–473, Oct. 12, 1984, 98 Stat. 2131.

(g) Compliance with the restrictions contained in subsection (c)(5)(B) upon contributions to trust funds, otherwise lawful, shall not be applicable to contributions to such trust funds established by collective agreement prior to January 1, 1946, nor shall subsection (c)(5)(A) be construed as prohibiting contributions to such trust funds if prior to January 1, 1947, such funds contained provisions for pooled vacation benefits.

BOYCOTTS AND OTHER UNLAWFUL COMBINATIONS

Sec. 303.   (a) It shall be unlawful, for the purpose of this section only, in an industry or activity affecting commerce, for any labor organization to engage in any activity or conduct defined as an unfair labor practice in section 8(b)(4) of the National Labor Relations Act, as amended.

(b) Whoever shall be injured in his business or property by reason of any violation of subsection (a) may sue therefor in any district court of the United States subject to the limitations and provisions of section 301 hereof without respect to the amount in controversy, or in any other court having jurisdiction of the parties, and shall recover the damages by him sustained and the cost of the suit.

Sec. 304.   [Repealed.]

Sec. 305.   [Repealed.]

TITLE IV

CREATION OF JOINT COMMITTEE TO STUDY AND REPORT ON BASIC PROBLEMS AFFECTING FRIENDLY LABOR RELATIONS AND PRODUCTIVITY

* * *

TITLE V

DEFINITIONS

Sec. 501.   When used in this Act—

(1) The term "industry affecting commerce" means any industry or activity in commerce or in which a labor dispute would burden or obstruct commerce or tend to burden or obstruct commerce or the free flow of commerce.

(2) The term "strike" includes any strike or other concerted stoppage of work by employees (including a stoppage by reason of the expiration of a collective-bargaining agreement) and any concerted slow-down or other concerted interruption of operations by employees.

(3) The terms "commerce", "labor disputes", "employer", "employee", "labor organization", "representative", "person", and "supervisor" shall have the same meaning as when used in the National Labor Relations Act as amended by this Act.

SAVING PROVISION

Sec. 502. Nothing in this Act shall be construed to require an individual employee to render labor or service without his consent, nor shall anything in this Act be construed to make the quitting of his labor by an individual employee an illegal act; nor shall any court issue any process to compel the performance by an individual employee of such labor or service, without his consent; nor shall the quitting of labor by an employee or employees in good faith because of abnormally dangerous conditions for work at the place of employment of such employee or employees be deemed a strike under this Act.

SEPARABILITY

Sec. 503. If any provision of this Act, or the application of such provision to any person or circumstance, shall be held invalid, the remainder of this Act, or the application of such provision to persons or circumstances other than those as to which it is held invalid, shall not be affected thereby.

LABOR–MANAGEMENT REPORTING AND DISCLOSURE ACT OF 1959

73 Stat. 519 (1959), as amended; 29 U.S.C. §§ 401–531 (1988).

SHORT TITLE

Sec. 1. This Act may be cited as the "Labor-Management Reporting and Disclosure Act of 1959".

DECLARATION OF FINDINGS, PURPOSES, AND POLICY

Sec. 2. (a) The Congress finds that, in the public interest, it continues to be the responsibility of the Federal Government to protect employees' rights to organize, choose their own representatives, bargain collectively, and otherwise engage in concerted activities for their mutual aid or protection; that the relations between employers and labor organizations and the millions of workers they represent have a substantial impact on the commerce of the Nation; and that in order to accomplish the objective of a free flow of commerce it is essential that labor organizations, employers, and their officials adhere to the highest standards of responsibility and ethical conduct in administering the affairs of their organizations, particularly as they affect labor-management relations.

(b) The Congress further finds, from recent investigations in the labor and management fields, that there have been a number of instances of breach of trust, corruption, disregard of the rights of individual employees, and other failures to observe high standards of responsibility and ethical conduct which require further and supplementary legislation that will afford necessary protection of the rights and interests of employees and the public generally as they relate to the activities of labor organizations, employers, labor relations consultants, and their officers and representatives.

(c) The Congress, therefore, further finds and declares that the enactment of this Act is necessary to eliminate or prevent improper practices on the part of labor organizations, employers, labor relations consultants, and their officers and representatives which distort and defeat the policies of the Labor Management Relations Act, 1947, as amended, and the Railway Labor Act, as amended, and have the tendency or necessary effect of burdening or obstructing commerce by (1) impairing the efficiency, safety, or operation of the instrumentalities of commerce; (2) occurring in the current of commerce; (3) materially affecting, restraining, or controlling the flow of raw materials or manufactured or processed goods into or from the channels of commerce, or the prices of such materials or goods in commerce; or (4) causing diminution of employment and wages in such volume as substantially to impair or disrupt the market for goods flowing into or from the channels of commerce.

DEFINITIONS

Sec. 3. For the purposes of titles I, II, III, IV, V (except section 505), and VI of this Act—

(a) "Commerce" means trade, traffic, commerce, transportation, transmission, or communication among the several States or between any State and any place outside thereof.

(b) "State" includes any State of the United States, the District of Columbia, Puerto Rico, the Virgin Islands, American Samoa, Guam, Wake Island, the Canal Zone, and Outer Continental Shelf lands defined in the Outer Continental Shelf Lands Act (43 U.S.C. §§ 1331–1343).

(c) "Industry affecting commerce" means any activity, business, or industry in commerce or in which a labor dispute would hinder or obstruct commerce or the free flow of commerce and includes any activity or industry "affecting commerce" within the meaning of the Labor Management Relations Act, 1947, as amended, or the Railway Labor Act, as amended.

(d) "Person" includes one or more individuals, labor organizations, partnerships, associations, corporations, legal representatives, mutual companies, joint-stock companies, trusts, unincorporated organizations, trustees, trustees in bankruptcy, or receivers.

(e) "Employer" means any employer or any group or association of employers engaged in an industry affecting commerce (1) which is, with respect to employees engaged in an industry affecting commerce, an employer within the meaning of any law of the United States relating to the employment of any employees or (2) which may deal with any labor organization concerning grievances, labor disputes, wages, rates of pay, hours of employment, or conditions of work, and includes any person acting directly or indirectly as an employer or as an agent of an employer in relation to an employee but does not include the United States or any corporation wholly owned by the Government of the United States or any State or political subdivision thereof.

(f) "Employee" means any individual employed by an employer, and includes any individual whose work has ceased as a consequence of, or in connection with, any current labor dispute or because of any unfair labor practice or because of exclusion or expulsion from a labor organization in any manner or for any reason inconsistent with the requirements of this Act.

(g) "Labor dispute" includes any controversy concerning terms, tenure, or conditions of employment, or concerning the association or representation of persons in negotiating, fixing, maintaining, changing or seeking to arrange terms or conditions of employment, regardless of whether the disputants stand in the proximate relation of employer and employee.

(h) "Trusteeship" means any receivership, trusteeship, or other method of supervision or control whereby a labor organization suspends the autonomy otherwise available to a subordinate body under its constitution or bylaws.

(i) "Labor organization" means a labor organization engaged in an industry affecting commerce and includes any organization of any kind, any agency, or employee representation committee, group, association, or plan so engaged in which employees participate and which exists for the purpose, in whole or in part, of dealing with employers concerning grievances, labor disputes, wages, rates of pay, hours, or other terms or conditions of employment, and any conference, general committee, joint or system board, or joint council so engaged which is subordinate to a national or international labor organization, other than a State or local central body.

(j) A labor organization shall be deemed to be engaged in an industry affecting commerce if it—

(1) is the certified representative of employees under the provisions of the National Labor Relations Act, as amended, or the Railway Labor Act, as amended; or

(2) although not certified, is a national or international labor organization or a local labor organization recognized or acting as the representative of employees of an employer or employers engaged in an industry affecting commerce; or

(3) has chartered a local labor organization or subsidiary body which is representing or actively seeking to represent employees of employers within the meaning of paragraph (1) or (2); or

(4) has been chartered by a labor organization representing or actively seeking to represent employees within the meaning of paragraph (1) or (2) as the local or subordinate body through which such employees may enjoy membership or become affiliated with such labor organization; or

(5) is a conference, general committee, joint or system board, or joint council, subordinate to a national or international labor organization, which includes a labor organization engaged in an industry affecting commerce within the meaning of any of the preceding paragraphs of this subsection, other than a State or local central body.

(k) "Secret ballot" means the expression by ballot, voting machine, or otherwise, but in no event by proxy, of a choice with respect to any election or vote taken upon any matter, which is cast in such a manner that the person expressing such choice cannot be identified with the choice expressed.

(l) "Trust in which a labor organization is interested" means a trust or other fund or organization (1) which was created or established by a labor organization, or one or more of the trustees or one or more members of the governing body of which is selected or appointed by a labor organization, and (2) a primary purpose of which is to provide benefits for the members of such labor organization or their beneficiaries.

(m) "Labor relations consultant" means any person who, for compensation, advises or represents an employer, employer organization, or labor organization concerning employee organizing, concerted activities, or collective bargaining activities.

(n) "Officer" means any constitutional officer, any person authorized to perform the functions of president, vice president, secretary, treasurer, or other executive functions of a labor organization, and any member of its executive board or similar governing body.

(o) "Member" or "member in good standing", when used in reference to a labor organization, includes any person who has fulfilled the requirements for membership in such organization, and who neither has voluntarily withdrawn from membership nor has been expelled or suspended from membership after appropriate proceedings consistent with lawful provisions of the constitution and bylaws of such organization.

(p) "Secretary" means the Secretary of Labor.

(q) "Officer, agent, shop steward, or other representative", when used with respect to a labor organization, includes elected officials and key administrative personnel, whether elected or appointed (such as business agents, heads of departments or major units, and organizers who exercise substantial independent authority), but does not include salaried nonsupervisory professional staff, stenographic, and service personnel.

(r) "District court of the United States" means a United States district court and a United States court of any place subject to the jurisdiction of the United States.

TITLE I—BILL OF RIGHTS OF MEMBERS OF LABOR ORGANIZATIONS

BILL OF RIGHTS

Sec. 101. (a)(1) EQUAL RIGHTS.—Every member of a labor organization shall have equal rights and privileges within such organization to nominate candidates, to vote in elections or referendums of the labor organization, to attend membership meetings, and to participate in the deliberations and voting upon the business of such meetings, subject to reasonable rules and regulations in such organization's constitution and bylaws.

(2) FREEDOM OF SPEECH AND ASSEMBLY.—Every member of any labor organization shall have the right to meet and assemble freely with other members; and to express any views, arguments, or opinions; and to express at meetings of the labor organization his views, upon candidates in an election of the labor organization or upon any business properly before the meeting, subject to the organization's established and reasonable rules pertaining to the conduct of meetings: *Provided,* That nothing herein shall be construed to impair the right of a labor organization to adopt and enforce reasonable rules as to the responsibility of every member toward the organization as an institution and to his refraining

from conduct that would interfere with its performance of its legal or contractual obligations.

(3) DUES, INITIATION FEES, AND ASSESSMENTS.—Except in the case of a federation of national or international labor organizations, the rates of dues and initiation fees payable by members of any labor organization in effect on the date of enactment of this Act shall not be increased, and no general or special assessment shall be levied upon such members, except—

(A) in a case of a local labor organization, (i) by majority vote by secret ballot of the members in good standing voting at a general or special membership meeting, after reasonable notice of the intention to vote upon such question, or (ii) by majority vote of the members in good standing voting in a membership referendum conducted by secret ballot; or

(B) in the case of a labor organization, other than a local labor organization or a federation of national or international labor organizations, (i) by majority vote of the delegates voting at a regular convention, or at a special convention of such labor organization held upon not less than thirty days' written notice to the principal office of each local or constituent labor organization entitled to such notice, or (ii) by majority vote of the members in good standing of such labor organization voting in a membership referendum conducted by secret ballot, or (iii) by majority vote of the members of the executive board or similar governing body of such labor organization, pursuant to express authority contained in the constitution and bylaws of such labor organization: *Provided,* That such action on the part of the executive board or similar governing body shall be effective only until the next regular convention of such labor organization.

(4) PROTECTION OF THE RIGHT TO SUE.—No labor organization shall limit the right of any member thereof to institute an action in any court, or in a proceeding before any administrative agency, irrespective of whether or not the labor organization or its officers are named as defendants or respondents in such action or proceeding, or the right of any member of a labor organization to appear as a witness in any judicial, administrative, or legislative proceeding, or to petition any legislature or to communicate with any legislator: *Provided,* That any such member may be required to exhaust reasonable hearing procedures (but not to exceed a four-month lapse of time) within such organization, before instituting legal or administrative proceedings against such organizations or any officer thereof: *And provided further,* That no interested employer or employer association shall directly or indirectly finance, encourage, or participate in, except as a party, any such action, proceeding, appearance, or petition.

(5) SAFEGUARDS AGAINST IMPROPER DISCIPLINARY ACTION.—No member of any labor organization may be fined, suspended, expelled, or otherwise disciplined except for nonpayment of dues by such organization or by any officer thereof unless such member has been (A)

served with written specific charges; (B) given a reasonable time to prepare his defense; (C) afforded a full and fair hearing.

(b) Any provision of the constitution and bylaws of any labor organization which is inconsistent with the provisions of this section shall be of no force or effect.

CIVIL ENFORCEMENT

Sec. 102. Any person whose rights secured by the provisions of this title have been infringed by any violation of this title may bring a civil action in a district court of the United States for such relief (including injunctions) as may be appropriate. Any such action against a labor organization shall be brought in the district court of the United States for the district where the alleged violation occurred, or where the principal office of such labor organization is located.

RETENTION OF EXISTING RIGHTS

Sec. 103. Nothing contained in this title shall limit the rights and remedies of any member of a labor organization under any State or Federal law or before any court or other tribunal, or under the constitution and bylaws of any labor organization.

RIGHT TO COPIES OF COLLECTIVE BARGAINING AGREEMENTS

Sec. 104. It shall be the duty of the secretary or corresponding principal officer of each labor organization, in the case of a local labor organization, to forward a copy of each collective bargaining agreement made by such labor organization with any employer to any employee who requests such a copy and whose rights as such employee are directly affected by such agreement, and in the case of a labor organization other than a local labor organization, to forward a copy of any such agreement to each constituent unit which has members directly affected by such agreement; and such officer shall maintain at the principal office of the labor organization of which he is an officer copies of any such agreement made or received by such labor organization, which copies shall be available for inspection by any member or by any employee whose rights are affected by such agreement. The provisions of section 210 shall be applicable in the enforcement of this section.

INFORMATION AS TO ACT

Sec. 105. Every labor organization shall inform its members concerning the provisions of this Act.

TITLE II—REPORTING BY LABOR ORGANIZATIONS, OFFICERS AND EMPLOYEES OF LABOR ORGANIZATIONS, AND EMPLOYERS

REPORT OF LABOR ORGANIZATIONS

Sec. 201. (a) Every labor organization shall adopt a constitution and bylaws and shall file a copy thereof with the Secretary, together with a report, signed by its president and secretary or corresponding principal officers, containing the following information—

(1) the name of the labor organization, its mailing address, and any other address at which it maintains its principal office or at which it keeps the records referred to in this title;

(2) the name and title of each of its officers;

(3) the initiation fee or fees required from a new or transferred member and fees for work permits required by the reporting labor organization;

(4) the regular dues or fees or other periodic payments required to remain a member of the reporting labor organization; and

(5) detailed statements, or references to specific provisions of documents filed under this subsection which contain such statements, showing the provision made and procedures followed with respect to each of the following: (A) qualifications for or restrictions on membership, (B) levying of assessments, (C) participation in insurance or other benefit plans, (D) authorization for disbursement of funds of the labor organization, (E) audit of financial transactions of the labor organization, (F) the calling of regular and special meetings, (G) the selection of officers and stewards and of any representatives to other bodies composed of labor organizations' representatives, with a specific statement of the manner in which each officer was elected, appointed, or otherwise selected, (H) discipline or removal of officers or agents for breaches of their trust, (I) imposition of fines, suspensions and expulsions of members, including the grounds for such action and any provision made for notice, hearing, judgment on the evidence, and appeal procedures, (J) authorization for bargaining demands, (K) ratification of contract terms, (L) authorization for strikes, and (M) issuance of work permits. Any change in the information required by this subsection shall be reported to the Secretary at the time the reporting labor organization files with the Secretary the annual financial report required by subsection (b).

(b) Every labor organization shall file annually with the Secretary a financial report signed by its president and treasurer or corresponding principal officers containing the following information in such detail as may be necessary accurately to disclose its financial condition and operations for its preceding fiscal year—

(1) assets and liabilities at the beginning and end of the fiscal year;

(2) receipts of any kind and the sources thereof;

(3) salary, allowances, and other direct or indirect disbursements (including reimbursed expenses) to each officer and also to each employee who, during such fiscal year, received more than $10,000 in the aggregate from such labor organization and any other labor organi-

zation affiliated with it or with which it is affiliated, or which is affiliated with the same national or international labor organization;

(4) direct and indirect loans made to any officer, employee, or member, which aggregated more than $250 during the fiscal year, together with a statement of the purpose, security, if any, and arrangements for repayment;

(5) direct and indirect loans to any business enterprise, together with a statement of the purpose, security, if any, and arrangements for repayment; and

(6) other disbursements made by it including the purposes thereof;

all in such categories as the Secretary may prescribe.

(c) Every labor organization required to submit a report under this title shall make available the information required to be contained in such report to all of its members, and every such labor organization and its officers shall be under a duty enforceable at the suit of any member of such organization in any State court of competent jurisdiction or in the district court of the United States for the district in which such labor organization maintains its principal office, to permit such member for just cause to examine any books, records, and accounts necessary to verify such report. The court in such action may, in its discretion, in addition to any judgment awarded to the plaintiff or plaintiffs, allow a reasonable attorney's fee to be paid by the defendant, and costs of the action.

REPORT OF OFFICERS AND EMPLOYEES
OF LABOR ORGANIZATIONS

Sec. 202. (a) Every officer of a labor organization and every employee of a labor organization (other than an employee performing exclusively clerical or custodial services) shall file with the Secretary a signed report listing and describing for his preceding fiscal year—

(1) any stock, bond, security, or other interest, legal or equitable, which he or his spouse or minor child directly or indirectly held in, and any income or any other benefit with monetary value (including reimbursed expenses) which he or his spouse or minor child derived directly or indirectly from, an employer whose employees such labor organization represents or is actively seeking to represent, except payments and other benefits received as a bona fide employee of such employer;

(2) any transaction in which he or his spouse or minor child engaged, directly or indirectly, involving any stock, bond, security, or loan to or from, or other legal or equitable interest in the business of an employer whose employees such labor organization represents or is actively seeking to represent;

(3) any stock, bond, security, or other interest, legal or equitable, which he or his spouse or minor child directly or indirectly held in, and

any income or any other benefit with monetary value (including reimbursed expenses) which he or his spouse or minor child directly or indirectly derived from, any business a substantial part of which consists of buying from, selling or leasing to, or otherwise dealing with, the business of an employer whose employees such labor organization represents or is actively seeking to represent;

(4) any stock, bond, security, or other interest, legal or equitable, which he or his spouse or minor child directly or indirectly held in, and any income or any other benefit with monetary value (including reimbursed expenses) which he or his spouse or minor child directly or indirectly derived from, a business any part of which consists of buying from, or selling or leasing directly or indirectly to, or otherwise dealing with such labor organization;

(5) any direct or indirect business transaction or arrangement between him or his spouse or minor child and any employer whose employees his organization represents or is actively seeking to represent, except work performed and payments and benefits received as a bona fide employee of such employer and except purchases and sales of goods or services in the regular course of business at prices generally available to any employee of such employer; and

(6) any payment of money or other thing of value (including reimbursed expenses) which he or his spouse or minor child received directly or indirectly from any employer or any person who acts as a labor relations consultant to an employer, except payments of the kinds referred to in section 302(c) of the Labor Management Relations Act, 1947, as amended.

(b) The provisions of paragraphs (1), (2), (3), (4), and (5) of subsection (a) shall not be construed to require any such officer or employee to report his bona fide investments in securities traded on a securities exchange registered as a national securities exchange under the Securities Exchange Act of 1934, in shares in an investment company registered under the Investment Company Act of 1940, or in securities of a public utility holding company registered under the Public Utility Holding Company Act of 1935, or to report any income derived therefrom.

(c) Nothing contained in this section shall be construed to require any officer or employee of a labor organization to file a report under subsection (a) unless he or his spouse or minor child holds or has held an interest, has received income or any other benefit with monetary value or a loan, or has engaged in a transaction described therein.

REPORT OF EMPLOYERS

Sec. 203. (a) Every employer who in any fiscal year made—

(1) any payment or loan, direct or indirect, of money or other thing of value (including reimbursed expenses), or any promise or agreement therefor, to any labor organization or officer, agent, shop steward, or other representative of a labor organization, or employee of

any labor organization, except (A) payments or loans made by any national or State bank, credit union, insurance company, savings and loan association or other credit institution and (B) payments of the kind referred to in section 302(c) of the Labor Management Relations Act, 1947, as amended;

(2) any payment (including reimbursed expenses) to any of his employees, or any group or committee of such employees, for the purpose of causing such employee or group or committee of employees to persuade other employees to exercise or not to exercise, or as the manner of exercising, the right to organize and bargain collectively through representatives of their own choosing unless such payments were contemporaneously or previously disclosed to such other employees;

(3) any expenditure, during the fiscal year, where an object thereof, directly or indirectly, is to interfere with, restrain, or coerce employees in the exercise of the right to organize and bargain collectively through representatives of their own choosing, or is to obtain information concerning the activities of employees or a labor organization in connection with a labor dispute involving such employer, except for use solely in conjunction with an administrative or arbitral proceeding or a criminal or civil judicial proceeding;

(4) any agreement or arrangement with a labor relations consultant or other independent contractor or organization pursuant to which such person undertakes activities where an object thereof, directly or indirectly, is to persuade employees to exercise or not to exercise, or persuade employees as to the manner of exercising, the right to organize and bargain collectively through representatives of their own choosing, or undertakes to supply such employer with information concerning the activities of employees or a labor organization in connection with a labor dispute involving such employer, except information for use solely in conjunction with an administrative or arbitral proceeding or a criminal or civil judicial proceeding; or

(5) any payment (including reimbursed expenses) pursuant to an agreement or arrangement described in subdivision (4);

shall file with the Secretary a report, in a form prescribed by him, signed by its president and treasurer or corresponding principal officers showing in detail the date and amount of each such payment, loan, promise, agreement, or arrangement and the name, address, and position, if any, in any firm or labor organization of the person to whom it was made and a full explanation of the circumstances of all such payments, including the terms of any agreement or understanding pursuant to which they were made.

(b) Every person who pursuant to any agreement or arrangement with an employer undertakes activities where an object thereof is, directly or indirectly—

(1) to persuade employees to exercise or not to exercise, or persuade employees as to the manner of exercising, the right to organize and bargain collectively through representatives of their own choosing; or

(2) to supply an employer with information concerning the activities of employees or a labor organization in connection with a labor dispute involving such employer, except information for use solely in conjunction with an administrative or arbitral proceeding or a criminal or civil judicial proceeding;

shall file within thirty days after entering into such agreement or arrangement a report with the Secretary, signed by its president and treasurer or corresponding principal officers, containing the name under which such person is engaged in doing business and the address of its principal office, and a detailed statement of the terms and conditions of such agreement or arrangement. Every such person shall file annually, with respect to each fiscal year during which payments were made as a result of such an agreement or arrangement, a report with the Secretary, signed by its president and treasurer or corresponding principal officers, containing a statement (A) of its receipts of any kind from employers on account of labor relations advice or services, designating the sources thereof, and (B) of its disbursements of any kind, in connection with such services and the purposes thereof. In each such case such information shall be set forth in such categories as the Secretary may prescribe.

(c) Nothing in this section shall be construed to require any employer or other person to file a report covering the services of such person by reason of his giving or agreeing to give advice to such employer or representing or agreeing to represent such employer before any court, administrative agency, or tribunal of arbitration or engaging or agreeing to engage in collective bargaining on behalf of such employer with respect to wages, hours, or other terms or conditions of employment or the negotiation of an agreement or any question arising thereunder.

(d) Nothing contained in this section shall be construed to require an employer to file a report under subsection (a) unless he has made an expenditure, payment, loan, agreement, or arrangement of the kind described therein. Nothing contained in this section shall be construed to require any other person to file a report under subsection (b) unless he was a party to an agreement or arrangement of the kind described therein.

(e) Nothing contained in this section shall be construed to require any regular officer, supervisor, or employee of an employer to file a report in connection with services rendered to such employer nor shall any employer be required to file a report covering expenditures made to any regular officer, supervisor, or employee of an employer as compensation for service as a regular officer, supervisor, or employee of such employer.

(f) Nothing contained in this section shall be construed as an amendment to, or modification of the rights protected by, section 8(c) of the National Labor Relations Act, as amended.

(g) The term "interfere with, restrain, or coerce" as used in this section means interference, restraint, and coercion which, if done with respect to the exercise of rights guaranteed in section 7 of the National Labor Relations Act, as amended, would, under section 8(a) of such Act, constitute an unfair labor practice.

ATTORNEY–CLIENT COMMUNICATIONS EXEMPTED

Sec. 204. Nothing contained in this Act shall be construed to require an attorney who is a member in good standing of the bar of any State, to include in any report required to be filed pursuant to the provisions of this Act any information which was lawfully communicated to such attorney by any of his clients in the course of a legitimate attorney-client relationship.

REPORTS MADE PUBLIC INFORMATION

Sec. 205. (a) The contents of the reports and documents filed with the Secretary pursuant to sections 201, 202, 203, and 211 shall be public information, and the Secretary may publish any information and data which he obtains pursuant to the provisions of this title. The Secretary may use the information and data for statistical and research purposes, and compile and publish such studies, analyses, reports, and surveys based thereon as he may deem appropriate.

(b) The Secretary shall by regulation make reasonable provision for the inspection and examination, on the request of any person, of the information and data contained in any report or other document filed with him pursuant to section 201, 202, 203, or 211.

(c) The Secretary shall by regulation provide for the furnishing by the Department of Labor of copies of reports or other documents filed with the Secretary pursuant to this title, upon payment of a charge based upon the cost of the service. The Secretary shall make available without payment of a charge, or require any person to furnish, to such State agency as is designated by law or by the Governor of the State in which such person has his principal place of business or headquarters, upon request of the Governor of such State, copies of any reports and documents filed by such person with the Secretary pursuant to section 201, 202, 203, or 211, or of information and data contained therein. No person shall be required by reason of any law of any State to furnish to any officer or agency of such State any information included in a report filed by such person with the Secretary pursuant to the provisions of this title, if a copy of such report, or of the portion thereof containing such information, is furnished to such officer or agency. All moneys received in payment of such charges fixed by the Secretary pursuant to this subsection shall be deposited in the general fund of the Treasury.

RETENTION OF RECORDS

Sec. 206. Every person required to file any report under this title shall maintain records on the matters required to be reported which will provide in sufficient detail the necessary basic information and data from which the documents filed with the Secretary may be verified, explained or clarified, and checked for accuracy and completeness, and shall include vouchers, worksheets, receipts, and applicable resolutions, and shall keep such records available for examination for a period of not less than five years after the filing of the documents based on the information which they contain.

EFFECTIVE DATE

Sec. 207.   (a) Each labor organization shall file the initial report required under section 201(a) within ninety days after the date on which it first becomes subject to this Act.

(b) Each person required to file a report under section 201(b), 202, 203(a), or the second sentence of 203(b), or section 211 shall file such report within ninety days after the end of each of its fiscal years; except that where such person is subject to section 201(b), 202, 203(a), the second sentence of 203(b), or section 211, as the case may be, for only a portion of such a fiscal year (because the date of enactment of this Act occurs during such person's fiscal year or such person becomes subject to this Act during its fiscal year) such person may consider that portion as the entire fiscal year in making such report.

RULES AND REGULATIONS

Sec. 208.   The Secretary shall have authority to issue, amend, and rescind rules and regulations prescribing the form and publication of reports required to be filed under this title and such other reasonable rules and regulations (including rules prescribing reports concerning trusts in which a labor organization is interested) as he may find necessary to prevent the circumvention or evasion of such reporting requirements. In exercising his power under this section the Secretary shall prescribe by general rule simplified reports for labor organizations or employers for whom he finds that by virtue of their size a detailed report would be unduly burdensome, but the Secretary may revoke such provision for simplified forms of any labor organization or employer if he determines, after such investigation as he deems proper and due notice and opportunity for a hearing, that the purposes of this section would be served thereby.

CRIMINAL PROVISIONS

Sec. 209.   (a) Any person who willfully violates this title shall be fined not more than $10,000 or imprisoned for not more than one year, or both.

(b) Any person who makes a false statement or representation of a material fact, knowing it to be false, or who knowingly fails to disclose a material fact, in any document, report, or other information required under the provisions of this title shall be fined not more than $10,000 or imprisoned for not more than one year, or both.

(c) Any person who willfully makes a false entry in or willfully conceals, withholds, or destroys any books, records, reports, or statements required to be kept by any provision of this title shall be fined not more than $10,000 or imprisoned for not more than one year, or both.

(d) Each individual required to sign reports under sections 201 and 203 shall be personally responsible for the filing of such reports and for any statement contained therein which he knows to be false.

CIVIL ENFORCEMENT

Sec. 210.   Whenever it shall appear that any person has violated or is about to violate any of the provisions of this title, the Secretary may bring a civil action for such relief (including injunctions) as may be appropriate. Any such action may be brought in the district court of the United States where the violation occurred or, at the option of the parties, in the United States District Court for the District of Columbia.

SURETY COMPANY REPORTS

Sec. 211.   Each surety company which issues any bond required by this Act or the Employee Retirement Income Security Act of 1974 shall file annually with the Secretary, with respect to each fiscal year during which any such bond was in force, a report, in such form and detail as he may prescribe by regulation, filed by the president and treasurer or corresponding principal officers of the surety company, describing its bond experience under each such Act, including information as to the premiums received, total claims paid, amounts recovered by way of subrogation, administrative and legal expenses and such related data and information as the Secretary shall determine to be necessary in the public interest and to carry out the policy of the Act. Notwithstanding the foregoing, if the Secretary finds that any such specific information cannot be practicably ascertained or would be uninformative, the Secretary may modify or waive the requirement for such information.

TITLE III—TRUSTEESHIPS

REPORTS

Sec. 301.   (a) Every labor organization which has or assumes trusteeship over any subordinate labor organization shall file with the Secretary within thirty days after the date of the enactment of this Act or the imposition of any such trusteeship, and semiannually thereafter, a report, signed by its president and treasurer or corresponding principal officers, as well as by the trustees of such subordinate labor organization, containing the following information: (1) the name and address of the subordinate organization; (2) the date of establishing the trusteeship; (3) a detailed statement of the reason or reasons for establishing or continuing the trusteeship; and (4) the nature and extent of participation by the membership of the subordinate organization in the selection of delegates to represent such organization in regular or special conventions or other policy-determining bodies and in the election of officers of the labor organization which has assumed trusteeship over such subordinate organization. The initial report shall also include a full and complete account of the financial condition of such subordinate organization as of the time trusteeship was assumed over it. During the continuance of a trusteeship the labor organization which has assumed trusteeship over a subordinate labor organization shall file on behalf of the subordinate labor organization the annual financial report required by section 201(b) signed by the president and treasurer or corresponding principal officers of the labor organization which has assumed such trusteeship and the trustees of the subordinate labor organization.

(b) The provisions of sections 201(c), 205, 206, 208, and 210 shall be applicable to reports filed under this title.

(c) Any person who willfully violates this section shall be fined not more than $10,000 or imprisoned for not more than one year, or both.

(d) Any person who makes a false statement or representation of a material fact, knowing it to be false, or who knowingly fails to disclose a material fact, in any report required under the provisions of this section or willfully makes any false entry in or willfully withholds, conceals, or destroys any documents, books, records, reports, or statements upon which such report is based, shall be fined not more than $10,000 or imprisoned for not more than one year, or both.

(e) Each individual required to sign a report under this section shall be personally responsible for the filing of such report and for any statement contained therein which he knows to be false.

PURPOSES FOR WHICH A TRUSTEESHIP MAY BE ESTABLISHED

Sec. 302.   Trusteeships shall be established and administered by a labor organization over a subordinate body only in accordance with the constitution and bylaws of the organization which has assumed trusteeship over the subordinate body and for the purpose of correcting corruption or financial malpractice, assuring the performance of collective bargaining agreements or other duties of a bargaining representative, restoring democratic procedures, or otherwise carrying out the legitimate objects of such labor organization.

UNLAWFUL ACTS RELATING TO LABOR ORGANIZATION UNDER TRUSTEESHIP

Sec. 303.   (a) During any period when a subordinate body of a labor organization is in trusteeship, it shall be unlawful (1) to count the vote of delegates from such body in any convention or election of officers of the labor organization unless the delegates have been chosen by secret ballot in an election in which all the members in good standing of such subordinate body were eligible to participate, or (2) to transfer to such organization any current receipts or other funds of the subordinate body except the normal per capita tax and assessments payable by subordinate bodies not in trusteeship: *Provided,* That nothing herein contained shall prevent the distribution of the assets of a labor organization in accordance with its constitution and bylaws upon the bona fide dissolution thereof.

(b) Any person who willfully violates this section shall be fined not more than $10,000 or imprisoned for not more than one year, or both.

ENFORCEMENT

Sec. 304. (a) Upon the written complaint of any member or subordinate body of a labor organization alleging that such organization has violated the provisions of this title (except section 301) the Secretary shall investigate the complaint and if the Secretary finds probable cause to believe that such violation has occurred and has not been remedied he shall, without disclosing the identity of the complainant, bring a civil action in any district court of the United States having jurisdiction of the labor organization for such relief (including injunctions) as may be appropriate. Any member or subordinate body of a labor organization affected by any violation of this title (except section 301) may bring a civil action in any district court of the United States having jurisdiction of the labor organization for such relief (including injunctions) as may be appropriate.

(b) For the purpose of actions under this section, district courts of the United States shall be deemed to have jurisdiction of a labor organization (1) in the district in which the principal office of such labor organization is located, or (2) in any district in which its duly authorized officers or agents are engaged in conducting the affairs of the trusteeship.

(c) In any proceeding pursuant to this section a trusteeship established by a labor organization in conformity with the procedural requirements of its constitution and bylaws and authorized or ratified after a fair hearing either before the executive board or before such other body as may be provided in accordance with its constitution or bylaws shall be presumed valid for a period of eighteen months from the date of its establishment and shall not be subject to attack during such period except upon clear and convincing proof that the trusteeship was not established or maintained in good faith for a purpose allowable under section 302. After the expiration of eighteen months the trusteeship shall be presumed invalid in any such proceeding and its discontinuance shall be decreed unless the labor organization shall show by clear and convincing proof that the continuation of the trusteeship is necessary for a purpose allowable under section 302. In the latter event the court may dismiss the complaint or retain jurisdiction of the cause on such conditions and for such period as it deems appropriate.

REPORT TO CONGRESS

Sec. 305. The Secretary shall submit to the Congress at the expiration of three years from the date of enactment of this Act a report upon the operation of this title.

COMPLAINT BY SECRETARY

Sec. 306. The rights and remedies provided by this title shall be in addition to any and all other rights and remedies at law or in equity: *Provided,* That upon the filing of a complaint by the Secretary the jurisdiction of the district court over such trusteeship shall be exclusive and the final judgment shall be res judicata.

TITLE IV—ELECTIONS
TERMS OF OFFICE; ELECTION PROCEDURES

Sec. 401. (a) Every national or international labor organization, except a federation of national or international labor organizations, shall elect its officers not less often than once every five years either by secret ballot among the members in good standing or at a convention of delegates chosen by secret ballot.

(b) Every local labor organization shall elect its officers not less often than once every three years by secret ballot among the members in good standing.

(c) Every national or international labor organization, except a federation of national or international labor organizations, and every local labor organization, and its officers, shall be under a duty, enforceable at the suit of any bona fide candidate for office in such labor organization in the district court of the United States in which such labor organization maintains its principal office, to comply with all reasonable requests of any candidate to distribute by mail or otherwise at the candidate's expense campaign literature in aid of such person's candidacy to all members in good standing of such labor organization and to refrain from discrimination in favor of or against any candidate with respect to the use of lists of members, and whenever such labor organizations or its officers authorize the distribution by mail or otherwise to members of campaign literature on behalf of any candidate or of the labor organization itself with reference to such election, similar distribution at the request of any other bona fide candidate shall be made by such labor organization and its officers, with equal treatment as to the expense of such distribution. Every bona fide candidate shall have the right, once within 30 days prior to an election of a labor organization in which he is a candidate, to inspect a list containing the names and last known addresses of all members of the labor organization who are subject to a collective bargaining agreement requiring membership therein as a condition of employment, which list shall be maintained and kept at the principal office of such labor organization by a designated official thereof. Adequate safeguards to insure a fair election shall be provided, including the right of any candidate to have an observer at the polls and at the counting of the ballots.

(d) Officers of intermediate bodies, such as general committees, system boards, joint boards, or joint councils, shall be elected not less often than once every four years by secret ballot among the members in good standing or by labor organization officers representative of such members who have been elected by secret ballot.

(e) In any election required by this section which is to be held by secret ballot a reasonable opportunity shall be given for the nomination of candidates and every member in good standing shall be eligible to be a candidate and to hold office (subject to section 504 and to reasonable qualifications uniformly imposed) and shall have the right to vote for or otherwise support the candidate or candidates of his choice, without being subject to penalty, discipline, or improper interference or reprisal of any kind by such organization or any member thereof. Not less than fifteen days prior to the election notice thereof shall be mailed to each member at his last known home address. Each member in good standing shall be entitled to one vote. No member whose dues have been withheld by his employer for payment to such organization pursuant to his voluntary authorization provided for in a collective bargaining agreement, shall be declared ineligible to vote or be a candidate for office in such organization by reason of alleged delay or default in the payment of dues. The votes cast by members of each local labor organization shall be counted, and the results published, separately. The election officials designated in the constitution and bylaws or the secretary, if no other official is designated, shall preserve for one year the ballots and all other records pertaining to the election. The election shall be conducted in accordance with the constitution and bylaws of such organization insofar as they are not inconsistent with the provisions of this title.

(f) When officers are chosen by a convention of delegates elected by secret ballot, the convention shall be conducted in accordance with the constitution and bylaws of the labor organization insofar as they are not inconsistent with the provisions of this title. The officials designated in the constitution and bylaws or the secretary, if no other is designated, shall preserve for one year the credentials of the delegates and all minutes and other records of the convention pertaining to the election of officers.

(g) No moneys received by any labor organization by way of dues, assessment, or similar levy, and no moneys of an employer shall be contributed or applied to promote the candidacy of any person in an election subject to the provisions of this title. Such moneys of a labor organization may be utilized for notices, factual statements of issues not involving candidates, and other expenses necessary for the holding of an election.

(h) If the Secretary, upon application of any member of a local labor organization, finds after hearing in accordance with the Administrative Procedure Act that the constitution and bylaws of such labor organization do not provide an adequate procedure for the removal of an elected officer guilty of serious misconduct, such officer may be removed, for cause shown and after notice and hearing, by the members in good standing voting in a secret ballot conducted by the officers of such labor organization in accordance with its constitution and bylaws insofar as they are not inconsistent with the provisions of this title.

(i) The Secretary shall promulgate rules and regulations prescribing minimum standards and procedures for determining the adequacy of the removal procedures to which reference is made in subsection (h).

ENFORCEMENT

Sec. 402. (a) A member of a labor organization—

(1) who has exhausted the remedies available under the constitution and bylaws of such organization and of any parent body or

(2) who has invoked such available remedies without obtaining a final decision within three calendar months after their invocation,

may file a complaint with the Secretary within one calendar month thereafter alleging the violation of any provision of section 401 (including violation of the constitution and bylaws of the labor organization pertaining to the election and removal of officers). The challenged election shall be presumed valid pending a final decision thereon (as hereinafter provided) and in the interim the affairs of the organization shall be conducted by the officers elected or in such other manner as its constitution and bylaws may provide.

(b) The Secretary shall investigate such complaint and, if he finds probable cause to believe that a violation of this title has occurred and has not been remedied, he shall, within sixty days after the filing of such complaint, bring a civil action against the labor organization as an entity in the district court of the United States in which such labor organization maintains its principal office to set aside the invalid election, if any, and to direct the conduct of an election or hearing and vote upon the removal of officers under the supervision of the Secretary and in accordance with the provisions of this title and such rules and regulations as the Secretary may prescribe. The court shall have power to take such action as it deems proper to preserve the assets of the labor organization.

(c) If, upon a preponderance of the evidence after a trial upon the merits, the court finds—

(1) that an election has not been held within the time prescribed by section 401, or

(2) that the violation of section 401 may have affected the outcome of an election

the court shall declare the election, if any, to be void and direct the conduct of a new election under supervision of the Secretary and, so far as lawful and practicable, in conformity with the constitution and bylaws of the labor organization. The Secretary shall promptly certify to the court the names of the persons elected, and the court shall thereupon enter a decree declaring such persons to be the officers of the labor organization. If the proceeding is for the removal of officers pursuant to subsection (h) of section 401, the Secretary shall certify the results of the vote and the court shall enter a decree declaring whether such persons have been removed as officers of the labor organization.

(d) An order directing an election, dismissing a complaint, or designating elected officers of a labor organization shall be appealable in the same manner as the final judgment in a civil action, but an order directing an election shall not be stayed pending appeal.

APPLICATION OF OTHER LAWS

Sec. 403. No labor organization shall be required by law to conduct elections of officers with greater frequency or in a different form or manner than is required by its own constitution or bylaws, except as otherwise provided by this title. Existing rights and remedies to enforce the constitution and bylaws of a labor organization with respect to elections prior to the conduct thereof shall not be affected by the provisions of this title. The remedy provided by this title for challenging an election already conducted shall be exclusive.

EFFECTIVE DATE

Sec. 404. The provisions of this title shall become applicable—

(1) ninety days after the date of enactment of this Act in the case of a labor organization whose constitution and bylaws can lawfully be modified or amended by action of its constitutional officers or governing body, or

(2) where such modification can only be made by a constitutional convention of the labor organization, not later than the next constitutional convention of such labor organization after the date of enactment of this Act, or one year after such date, whichever is sooner. If no such convention is held within such one-year period, the executive board or similar governing body empowered to act for such labor organization between conventions is empowered to make such interim constitutional changes as are necessary to carry out the provisions of this title.

TITLE V—SAFEGUARDS FOR LABOR ORGANIZATIONS
FIDUCIARY RESPONSIBILITY OF OFFICERS OF LABOR ORGANIZATIONS

Sec. 501. (a) The officers, agents, shop stewards, and other representatives of a labor organization occupy positions of trust in relation to such organization and its members as a group. It is, therefore, the duty of each such person, taking into account the special problems and functions of a labor organization, to hold its money and property solely for the benefit of the organization and its members and to manage, invest, and expend the same in accordance with its constitution and bylaws and any resolutions of the governing bodies adopted thereunder, to refrain from dealing with such organization as an adverse party or in behalf of an adverse party in any matter connected with his duties and from holding or acquiring any pecuniary or personal interest which conflicts with the interests of such organization, and to account to the organization for any profit received by him in whatever capacity in connection with transactions conducted by him or under his direction on behalf of the organization. A general exculpatory provision in the constitution and bylaws of such a labor organization or a general exculpatory resolution of a governing body purporting to relieve any such person of liability for breach of the duties declared by this section shall be void as against public policy.

(b) When any officer, agent, shop steward, or representative of any labor organization is alleged to have violated the duties declared in subsection (a) and the labor organization or its governing board or officers refuse or fail to sue or recover damages or secure an accounting or other appropriate relief within a reasonable time after being requested to do so by any member of the labor organization, such member may sue such officer, agent, shop steward, or representative in any district court of the United States or in any State court of competent jurisdiction to recover damages or secure an accounting or other appropriate relief for the benefit of the labor organization. No such proceeding shall be brought except upon leave of the court obtained upon verified application and for good cause shown which application may be made ex parte. The trial judge may allot a reasonable part of the recovery in any action under this subsection to pay the fees of counsel prosecuting the suit at the instance of the member of the labor organization and to compensate such member for any expenses necessarily paid or incurred by him in connection with the litigation.

(c) Any person who embezzles, steals, or unlawfully and willfully abstracts or converts to his own use, or the use of another, any of the moneys, funds, securities, property, or other assets of a labor organization of which he is an officer, or by which he is employed, directly or indirectly, shall be fined not more than $10,000 or imprisoned for not more than five years, or both.

BONDING

Sec. 502. (a) Every officer, agent, shop steward, or other representative or employee of any labor organization (other than a labor organization whose property and annual financial receipts do not exceed $5,000 in value), or of a trust in which a labor organization is interested, who handles funds or other property thereof shall be bonded to provide protection against loss by reason of acts of fraud or dishonesty on his part directly or through connivance with others. The bond of each such person shall be fixed at the beginning of the organization's fiscal year and shall be in an amount not less than 10 per centum of the funds handled by him and his predecessor or predecessors, if any, during the preceding fiscal year, but in no case more than $500,000. If the labor organization or the trust in which a labor organization is interested does not have a preceding fiscal year, the amount of the bond shall be, in the case of a local labor organization, not less than $1,000, and in the case of any other labor organization or of a trust in which a labor organization is interested, not less than $10,000. Such bonds shall be individual or schedule in form, and shall have a corporate surety company as surety thereon. Any person who is not covered by such bonds shall not be permitted to receive, handle, disburse, or otherwise exercise custody or control of the funds or other property of a labor organization or of a trust in which a labor organization is interested. No such bond shall be placed through an agent or broker or with a surety company in which any labor organization or any officer, agent, shop steward, or other representative of a labor organization has any direct or indirect interest. Such surety company shall be a corporate surety which holds a grant of authority from the Secretary of the Treasury under the Act of July 30, 1947 (6 U.S.C. 6–13), as an acceptable surety on Federal bonds: *Provided,* That when in the opinion of the Secretary a labor organization has made other bonding arrangements which would provide the protection required by this section at comparable cost or less, he may exempt such labor organization from placing a bond through a surety company holding such grant of authority.

(b) Any person who willfully violates this section shall be fined not more than $10,000 or imprisoned for not more than one year, or both.

MAKING OF LOANS; PAYMENT OF FINES

Sec. 503. (a) No labor organization shall make directly or indirectly any loan or loans to any officer or employee of such organization which results in a total indebtedness on the part of such officer or employee to the labor organization in excess of $2,000.

(b) No labor organization or employer shall directly or indirectly pay the fine of any officer or employee convicted of any willful violation of this Act.

(c) Any person who willfully violates this section shall be fined not more than $5,000 or imprisoned for not more than one year, or both.

PROHIBITION AGAINST CERTAIN PERSONS HOLDING OFFICE

Sec. 504.* (a) No person who is or has been a member of the Communist Party or who has been convicted of, or served any part of a prison term resulting from his conviction of, robbery, bribery, extortion, embezzlement, grand larceny, burglary, arson, violation of narcotics laws, murder, rape, assault with intent to kill, assault which inflicts grievous bodily injury, or a violation of subchapter III or IV of this chapter, any felony involving abuse or misuse of such person's position or employment in a labor organization or employee benefit plan to seek or obtain an illegal gain at the expense of the members of the labor organization or the beneficiaries of the employee benefit plan, or conspiracy to commit any such crimes or attempt to commit any such crimes, or a crime in which any of the foregoing crimes is an element, shall serve or be permitted to serve—

(1) as a consultant or adviser to any labor organization,

(2) as an officer, director, trustee, member of any executive board or similar governing body, business agent, manager, organizer, employee, or representative in any capacity of any labor organization,

(3) as a labor relations consultant or adviser to a person engaged in an industry or activity affecting commerce, or as an officer, director, agent, or employee of any group or association of employers dealing with any labor organization, or in a position having specific collective

* This section was amended by Pub.L. Stat. 2133. 98–473, Title II, § 803, Oct. 12, 1984, 98

bargaining authority or direct responsibility in the area of labor-management relations in any corporation or association engaged in an industry or activity affecting commerce, or

(4) in a position which entitles its occupant to a share of the proceeds of, or as an officer or executive or administrative employee of, any entity whose activities are in whole or substantial part devoted to providing goods or services to any labor organization, or

(5) in any capacity, other than in his capacity as a member of such labor organization, that involves decisionmaking authority concerning, or decisionmaking authority over, or custody of, or control of the moneys, funds, assets, or property of any labor organization,

during or for the period of thirteen years after such conviction or after the end of such imprisonment, whichever is later, unless the sentencing court on the motion of the person convicted sets a lesser period of at least three years after such conviction or after the end of such imprisonment, whichever is later, or unless prior to the end of such period, in the case of a person so convicted or imprisoned, (A) his citizenship rights, having been revoked as a result of such conviction, have been fully restored, or (B) the United States Parole Commission determines that such person's service in any capacity referred to in clauses (1) through (5) would not be contrary to the purposes of this chapter. Prior to making any such determination the Commission shall hold an administrative hearing and shall give notice of such proceeding by certified mail to the Secretary of Labor and to State, county, and Federal prosecuting officials in the jurisdiction or jurisdictions in which such person was convicted. The Commission's determination in any such proceeding shall be final. No person shall knowingly hire, retain, employ, or otherwise place any other person to serve in any capacity in violation of this subsection.

(b) Any person who willfully violates this section shall be fined not more than $10,000 or imprisoned for not more than five years, or both.

(c) For the purpose of this section—

(1) A person shall be deemed to have been "convicted" and under the disability of "conviction" from the date of the judgment of the trial court, regardless of whether that judgment remains under appeal.

(2) A period of parole shall not be considered as part of a period of imprisonment.

(d) Whenever any person—

(1) by operation of this section, has been barred from office or other position in a labor organization as a result of a conviction, and

(2) has filed an appeal of that conviction,

any salary which would be otherwise due such person by virtue of such office or position, shall be placed in escrow by the individual employer or organization responsible for payment of such salary. Payment of such salary into escrow shall continue for the duration of the appeal or for the period of time during which such salary would be otherwise due, whichever period is shorter. Upon the final reversal of such person's conviction on appeal, the amounts in escrow shall be paid to such person. Upon the final sustaining of such person's conviction on appeal, the amounts in escrow shall be returned to the individual employer or organization responsible for payments of those amounts. Upon final reversal of such person's conviction, such person shall no longer be barred by this statute from assuming any position from which such person was previously barred.

TITLE VI—MISCELLANEOUS PROVISIONS
INVESTIGATIONS

Sec. 601. (a) The Secretary shall have power when he believes it necessary in order to determine whether any person has violated or is about to violate any provision of this Act (except title I or amendments made by this Act to other statutes) to make an investigation and in connection therewith he may enter such places and inspect such records and accounts and question such persons as he may deem necessary to enable him to determine the facts relative thereto. The Secretary may report to interested persons or officials concerning the facts required to be shown in any report required by this Act and concerning the reasons for failure or refusal to file such a report or any other matter which he deems to be appropriate as a result of such an investigation.

(b) For the purpose of any investigation provided for in this Act, the provisions of sections 9 and 10 (relating to the attendance of witnesses and the production of books, papers, and documents) of the Federal Trade Commission Act of September 16, 1914, as amended (15 U.S.C. 49, 50), are hereby made applicable to the jurisdiction, powers, and duties of the Secretary or any officers designated by him.

EXTORTIONATE PICKETING

Sec. 602. (a) It shall be unlawful to carry on picketing on or about the premises of any employer for the purpose of, or as part of any conspiracy or in furtherance of any plan or purpose for, the personal profit or enrichment of any individual (except a bona fide increase in wages or other employee benefits) by taking or obtaining any money or other thing of value from such employer against his will or with his consent.

(b) Any person who willfully violates this section shall be fined not more than $10,000 or imprisoned not more than twenty years, or both.

RETENTION OF RIGHTS UNDER OTHER
FEDERAL AND STATE LAWS

Sec. 603. (a) Except as explicitly provided to the contrary, nothing in this Act shall reduce or limit the responsibilities of any labor organization or any officer, agent, shop steward, or other representative of a labor organization, or of any trust in which a labor organization is interested, under any other Federal law or under the laws of any State, and, except as explicitly provided to the contrary, nothing in this Act shall take away any right or bar any remedy to which members of a labor organization are entitled under such other Federal law or law of any State.

(b) Nothing contained in titles I, II, III, IV, V, or VI of this Act shall be construed to supersede or impair or otherwise affect the provisions of the Railway Labor Act, as amended, or any of the obligations, rights, benefits, privileges, or immunities of any carrier, employee, organization, representative, or person subject thereto; nor shall anything contained in said titles (except section 505) of this Act be construed to confer any rights, privileges, immunities, or defenses upon employers, or to impair or otherwise affect the rights of any person under the National Labor Relations Act, as amended.

EFFECT ON STATE LAWS

Sec. 604. Nothing in this Act shall be construed to impair or diminish the authority of any State to enact and enforce general criminal laws with respect to robbery, bribery, extortion, embezzlement, grand larceny, burglary, arson, violation of narcotics laws, murder, rape, assault with intent to kill, or assault which inflicts grievous bodily injury, or conspiracy to commit any of such crimes.

STATE AUTHORITY TO ENACT AND ENFORCE LEGISLATION

Sec. 604a. Notwithstanding this or any other Act regulating labor-management relations, each State shall have the authority to enact and enforce, as part of a comprehensive statutory system to eliminate the threat of pervasive racketeering activity in an industry that is, or over time has been, affected by such activity, a provision of law that applies equally to employers, employees, and collective bargaining representatives, which provision of law governs service in any position in a local labor organization which acts or seeks to act in that State as a collective bargaining representative pursuant to the National Labor Relations Act [29 U.S.C.A. § 151 et seq.], in the industry that is subject to that program.*

SERVICE OF PROCESS

Sec. 605. For the purposes of this Act, service of summons, subpena, or other legal process of a court of the United States upon an officer or agent of a labor organization in his capacity as such shall constitute service upon the labor organization.

ADMINISTRATIVE PROCEDURE ACT

Sec. 606. The provisions of the Administrative Procedure Act shall be applicable to the issuance, amendment, or rescission of any rules or regulations, or any adjudication, authorized or required pursuant to the provisions of this Act.

* Pub.L. 98–473, Title II, § 2201, Oct. 12, 1984, 98 Stat. 2192.

OTHER AGENCIES AND DEPARTMENTS

Sec. 607. In order to avoid unnecessary expense and duplication of functions among Government agencies, the Secretary may make such arrangements or agreements for cooperation or mutual assistance in the performance of his functions under this Act and the functions of any such agency as he may find to be practicable and consistent with law. The Secretary may utilize the facilities or services of any department, agency, or establishment of the United States or of any State or political subdivision of a State, including the services of any of its employees, with the lawful consent of such department, agency, or establishment; and each department, agency, or establishment of the United States is authorized and directed to cooperate with the Secretary and, to the extent permitted by law, to provide such information and facilities as he may request for his assistance in the performance of his functions under this Act. The Attorney General or his representative shall receive from the Secretary for appropriate action such evidence developed in the performance of his functions under this Act as may be found to warrant consideration for criminal prosecution under the provisions of this Act or other Federal law.

CRIMINAL CONTEMPT

Sec. 608. No person shall be punished for any criminal contempt allegedly committed outside the immediate presence of the court in connection with any civil action prosecuted by the Secretary or any other person in any court of the United States under the provisions of this Act unless the facts constituting such criminal contempt are established by the verdict of the jury in a proceeding in the district court of the United States, which jury shall be chosen and empaneled in the manner prescribed by the law governing trial juries in criminal prosecutions in the district courts of the United States.

PROHIBITION ON CERTAIN DISCIPLINE
BY LABOR ORGANIZATION

Sec. 609. It shall be unlawful for any labor organization, or any officer, agent, shop steward, or other representative of a labor organization, or any employee thereof to fine, suspend, expel, or otherwise discipline any of its members for exercising any right to which he is entitled under the provisions of this Act. The provisions of section 102 shall be applicable in the enforcement of this section.

DEPRIVATION OF RIGHTS UNDER ACT BY VIOLENCE

Sec. 610. It shall be unlawful for any person through the use of force or violence, or threat of the use of force or violence, to restrain, coerce, or intimidate, or attempt to restrain, coerce, or intimidate any member of a labor organization for the purpose of interfering with or preventing the exercise of any right to which he is entitled under the provisions of this Act. Any person who willfully violates this section shall be fined not more than $1,000 or imprisoned for not more than one year, or both.

SEPARABILITY PROVISIONS

Sec. 611. If any provision of this Act, or the application of such provision to any person or circumstances, shall be held invalid, the remainder of this Act or the application of such provision to persons or circumstances other than those as to which it is held invalid, shall not be affected thereby.

CIVIL RIGHTS ACT OF 1964

78 Stat. 253 (1964), as amended; 42 U.S.C. § 2000e et seq.
(1988); as amended Pub.L. 102–166 (Nov. 21, 1991).

TITLE VII—EQUAL EMPLOYMENT OPPORTUNITY

DEFINITIONS

Sec. 701. (§ 2000e) For the purposes of this title—

(a) The term "person" includes one or more individuals, governments, governmental agencies, political subdivisions, labor unions, partnerships, associations, corporations, legal representatives, mutual companies, joint-stock companies, trusts, unincorporated organizations, trustees, trustees in bankruptcy, or receivers.

(b) The term "employer" means a person engaged in an industry affecting commerce who has fifteen or more employees for each working day in each of twenty or more calendar weeks in the current or preceding calendar year, and any agent of such a person, but such term does not include (1) the United States, a corporation wholly owned by the Government of the United States, an Indian tribe, or any department or agency of the District of Columbia subject by statute to procedures of the competitive service (as defined in section 2102 of Title 5), or (2) a bona fide private membership club (other than a labor organization) which is exempt from taxation under section 501(c) of Title 26, except that during the first year after March 24, 1972, persons having fewer than twenty-five employees (and their agents) shall not be considered employers.

(c) The term "employment agency" means any person regularly undertaking with or without compensation to procure employees for an employer or to procure for employees opportunities to work for an employer and includes an agent of such a person.

(d) The term "labor organization" means a labor organization engaged in an industry affecting commerce, and any agent of such an organization, and includes any organization of any kind, any agency, or employee representation committee, group, association, or plan so engaged in which employees participate and which exists for the purpose, in whole or in part, of dealing with employers concerning grievances, labor disputes, wages, rates of pay, hours, or other terms or conditions of employment, and any conference, general committee, joint or system board, or joint council so engaged which is subordinate to a national or international labor organization.

(e) A labor organization shall be deemed to be engaged in an industry affecting commerce if (1) it maintains or operates a hiring hall or hiring office which procures employees for an employer or procures for employees opportunities to work for an employer, or (2) the number of its members (or, where it is a labor organization composed of other labor organizations or their representatives, if the aggregate number of the members of such other labor organization) is (A) twenty-five or more during the first year after March 24, 1972, or (B) fifteen or more thereafter, and such labor organization—

(1) is the certified representative of employees under the provisions of the National Labor Relations Act, as amended, or the Railway Labor Act, as amended;

(2) although not certified, is a national or international labor organization or a local labor organization recognized or acting as the representative of employees of an employer or employers engaged in an industry affecting commerce; or

(3) has chartered a local labor organization or subsidiary body which is representing or actively seeking to represent employees of employers within the meaning of paragraph (1) or (2); or

(4) has been chartered by a labor organization representing or actively seeking to represent employees within the meaning of paragraph (1) or (2) as the local or subordinate body through which such employees may enjoy membership or become affiliated with such labor organization; or

(5) is a conference, general committee, joint or system board, or joint council subordinate to a national or international labor organization, which includes a labor organization engaged in an industry affecting commerce within the meaning of any of the preceding paragraphs of this subsection.

(f) The term "employee" means an individual employed by an employer, except that the term "employee" shall not include any person elected to public office in any State or political subdivision of any State by the qualified voters thereof, or any person chosen by such officer to be on such officer's personal staff, or an appointee on the policy making level or an immediate adviser with respect to the exercise of the constitutional or legal powers of the office. The exemption set forth in the preceding sentence shall not include employees subject to the civil service laws of a State government, governmental agency or political subdivision. With respect to employment in a foreign country, such term includes an individual who is a citizen of the United States.

(g) The term "commerce" means trade, traffic, commerce, transportation, transmission, or communication among the several States; or between a State and any place outside thereof; or within the District of Columbia, or a possession of the United States; or between points in the same State but through a point outside thereof.

(h) The term "industry affecting commerce" means any activity, business, or industry in commerce or in which a labor dispute would hinder or obstruct commerce or the free flow of commerce and includes any activity or industry "affecting commerce" within the meaning of the Labor-Management Reporting and Disclosure Act of 1959, and further includes any governmental industry, business, or activity.

(i) The term "State" includes a State of the United States, the District of Columbia, Puerto Rico, the Virgin Islands, American Samoa, Guam, Wake Island, the Canal Zone, and Outer Continental Shelf lands defined in the Outer Continental Shelf Lands Act.

(j) The term "religion" includes all aspects of religious observance and practice, as well as belief, unless an employer demonstrates that he is unable to reasonably accommodate to an employee's or prospective employee's religious observance or practice without undue hardship on the conduct of the employer's business.

(k) The terms "because of sex" or "on the basis of sex" include, but are not limited to, because of or on the basis of pregnancy, childbirth, or related medical conditions; and women affected by pregnancy, childbirth, or related medical conditions shall be treated the same for all employment-related purposes, including receipt of benefits under fringe benefit programs, as other persons not so affected but similar in their ability or inability to work, and nothing in section 2(h) of this Act shall be interpreted to permit otherwise. This subsection shall not require an employer to pay for health insurance benefits for abortion, except where the life of the mother would be endangered if the fetus were carried to term, or except where medical complications have arisen from an abortion: *Provided,* That nothing herein shall preclude an employer from providing abortion benefits or otherwise affect bargaining agreements in regard to abortion.

(*l*) The term "complaining party" means the Commission, the Attorney General, or a person who may bring an action or proceeding under this subchapter.

(m) The term "demonstrates" means meets the burdens of production and persuasion.

(n) The term "respondent" means an employer, employment agency, labor organization, joint labor-management committee controlling apprenticeship or other training or retraining program, including an on-the-job training program, or Federal entity subject to section 2000e-16 of this title.

FOREIGN AND RELIGIOUS EMPLOYMENT

Sec. 702. (§ 2000e-1) (a) This Subchapter shall not apply to an employer with respect to the employment of aliens outside any State, or to a religious corporation, association, educational institution, or society with respect to the employment of individuals of a particular religion to perform work connected with the carrying on by such corporation, association, educational institution, or society of its activities.

(b) It shall not be unlawful under section 2000e-2 or 2000e-3 of this title for an employer (or a corporation controlled by an employer), labor organization, employment agency, or joint labor-management committee controlling apprenticeship or other training or retraining (including on-the-job training programs) to take any action otherwise prohibited by such section, with respect to an employee in a workplace in a foreign country if compliance with such section would cause such employer (or such corporation), such organization, such agency, or such committee to violate the law of the foreign country in which such workplace is located.

(c)(1) If an employer controls a corporation whose place of incorporation is a foreign country, any practice prohibited by section 2000e-2 or 2000e-3 of this title engaged in by such corporation shall be presumed to be engaged in by such employer.

(2) Sections 2000e-2 and 2000e-3 of this title shall not apply with respect to the foreign operations of an employer that is a foreign person not controlled by an American employer.

(3) For purposes of this subsection, the determination of whether an employer controls a corporation shall be based on—

(A) the interrelation of operations;

(B) the common management;

(C) the centralized control of labor relations; and

(D) the common ownership or financial control,

of the employer and the corporation.

DISCRIMINATION BECAUSE OF RACE, COLOR, RELIGION, SEX, OR NATIONAL ORIGIN

Sec. 703. (§ 2000e-2) (a) It shall be an unlawful employment practice for an employer—

(1) to fail or refuse to hire or to discharge any individual, or otherwise to discriminate against any individual with respect to his compensation, terms, conditions, or privileges of employment, because of such individual's race, color, religion, sex, or national origin; or

(2) to limit, segregate, or classify his employees or applicants for employment in any way which would deprive or tend to deprive any individual of employment opportunities or otherwise adversely affect his status as an employee, because of such individual's race, color, religion, sex, or national origin.

(b) It shall be an unlawful employment practice for an employment agency to fail or refuse to refer for employment, or otherwise to discriminate against, any individual because of his race, color, religion, sex, or national origin, or to classify or refer for employment any individual on the basis of his race, color, religion, sex, or national origin.

(c) It shall be an unlawful employment practice for a labor organization—

(1) to exclude or to expel from its membership, or otherwise to discriminate against, any individual because of his race, color, religion, sex, or national origin;

(2) to limit, segregate, or classify its membership or applicants for membership, or to classify or fail or refuse to refer for employment any individual, in any way which would deprive or tend to deprive any

individual of employment opportunities, or would limit such employment opportunities or otherwise adversely affect his status as an employee or as an applicant for employment, because of such individual's race, color, religion, sex, or national origin; or

(3) to cause or attempt to cause an employer to discriminate against an individual in violation of this section.

(d) It shall be an unlawful employment practice for any employer, labor organization, or joint labor-management committee controlling apprenticeship or other training or retraining, including on-the-job training programs to discriminate against any individual because of his race, color, religion, sex, or national origin in admission to, or employment in, any program established to provide apprenticeship or other training.

(e) Notwithstanding any other provision of this Subchapter (1) it shall not be an unlawful employment practice for an employer to hire and employ employees, for an employment agency to classify, or refer for employment any individual, for a labor organization to classify its membership or to classify or refer for employment any individual, or for an employer, labor organization, or joint labor-management committee controlling apprenticeship or other training or retraining programs to admit or employ any individual in any such program, on the basis of his religion, sex, or national origin in those certain instances where religion, sex, or national origin is a bona fide occupational qualification reasonably necessary to the normal operation of that particular business or enterprise, and (2) it shall not be an unlawful employment practice for a school, college, university, or other educational institution or institution of learning to hire and employ employees of a particular religion if such school, college, university, or other educational institution or institution of learning is, in whole or in substantial part, owned, supported, controlled, or managed by a particular religion or by a particular religious corporation, association, or society, or if the curriculum of such school, college, university, or other educational institution or institution of learning is directed toward the propagation of a particular religion.

(f) As used in this Subchapter, the phrase "unlawful employment practice" shall not be deemed to include any action or measure taken by an employer, labor organization, joint labor-management committee, or employment agency with respect to an individual who is a member of the Communist Party of the United States or of any other organization required to register as a Communist-action or Communist-front organization by final order of the Subversive Activities Control Board pursuant to the Subversive Activities Control Act of 1950.

(g) Notwithstanding any other provision of this Subchapter, it shall not be an unlawful employment practice for an employer to fail or refuse to hire and employ any individual for any position, for an employer to discharge any individual from any position, or for an employment agency to fail or refuse to refer any individual for employment in any position, or for a labor organization to fail or refuse to refer any individual for employment in any position, if—

(1) the occupancy of such position, or access to the premises in or upon which any part of the duties of such position is performed or is to be performed, is subject to any requirement imposed in the interest of the national security of the United States under any security program in effect pursuant to or administered under any statute of the United States or any Executive order of the President; and

(2) such individual has not fulfilled or has ceased to fulfill that requirement.

(h) Notwithstanding any other provision of this Subchapter, it shall not be an unlawful employment practice for an employer to apply different standards of compensation, or different terms, conditions, or privileges of employment pursuant to a bona fide seniority or merit system, or a system which measures earnings by quantity or quality of production or to employees who work in different locations, provided that such differences are not the result of an intention to discriminate because of race, color, religion, sex, or national origin, nor shall it be an unlawful employment practice for an employer to give and to act upon the results of any professionally developed ability test provided that such test, its administration or action upon the results is not designed, intended or used to discriminate because of race, color, religion, sex or national origin. It shall not be an unlawful employment practice under this subchapter for any employer to differentiate upon the basis of sex in determining the amount of the wages or compensation paid or to be paid to employees of such employer if such differentiation is authorized by the provisions of section 206(d) of Title 29.

(i) Nothing contained in this Subchapter shall apply to any business or enterprise on or near an Indian reservation with respect to any publicly announced employment practice of such business or enterprise under which a preferential treatment is given to any individual because he is an Indian living on or near a reservation.

(j) Nothing contained in this Subchapter shall be interpreted to require any employer, employment agency, labor organization, or joint labor-management committee subject to this subchapter to grant preferential treatment to any individual or to any group because of the race, color, religion, sex, or national origin of such individual or group on account of an imbalance which may exist with respect to the total number of percentage of persons of any race, color, religion, sex, or national origin employed by any employer, referred or classified for employment by any employment agency or labor organization, admitted to membership or classified by any labor organization, or admitted to, or employed in, any apprenticeship or other training program, in comparison with the total number or percentage of persons of such race, color, religion, sex, or national origin in any community, State, section, or other area, or in the available work force in any community, State, section, or other area.

(k)(1)(**A**) An unlawful employment practice based on disparate impact is established under this subchapter only if—

(i) a complaining party demonstrates that a respondent uses a particular employment practice that causes a disparate impact on the basis of race, color, religion, sex, or national origin and the respondent fails to demonstrate that the challenged practice is job related for the position in question and consistent with business necessity; or

(ii) the complaining party makes the demonstration described in subparagraph (C) with respect to an alternative employment practice and the respondent refuses to adopt such alternative employment practice.

(B)(i) With respect to demonstrating that a particular employment practice causes a disparate impact as described in subparagraph (A)(i), the complaining party shall demonstrate that each particular challenged employment practice causes a disparate impact, except that if the complaining party can demonstrate to the court that the elements of a respondent's decisionmaking process are not capable of separation for analysis, the decisionmaking process may be analyzed as one employment practice.

(ii) If the respondent demonstrates that a specific employment practice does not cause the disparate impact, the respondent shall not be required to demonstrate that such practice is required by business necessity.

(C) The demonstration referred to by subparagraph (A)(ii) shall be in accordance with the law as it existed on June 4, 1989, with respect to the concept of "alternative employment practice".

(2) A demonstration that an employment practice is required by business necessity may not be used as a defense against a claim of intentional discrimination under this subchapter.

(3) Notwithstanding any other provision of this subchapter, a rule barring the employment of an individual who currently and knowingly uses or possesses a controlled substance, as defined in schedules I and II of section 102(6) of the Controlled Substances Act (21 U.S.C. 802(6)), other than the use or possession of a drug taken under the supervision of a licensed health care professional, or any other use or possession authorized by the Controlled Substances Act or any other provision of Federal law, shall be considered an unlawful employment practice under this subchapter only if such rule is adopted or applied with an intent to discriminate because of race, color, religion, sex, or national origin.

(*l*) It shall be an unlawful employment practice for a respondent, in connection with the selection or referral of applicants or candidates for employment or promotion, to adjust the scores of, use different cutoff scores for, or otherwise alter the results of, employment related tests on the basis of race, color, religion, sex, or national origin.

(m) Except as otherwise provided in this subchapter, an unlawful employment practice is established when the complaining party demonstrates that race, color, religion, sex, or national origin was a motivating factor for any employment practice, even though other factors also motivated the practice.

(n)(1)**(A)** Notwithstanding any other provision of law, and except as provided in paragraph (2), an employment practice that implements and is within the scope of a litigated or consent judgment or order that resolves a claim of employment discrimination under the Constitution or Federal civil rights laws may not be challenged under the circumstances described in subparagraph (B).

(B) A practice described in subparagraph (A) may not be challenged in a claim under the Constitution or Federal civil rights laws—

(i) by a person who, prior to the entry of the judgment or order described in subparagraph (A), had—

(I) actual notice of the proposed judgment or order sufficient to apprise such person that such judgment or order might adversely affect the interests and legal rights of such person and that an opportunity was available to present objections to such judgment or order by a future date certain; and

(II) a reasonable opportunity to present objections to such judgment or order; or

(ii) by a person whose interests were adequately represented by another person who had previously challenged the judgment or order on the same legal grounds and with a similar factual situation, unless there has been an intervening change in law or fact.

(2) Nothing in this subsection shall be construed to—

(A) alter the standards for intervention under rule 24 of the Federal Rules of Civil Procedure or apply to the rights of parties who have successfully intervened pursuant to such rule in the proceeding in which the parties intervened;

(B) apply to the rights of parties to the action in which a litigated or consent judgment or order was entered, or of members of a class represented or sought to be represented in such action, or of members of a group on whose behalf relief was sought in such action by the Federal Government;

(C) prevent challenges to a litigated or consent judgment or order on the ground that such judgment or order was obtained through collusion or fraud, or is transparently invalid or was entered by a court lacking subject matter jurisdiction; or

(D) authorize or permit the denial to any person of the due process of law required by the Constitution.

(3) Any action not precluded under this subsection that challenges an employment consent judgment or order described in paragraph (1)

shall be brought in the court, and if possible before the judge, that entered such judgment or order. Nothing in this subsection shall preclude a transfer of such action pursuant to section 1404 of Title 28.

OTHER UNLAWFUL EMPLOYMENT PRACTICES

Sec. 704.   (§ 2000e-3) (a) It shall be an unlawful employment practice for an employer to discriminate against any of his employees or applicants for employment, for an employment agency, or joint labor-management committee controlling apprenticeship or other training or retraining, including on-the-job training programs, to discriminate against any individual, or for a labor organization to discriminate against any member thereof or applicant for membership, because he has opposed any practice made an unlawful employment practice by this subchapter, or because he has made a charge, testified, assisted, or participated in any manner in an investigation, proceeding, or hearing under this subchapter.

(b) It shall be an unlawful employment practice for an employer, labor organization, employment agency, or joint labor-management committee controlling apprenticeship or other training or retraining; including on-the-job training programs, to print or publish or cause to be printed or published any notice or advertisement relating to employment by such an employer or membership in or any classification or referral for employment by such a labor organization, or relating to any classification or referral for employment by such an employment agency, or relating to admission to, or employment in, any program established to provide apprenticeship or other training by such a joint labor management committee, indicating any preference, limitation, specification, or discrimination, based on race, color, religion, sex, or national origin, except that such a notice or advertisement may indicate a preference, limitation, specification, or discrimination based on religion, sex, or national origin when religion, sex, or national origin is a bona fide occupational qualification for employment.

* * *

WORKER ADJUSTMENT AND RETRAINING NOTIFICATION ACT

102 Stat. 890 (1988), 29 U.S.C. §§ 2101–2109 (1988).

§ 2101. Definitions; exclusions from definition of loss of employment

(a) **Definitions.**—As used in this chapter—

(1) the term "employer" means any business enterprise that employs—

(A) 100 or more employees, excluding part-time employees; or

(B) 100 or more employees who in the aggregate work at least 4,000 hours per week (exclusive of hours of overtime);

(2) the term "plant closing" means the permanent or temporary shutdown of a single site of employment, or one or more facilities or operating units within a single site of employment, if the shutdown results in an employment loss at the single site of employment during any 30-day period for 50 or more employees excluding any part-time employees;

(3) the term "mass layoff" means a reduction in force which—

(A) is not the result of a plant closing; and

(B) results in an employment loss at the single site of employment during any 30-day period for—

(i)(I) at least 33 percent of the employees (excluding any part-time employees); and

(II) at least 50 employees (excluding any part-time employees); or

(ii) at least 500 employees (excluding any part-time employees);

(4) the term "representative" means an exclusive representative of employees within the meaning of section 158(f) or 159(a) of this title or section 152 of Title 45;

(5) the term "affected employees" means employees who may reasonably be expected to experience an employment loss as a consequence of a proposed plant closing or mass layoff by their employer;

(6) subject to subsection (b) of this section the term "employment loss" means (A) an employment termination, other than a discharge for cause, voluntary departure, or retirement, (B) a layoff exceeding 6 months, or (C) a reduction in hours of work of more than 50 percent during each month of any 6-month period;

(7) the term "unit of local government" means any general purpose political subdivision of a State which has the power to levy taxes and spend funds, as well as general corporate and police powers; and

(8) the term "part-time employee" means an employee who is employed for an average of fewer than 20 hours per week or who has been employed for fewer than 6 of the 12 months preceding the date on which notice is required.

(b) Exclusions from definition of employment loss.—**(1)** In the case of a sale of part or all of an employer's business, the seller shall be responsible for providing notice for any plant closing or mass layoff in accordance with section 2102 of this title, up to and including the effective date of the sale. After the effective date of the sale of part or all of an employer's business, the purchaser shall be responsible for providing notice for any plant closing or mass layoff in accordance with section 2102 of this title. Notwithstanding any other provision of this chapter, any person who is an employee of the seller (other than a part-time employee) as of the effective date of the sale shall be considered an employee of the purchaser immediately after the effective date of the sale.

(2) Notwithstanding subsection (a)(6) of this section, an employee may not be considered to have experienced an employment loss if the closing or layoff is the result of the relocation or consolidation of part or all of the employer's business and, prior to the closing or layoff—

(A) the employer offers to transfer the employee to a different site of employment within a reasonable commuting distance with no more than a 6-month break in employment; or

(B) the employer offers to transfer the employee to any other site of employment regardless of distance with no more than a 6-month break in employment, and the employee accepts within 30 days of the offer or of the closing or layoff, whichever is later.

§ 2102. Notice required before plant closings and mass layoffs

(a) Notice to employees, state dislocated worker units, and local governments.—An employer shall not order a plant closing or mass layoff until the end of a 60-day period after the employer serves written notice of such an order—

(1) to each representative of the affected employees as of the time of the notice or, if there is no such representative at that time, to each affected employee; and

(2) to the State dislocated worker unit (designated or created under title III of the Job Training Partnership Act [29 U.S.C.A. § 1651 et seq.]), and the chief elected official of the unit of local government within which such closing or layoff is to occur.

If there is more than one such unit, the unit of local government which the employer shall notify is the unit of local government to which the employer pays the highest taxes for the year preceding the year for which the determination is made.

(b) Reduction of notification period.—(1) An employer may order the shutdown of a single site of employment before the conclusion of the 60-day period if as of the time that notice would have been required the employer was actively seeking capital or business which, if obtained, would have enabled the employer to avoid or postpone the shutdown and the employer reasonably and in good faith believed that giving the notice required would have precluded the employer from obtaining the needed capital or business.

(2)(A) An employer may order a plant closing or mass layoff before the conclusion of the 60-day period if the closing or mass layoff is caused by business circumstances that were not reasonably foreseeable as of the time that notice would have been required.

(B) No notice under this chapter shall be required if the plant closing or mass layoff is due to any form of natural disaster, such as a flood, earthquake, or the drought currently ravaging the farmlands of the United States.

(3) An employer relying on this subsection shall give as much notice as is practicable and at that time shall give a brief statement of the basis for reducing the notification period.

(c) Extension of layoff period.—A layoff of more than 6 months which, at its outset, was announced to be a layoff of 6 months or less, shall be treated as an employment loss under this chapter unless—

(1) the extension beyond 6 months is caused by business circumstances (including unforeseeable changes in price or cost) not reasonably foreseeable at the time of the initial layoff; and

(2) notice is given at the time it becomes reasonably foreseeable, that the extension beyond 6 months will be required.

(d) Determinations with respect to employment loss.—For purposes of this section, in determining whether a plant closing or mass layoff has occurred or will occur, employment losses for 2 or more groups at a single site of employment, each of which is less than the minimum number of employees specified in section 2101(a)(2) or (3) of this title but which in the aggregate exceed that minimum number, and which occur within any 90-day period shall be considered to be a plant closing or mass layoff unless the employer demonstrates that the employment losses are the result of separate and distinct actions and causes and are not an attempt by the employer to evade the requirements of this chapter.

§ **2103.   Exemptions**

This chapter shall not apply to a plant closing or mass layoff if—

(1) the closing is of a temporary facility or the closing or layoff is the result of the completion of a particular project or undertaking, and the affected employees were hired with the understanding that their employment was limited to the duration of the facility or the project or undertaking; or

(2) the closing or layoff constitutes a strike or constitutes a lockout not intended to evade the requirements of this chapter. Nothing in this chapter shall require an employer to serve written notice pursuant to section 2102(a) of this title when permanently replacing a person who is deemed to be an economic striker under the National Labor Relations Act [29 U.S.C.A. § 151 et seq.]: *Provided,* That nothing in this chapter shall be deemed to validate or invalidate any judicial or administrative ruling relating to the hiring of permanent replacements for economic strikers under the National Labor Relations Act.

§ 2104. Administration and enforcement of requirements

(a) Civil actions against employers.—**(1)** Any employer who orders a plant closing or mass layoff in violation of section 2102 of this title shall be liable to each aggrieved employee who suffers an employment loss as a result of such closing or layoff for—

(A) back pay for each day of violation at a rate of compensation not less than the higher of—

(i) the average regular rate received by such employee during the last 3 years of the employee's employment; or

(ii) the final regular rate received by such employee; and

(B) benefits under an employee benefit plan described in section 1002(3) of this title, including the cost of medical expenses incurred during the employment loss which would have been covered under an employee benefit plan if the employment loss had not occurred.

Such liability shall be calculated for the period of the violation, up to a maximum of 60 days, but in no event for more than one-half the number of days the employee was employed by the employer.

(2) The amount for which an employer is liable under paragraph (1) shall be reduced by—

(A) any wages paid by the employer to the employee for the period of the violation;

(B) any voluntary and unconditional payment by the employer to the employee that is not required by any legal obligation; and

(C) any payment by the employer to a third party or trustee (such as premiums for health benefits or payments to a defined contribution pension plan) on behalf of and attributable to the employee for the period of the violation.

In addition, any liability incurred under paragraph (1) with respect to a defined benefit pension plan may be reduced by crediting the employee with service for all purposes under such a plan for the period of the violation.

(3) Any employer who violates the provisions of section 2102 of this title with respect to a unit of local government shall be subject to a civil penalty of not more than $500 for each day of such violation, except that such penalty shall not apply if the employer pays to each aggrieved employee the amount for which the employer is liable to that employee within 3 weeks from the date the employer orders the shutdown or layoff.

(4) If an employer which has violated this chapter proves to the satisfaction of the court that the act or omission that violated this chapter was in good faith and that the employer had reasonable grounds for believing that the act or omission was not a violation of this chapter the court may, in its discretion, reduce the amount of the liability or penalty provided for in this section.

(5) A person seeking to enforce such liability, including a representative of employees or a unit of local government aggrieved under paragraph (1) or (3), may sue either for such person or for other persons similarly situated, or both, in any district court of the United States for any district in which the violation is alleged to have occurred, or in which the employer transacts business.

(6) In any such suit, the court, in its discretion, may allow the prevailing party a reasonable attorney's fee as part of the costs.

(7) For purposes of this subsection, the term, ''aggrieved employee'' means an employee who has worked for the employer ordering the plant closing or mass layoff and who, as a result of the failure by the employer to comply with section 2102 of this title, did not receive timely notice either directly or through his or her representative as required by section 2102 of this title.

(b) Exclusivity of remedies.—The remedies provided for in this section shall be the exclusive remedies for any violation of this chapter. Under this chapter, a Federal court shall not have authority to enjoin a plant closing or mass layoff.

§ 2105. Procedures in addition to other rights of employees

The rights and remedies provided to employees by this chapter are in addition to, and not in lieu of, any other contractual or statutory rights and remedies of the employees, and are not intended to alter or affect such rights and remedies, except that the period of notification required by this chapter shall run concurrently with any period of notification required by contract or by any other statute.

§ 2106. Procedures encouraged where not required

It is the sense of Congress that an employer who is not required to comply with the notice requirements of section 2102 of this title should, to the extent possible, provide notice to its employees about a proposal to close a plant or permanently reduce its workforce.

§ 2107. Authority to prescribe regulations

(a) The Secretary of Labor shall prescribe such regulations as may be necessary to carry out this chapter. Such regulations shall, at a minimum, include interpretative regulations describing the methods by which employers may provide for appropriate service of notice as required by this chapter.

(b) The mailing of notice to an employee's last known address or inclusion of notice in the employee's paycheck will be considered acceptable methods for fulfillment of the employer's obligation to give notice to each affected employee under this chapter.

§ 2108. Effect on other laws

The giving of notice pursuant to this chapter, if done in good faith compliance with this chapter, shall not constitute a violation of the National Labor Relations Act [29 U.S.C.A. § 151 et seq.] or the Railway Labor Act [45 U.S.C.A. 151 et seq.].

§ 2109. Report on employment and international competitiveness

Two years after Aug. 4, 1988, the Comptroller General shall submit to the Committee on Small Business of both the House and Senate, the Committee on Labor and Human Resources, and the Committee on Education and Labor a report containing a detailed and objective analysis of the effect of this chapter on employers (especially small- and medium-sized businesses), the economy (international competitiveness), and employees (in terms of levels and conditions of employment). The Comptroller General shall assess both costs and benefits, including the effect on productivity, competitiveness, unemployment rates and compensation, and worker retraining and readjustment.

MONTANA WRONGFUL DISCHARGE FROM EMPLOYMENT ACT

Montana Code §§ 39–2–901 to 39–2–915 (1987), as amended.

Sec. 39–2–902. Purpose. This part sets forth certain rights and remedies with respect to wrongful discharge. Except as limited in this part, employment having no specified term may be terminated at the will of either the employer or the employee on notice to the other for any reason considered sufficient by the terminating party. Except as provided in Sec. 39–2–912, this part provides the exclusive remedy for a wrongful discharge from employment.

Sec. 39–2–903. Definitions.

* * *

(2) "Discharge" includes a constructive discharge as defined in subsection (1) and any other termination of employment, including resignation, elimination of the job, layoff for lack of work, failure to recall or rehire, and any other cutback in the number of employees for a legitimate business reason.

* * *

(5) "Good cause" means reasonable job-related grounds for dismissal based on a failure to satisfactorily perform job duties, disruption of the employer's operation, or other legitimate business reason.

* * *

(7) "Public policy" means a policy in effect at the time of the discharge concerning the public health, safety, or welfare established by constitutional provision, statute, or administrative rule.

Sec. 39–2–904. Elements of wrongful discharge. A discharge is wrongful only if: (1) it was in retaliation for the employee's refusal to violate public policy or for reporting a violation of public policy; or

(2) The discharge was not for good cause and the employee had completed the employer's probationary period of employment; or

(3) The employer violated the express provisions of its own written personnel policy.

Sec. 34–2–905. Remedies. (1) If an employer has committed a wrongful discharge, the employee may be awarded lost wages and fringe benefits for a period not to exceed 4 years from the date of discharge, together with interest thereon. Interim earnings, including amounts the employee could have earned with reasonable diligence, must be deducted from the amount awarded for lost wages.

(2) The employee may recover punitive damages otherwise allowed by law if it is established by clear and convincing evidence that the employer

engaged in actual fraud or actual malice in the discharge of the employee in violation of 39–2–904(1).

(3) There is no right under any legal theory to damages for wrongful discharge under this part for pain and suffering, emotional distress, compensatory damages, punitive damages, or any other form of damages, except as provided for in subsections (1) and (2).

Sec. 39–2–911.   Limitation of actions. (1) An action under this part must be filed within 1 year after the date of discharge.

(2) If an employer maintains written internal procedures, other than those specified in 39–2–912, under which an employee may appeal a discharge within the organizational structure of the employer, the employee shall first exhaust those procedures prior to filing an action under this part. The employee's failure to initiate or exhaust available internal procedures is a defense to an action brought under this part. If the employer's internal procedures are not completed within 90 days from the date the employee initiates the internal procedures, the employee may file an action under this part and for purposes of this subsection the employer's internal procedures are considered exhausted. The limitation period in subsection (1) is tolled until the procedures are exhausted. In no case may the provisions of the employer's internal procedures extend the limitation period in subsection (1) more than 120 days.

(3) If the employer maintains written internal procedures under which an employee may appeal a discharge within the organizational structure of the employer, the employer shall within 7 days of the date of the discharge notify the discharged employee of the existence of such procedures and shall supply the discharged employee with a copy of them. If the employer fails to comply with this subsection, the discharged employee need not comply with subsection (2).

Sec. 39–2–912.   Exemptions. This part does not apply to a discharge

(1) that is subject to any other state or federal statute that provides a procedure or remedy for contesting the dispute. The statutes include those that prohibit discharge for filing complaints, charges, or claims with administrative bodies or that prohibit unlawful discrimination based on race, national origin, sex, age, disability, creed, religion, political belief, color, marital status, and other similar grounds.

(2) of an employee covered by a written collective bargaining agreement or a written contract of employment for a specific term.

Sec. 39–2–913.   Preemption of common-law remedies. Except as provided in this part, no claim for discharge may arise from tort or express or implied contract.

Sec. 39–2–914.   Arbitration. (1) A party may make a written offer to arbitrate a dispute that otherwise could be adjudicated under this part.

(2) An offer to arbitrate must be in writing and contain the following provisions:

(a) A neutral arbitrator must be selected by mutual agreement or, in the absence of agreement, as provided in 27–5–211.

(b) The arbitration must be governed by the Uniform Arbitration Act, Title 27, chapter 5. If there is a conflict between the Uniform Arbitration Act and this part, this part applies.

(c) The arbitrator is bound by this part.

(3) If complaint is filed under this part, the offer to arbitrate must be made within 60 days after service of the complaint and must be accepted in writing within 30 days after the date the offer is made.

(4) A discharged employee who makes a valid offer to arbitrate that is accepted by the employer and who prevails in such arbitration is entitled to have the arbitrator's fee and all costs of arbitration paid by the employer.

(5) If a valid offer to arbitrate is made and accepted, arbitration is the exclusive remedy for the wrongful discharge dispute and there is no right to bring or continue a lawsuit under this part. The arbitrator's award is final and binding, subject to review of the arbitrator's decision under the provisions of the Uniform Arbitration Act.

Sec. 39–2–915.   Effect of rejection of offer to arbitrate. A party who makes a valid offer to arbitrate that is not accepted by the other party and who prevails in an action under this part is entitled as an element of costs to reasonable attorney fees incurred subsequent to the date of the offer.

COLLECTIVE BARGAINING AGREEMENT

PREAMBLE

This Agreement is made and entered into by and between the MAJOR CONTAINER COMPANY ("Company"), their successors or assigns, and the UNITED PAPERWORKERS INTERNATIONAL UNION, AFL-CIO ("Union").

I. PURPOSE

Section 1. WITNESSETH, whereas the parties hereto have reached agreement as a result of collective bargaining for the purpose of facilitating the peaceful adjustment of differences which may arise from time to time between this Company and the Union, and to promote harmony and efficiency and to the end that the employees and the Company and the general public may mutually benefit, the parties hereto contract and agree with each other as follows:

II. RECOGNITION AND UNION SECURITY

Section 1. The Company recognizes the Union as the sole agency for collective bargaining on behalf of all employees, with the exception of timekeepers, clerks, office employees, watchmen and non-working foremen and non-working supervisors, in charge of any classes of labor.

Section 2. This recognition is interpreted by the parties to apply to any transfer or relocation of the Company's present facility to another location within or outside of the metropolitan area, which are an accretion to the existing bargaining unit, where the jobs performed are substantially the same as are covered by the present Agreement.

Section 3. All employees with the exceptions noted in Section 1 who are members of the Union in good standing on the effective date of this Agreement, shall as a condition of continued employment, maintain their membership in good standing in the Union. All employees, who on the effective date of this Agreement, are not as yet members in good standing of the Union, shall become members of the Union in good standing by no later than thirty (30) days following the effective date of this Agreement and shall maintain membership in good standing in the Union in order to continue in employment. All new employees, shall as a condition of continued employment, become members and maintain membership in good standing in the Union by no later than thirty (30) days following the date of their employment or the effective date of this Agreement, whichever is the later.

Section 4. The Company agrees to discharge any employee who does not join or maintain his membership in good standing in the Union within seven (7) calendar days after receipt of written notice from the Union that such employee is delinquent in initiation fee or dues. The Union will indemnify and save harmless the Company against any and all claims, demands, or suits that may arise out of the discharge of any employee under this section.

Section 5. During the term of this Agreement, and at the written request of the Union, the Company will deduct from their wages and remit promptly to the Union the regular monthly membership dues and/or initiation fees established by the Union in accordance with the Constitution and By–Laws of the Union for all employees who have executed and caused to be delivered to the Company a written authorization for such deductions, on a form in conformity with the applicable statutes, which shall not be irrevocable for a period of more than one (1) year, or the termination date of this Agreement, whichever occurs sooner.

III.   MANAGEMENT RIGHTS

Section 1.   It is understood and agreed that the management of the Plant and the direction of the work force, including but not limited to the right to hire, suspend, transfer or discharge for proper cause and the right to relieve employees from duty because of lack of work, the right to establish, determine, and maintain reasonable standards of production, to introduce new and improved methods, materials, equipment or facilities and change or eliminate methods, materials, equipment or facilities are vested exclusively in the Company, subject to the provisions of this Agreement.

IV.   DISCRIMINATION

Section 1. No employee shall be discriminated against by the Company for activity in or on behalf of the Union, but shall not be exempted from discipline that is not discriminatory.

Section 2. The Company and the Union agree that there shall be no discrimination in regard to hiring, tenure of employment or any condition of employment, or in regard to membership in the Union, because of race, color, religion, sex, age, disability, national origin, marital status, sexual orientation, veteran status, or any other classification protected by law.

Section 3. The parties recognize that in complying with this Article they are subject to the specific provisions and exemptions of Title VII of the Civil Rights Act of 1964, the Age Discrimination in Employment Act of 1967, the Americans with Disabilities Act, as well as the specific statutes of the various states and pertinent Executive Orders issued by the President of the United States.

V.   WAGES

Section 1.   The schedule of rates attached hereto as "Exhibit A" shall become a part of this Agreement and they shall be the minimum rates of pay to be paid by the Company to its employees for the duration of this Agreement.

Section 2.   All employees shall receive their pay weekly.

VI. HOURS OF WORK; OVERTIME

Section 1.   Eight (8) consecutive hours, shall constitute a normal day's work; five (5) days, shall constitute a normal work week. Employees assigned to work days will be granted an unpaid lunch period of thirty (30) minutes. Shift employees will be granted a paid twenty (20) minutes lunch period during the shift, when operating requirements permit. Any employee who works over eight (8) hours in any twenty-four (24) hour period, or forty (40) hours (for which overtime has not previously been paid) in any one work week, shall be paid at the rate of time and a half. This provision shall not be construed to guarantee any specific hours or days of work.

Any employee who works over sixty (60) hours (for which double-time has not previously been paid) in any one work week shall be paid at the rate of double-time.

Section 2.   Overtime shall be distributed as equitably as possible among the employees who can perform the work. The Company shall maintain open overtime records for the purpose of distributing over time equitably.

Section 3.   All work performed on Sundays and holidays shall be paid for at the rate of double time.

Section 4.   All work performed on Saturdays shall be paid for at the rate of time and one-half.

Section 5.   Employees working on second shift shall receive a shift premium of fifteen (15) cents per hour.

Section 6.   Employees working on third shift shall receive a shift premium of twenty-five (25) cents per hour.

VII. HOLIDAYS

Section 1.   The following holidays or days celebrated in place thereof shall be observed and shall be paid for even though not worked at eight hours of the regular hourly rate of pay for all employees who have worked sixty (60) days or more in the Company. Holidays falling on Sunday shall be observed on the following Monday.

New Year's Day.

Decoration Day

Fourth of July

Good Friday

Labor Day

Employee's Birthday

Thanksgiving Day

Day after Thanksgiving

Christmas Day

Christmas Eve Day

New Year's Eve Day

Section 2. Any employee entitled to a holiday with pay shall not be required to work on said holiday.

Section 3. It is agreed that to qualify for such holiday pay an employee shall have worked the regular scheduled work day immediately preceding and succeeding said holiday, provided work is available unless excused from such work by the plant management.

VIII. VACATIONS

Section 1. Vacation pay shall be computed on the basis of regular hourly rates of pay.

Section 2. The following schedule shall be the method of application of vacation periods and vacation pay.

Length of Service	Vacation Periods	Vacation Pay at Regular Hourly Rates of Pay
1 Year	1	42 Hours Pay
3 Years	2	84 Hours Pay
8 Years	3	126 Hours Pay
15 Years	4	168 Hours Pay
20 Years	5	210 Hours Pay
25 Years	6	252 Hours Pay

Section 3. The Company may shut down the plant completely or partially to grant vacations to all or part of the employees at one time provided it shall notify the employees of such a plan at least sixty (60) days before a vacation commences. Otherwise, vacations will be scheduled according to employees' desires, subject to the exclusive right of the Company to change vacation periods to assure orderly and efficient operation of the Plant. In the event of a dispute between two or more employees as to the time of their vacations, the employee with the greatest seniority with the Company shall receive the preference.

Section 4. Any employee eligible for a vacation, who is severed from the payroll of the Company in any calendar year before having taken his or her vacation, except one who is discharged for cause or who quits without two weeks notice, shall receive vacation pay.

IX. SENIORITY

Section 1. Seniority is defined as the length of an employee's service with the Company within the bargaining unit; it shall apply plant-wide.

Section 2. The Company agrees to draw up a plant-wide Seniority list as of June 1st of each year, which shall be posted in a location available to all employees.

Section 3. The Union may select from the employees covered by this Agreement a Steward who has been employed by the Company for a period of at least one (1) year, whose duty it is to see that this contract is not broken by either the employees or the Employer. The Union shall notify the Company, in writing, of the name of the Shop Steward.

Section 4. In the event of layoff, all Union officers, shop stewards, and shop committee members shall have seniority during their terms of office only, over other employees of the Company provided they have at least one (1) year service with the Company.

Section 5. Production foremen, or other non-bargaining unit employees, shall not do any work, the performance of which, would cause any employee to suffer lay-off or loss of overtime.

Section 6. An employee shall be terminated and shall lose all accumulated seniority when he or she:

a) quits

b) is discharged

c) is laid off for lack of work for a continuous period of 15 calendar months or a period of time equal to the employee's plant seniority, whichever comes first.

d) fails to return to work within four (4) days of notice to return to work, unless such failure to return is for reason satisfactory to the Company

e) engages in gainful employment during a leave of absence except in cases where such leave of absence is expressly granted for this purpose

f) fails to return to work within three (3) working days from the date of expiration of his leave of absence

g) is absent due to non-industrial accident or illness for a period of two (2) years

h) is retired under the Company's Pension Plan.

X.   PERMANENT VACANCIES

Section 1. Each permanent job vacancy and each permanent new job which falls within the scope of the Union's certification shall be filled as follows:

(a) Notice of such job shall be posted in the plant for two (2) days. Such job postings shall include the job classification, department, and the shift on which the new job or vacancy exists. Any employee who wishes to bid for such jobs shall sign the posting. Job postings shall be placed in three locations throughout the plant for official signing in the presence of a member of management, who will initial the posting. Two postings will be provided in the supervisory offices assigned in the plant; a third posting will be placed in the Human Resources office for signing. At all posting locations, job descriptions for all jobs will be available for review. At the end of the two (2) days, the Company shall remove the posting.

(b) Where skill and ability are relatively equal, seniority shall prevail, providing the employee is physically able to perform the work without endangering his or her health or safety. The most senior qualified employee will be awarded the job and be notified by the Human Resources office within five (5) days after removal of the posting. The Company will transfer the employee awarded the vacancy hereunder to the new job within fifteen (15) calendar days, provided the release of the employee does not interfere with the efficient operations of the department. Multiple postings will be awarded from the highest pay grade posting to the lowest pay grade posting.

(c) An employee awarded the vacancy hereunder shall be given up to sixteen (16) working days in which to demonstrate his or her ability to perform the work involved. In some circumstances, extensions may be required, not to exceed sixteen (16) additional workdays. During the qualifying period, employees are unable to bid. During this period, the Company may remove the employee from the job if the Company considers the employee's work to be unsatisfactory. The employee may then bid on any other vacancy. An employee disqualified from a job will be unable to bid that job for a period of three (3) months.

Section 2.   The Union and the Company may, by mutual agreement, provide rules whereby disabled employees may be assigned to jobs which they are able to satisfactorily perform without regard to this Article. When the Union and the Company agree to placement of an employee hereunder, the conditions pertaining to that placement shall be reduced to writing and signed by the parties.

XI.   LAYOFF AND RECALL

Section 1.   If the Company decides to reduce the number of employees in a job classification in a department, and the reduction is expected to continue for more than four (4) days, the reduction shall be made as follows:

(a) The least senior employee or employees shall be removed from the classification provided the skill and ability of the employees in the classification are relatively equal.

(b) An employee removed from his or her classification and/or shift pursuant to (a) shall be afforded the opportunity to move into a job classification in an equal or lower labor grade on any shift provided he or she has the proven skill and ability to perform such work which is held by an employee with less seniority. An employee displaced from his job classification by the exercise of the seniority rights granted in this paragraph shall also be afforded the opportunity to displace other employees in accordance with this paragraph and the exercise of seniority hereunder.

(c) In the operation of (a) and (b) above, a senior employee has the prerogative of accepting layoff instead of displacing a junior employee, if he or she so desires.

(d) The Company will post a notice of layoff expected to last more than four (4) days at least ten (10) days in advance of such layoff, unless the conditions leading to such layoff resulted from an Act of God, labor dispute, or other condition beyond the control of the Company.

Section 2. (a) Employees affected by a reduction of forces shall be recalled to their regular job classification and department in the inverse order of the force reduction. If the employee refuses such recall, he will be terminated as a voluntary quit. Employees recalled to their regular job classification and department, but not to their regular shift, shall be returned to their regular shift in order of seniority as openings occur.

(b) When a vacancy exists after exhausting paragraph (a), the job will be posted for bid according to the bidding procedure. If no employee is awarded such job vacancy, the most senior employee on layoff shall be afforded the vacancy providing he or she has the skill and ability to perform the work.

Section 3. Nothing in this Agreement shall prohibit the Company's laying off the employees for the purpose of taking inventory and offering the work available during such period to the senior qualified employees in the department.

XII.   EMPLOYEE SAFETY

Section 1. The Company agrees to provide a place of employment which shall be safe for the employees therein, shall furnish and use safety devices and safeguards, and shall adopt and use methods and processes adequate to render such places of employment safe. The term "safe" or "safety" as applied to employment or place of employment shall include conditions and methods of sanitation and hygiene necessary for the protection of life, health and safety of the employees.

Section 2. The Company agrees that all machinery, equipment and facilities the Company furnishes shall meet with all required legal standards of safety and sanitation. Accident records shall be kept and maintained by the Company and shall be made available on request to the Safety Committee

Section 3. The Company agrees to maintain a Joint Labor–Management Safety Committee. The Safety Committee shall be composed of at least two (2) representatives of Management and at least two (2) representatives of the Union. The Union representatives shall be selected by the local Union. The Safety Committee shall be able to sit in on any safety investigation when any employee is questioned and shall:

Meet at least once every month on definitely established dates;

Make inspections of the plant at least once every month;

Make recommendations for the correction of unsafe or harmful work practices;

Review and analyze all reports of industrial injury and illness, investigate causes of same and recommend rules and procedures for the prevention of accidents and disease and for the promotion of health and safety of employees;

Promote health and safety education.

Section 4.   All disputes and disagreements brought to the attention of the Safety Committee, arising under the Safety clause of this contract, if not disposed of by the Safety Committee, shall be subject to the Grievance Procedure.

Section 5.   In the event of special circumstances, the Safety Committee may seek advice, opinion and suggestions of experts and authorities on safety matters. Such experts shall have access to the plant for the purpose of applying this article at any time upon providing reasonable notice. The Personnel Manager or his/her designee and a Union designee shall accompany the Safety representative.

Section 6.   Employees injured in the plant shall be furnished medical aid or treatment on Company time, and shall receive full pay for the shift on which they were working when injured.

Section 7.   The Union agrees to participate on the Safety Committee and will endeavor to have its members observe all safety rules and use all equipment and safeguards provided. The Union representative on the Safety Committee, upon request, shall be allowed to leave his or her work during working hours for the purpose of performing his or duties as outlined in this Article without loss of time or pay.

XIII.   DISCIPLINE

Section 1.   The Employer may not discipline or discharge except for just cause and only after due regard for principles of progressive discipline, except as specified otherwise herein.

Section 2.   The following shall be causes for immediate discharge:

(a) Bringing intoxicants, narcotics or other dangerous drugs into or consuming intoxicants or such narcotics or drugs in the plant or on the plant premises.

(b) Reporting for duty under the influence of liquor, narcotics or drugs.

(c) Smoking while on duty or in prohibited areas.

(d) Deliberate destruction or removal of Company's or another employee's property.

(e) Refusal to comply with Company rules, provided that such rules shall be posted in a conspicuous place where they may be read by all employees; and further provided that no changes in present rules or no additional rules shall be made that are inconsistent with this Agreement.

(f) Disorderly conduct.

(g) Sleeping on duty.

(h) Giving or taking a bribe of any nature, as an inducement to obtaining work or retaining a position.

(i) Failure to report for duty without bona fide reasons.

(j) Reading of books, magazines or newspapers while on duty except where required in line of duty.

(k) Unsanitary practice endangering the health of others.

(l) Gambling during working hours.

Section 3.   Except for the infractions noted in Section 2, above, the Employer shall not discharge or suspend an employee without first having discussed such action with the employee and Shop Steward or, in absence of both, having given notice to the Union. Such notice may be by telephone, telegram, or letter, and such notice must include the reason or reasons for an employee's discharge or suspension.

Section 4.   No employee in the bargaining unit shall be required to take any polygraph test, but an employee may, of his own volition, take such a test.

XIV.   GRIEVANCE PROCEDURE

Section 1.   Should grievances arise, a diligent effort shall be made to settle all grievances as soon as possible after they have been presented either by the Union or an employee.

Any employee having a grievance shall submit same in writing as promptly as possible after its occurrence but no grievance shall be valid if not presented within fifteen (15) days from the time the cause for complaint became known to the employee.

If at any time a grievance remains at any step below Step 4 for more than seven (7) working days, the Local Union may, by written notice to local management, request that such grievance be heard at the next step.

Section 2.   When grievances arise, the following steps shall be followed, each to be exhausted before resorting to the next:

Step 1.   Between the immediate supervisor and the aggrieved employee; the appropriate Union representative shall be given an opportunity to be present.

Step 2.   Between the Production Superintendent and the Union Committee.

Step 3.   Between the Operations Manager and the Union Committee.

Step 4.   Between the Divisional Vice President of the Company, or his representative, and the President of the International Union, or his representative.

XV.   ARBITRATION

Section 1.   In the event that a grievance based upon the interpretation, application or compliance with the terms of this Agreement shall not have been satisfactorily settled, the Union within thirty (30) days after the Company's answer to the last step in the grievance procedure may submit the matter to the American Arbitration Association under their rules then in effect. Expenses of the arbitrator shall be shared equally by the Company and the Union. The decision of the arbitrator shall be binding upon both parties to this Agreement. Such decision shall be within the scope and terms of this Agreement, but shall not change any of its terms or conditions.

XVI.   STRIKES AND LOCKOUTS

Section 1.   The Union and the Company agree that there shall be no strikes, sympathy strikes, boycotts, lockouts or general slowing down of production by employees, during the life of this Agreement, and that in the event differences should arise between the Company and the Union or its members employed by the Company, as to the meaning and application of this Agreement, or should any local trouble of any kind arise in the plant, there shall be no suspension of work by the employees on account of such differences.

XVII.   EMPLOYEE BENEFITS

The benefits as shown in this section shall continue in effect during the life of this Agreement.

Medical Insurance: Blue Cross Preferred Comprehensive; Blue Shield, 100; and Major Medical Insurance shall continue to be provided at Company expense for employees until age 70. The Major Medical Insurance referred to herein shall be provided on the basis of $10,000 maximum; $100 deductible per person, and 80/20 participation.

A Blue Shield Eye Examination and Refraction Program shall be provided for employees and certain of their dependents at Company expense as promptly as arrangements can be made.

Dental Insurance: A dental insurance plan to be agreed upon by the parties shall be effective April 1, 2002. This plan shall provide dental benefits for employees and their covered dependents. Company shall contribute $20.00 per month per covered employee toward the cost of this coverage and any excess cost shall be made up by employee contributions.

Death in Family: Should death occur to the Mother, Father, Stepmother, Stepfather, Wife, Children, Stepchildren, Sister or Brother of any employee, he or she shall be entitled to a three-day leave of absence and should death occur to the Grandparent of any employee he or she shall be entitled to a one-day leave of absence. For all such leaves of absence the employee will be paid at his or her straight-time rate provided the leave is taken during the normal week, i.e., Monday through Friday.

Jury Duty: The Company agrees to pay to any employee who shall serve on a bona fide jury panel an amount equal to the difference between the employee's earnings from such service and his or her regular eight (8) hours straight time pay for the days, not in excess of fifteen days for any single period of jury service, during which the employee shall be absent and on jury service.

Sick Benefits: Provision is made for the payment of Sick Benefits to hourly paid employees who have been on the payroll for not less than one year immediately prior to the event of sickness.

On presentation of a licensed physician's, dentist's, chiropodist's, or chiropractor's certificate, an employee who has been ill seven (7) or more consecutive days is entitled to an amount equal to fifty (50) percent of his or her forty-hour weekly wages or the amount to which the employee would be entitled under the State Temporary Disability Law, whichever is greater, from the day he became ill, for a period not in excess of twenty-six weeks in any twelve-month period.

Sick benefits have no connection with illness due to injury in the plant. Disabilities due to injuries in the plant are compensated for under Employers' Liability Insurance in accordance with State regulations.

Retirement: All employees covered by this Agreement are also covered by the Pension Plan which went into operation July 1, 1985, as amended: This is a funded pension plan.

A copy of the Summary Plan Description will be regularly furnished to each new employee. Additional copies may be obtained upon request at the Personnel Office.

Life Insurance: A group life insurance policy will be purchased by the Company so that each employee with one or more years of continuous service with the Company shall have life insurance protection in the amount of $10,000 in the event such employee shall die while employed by the Company and before such employee's retirement. Beneficiary designations shall be made by each such employee in accordance with the provisions of such group policy.

XVIII.   NEW EMPLOYEES

Section 1.   New employees shall be considered probationary employees and shall not rank for seniority until they shall have been in the employ of the Company for sixty (60) calendar days, unless otherwise extended by mutual agreement. After the expiration of the sixty (60) day period, they shall cease to be probationary employees and rates of pay and all other provisions of this Agreement shall be applicable to them. They shall then rank for seniority from the date of original hiring in the plant. During the probationary period the Company may pay the employee the regular job wage rate.

XIX.   SCOPE OF WORK; NEW TECHNOLOGIES

Section 1. It is the intent of the parties to permit the Company to remain technologically competitive and to meet its customer's needs so long as work opportunities now and in the future are preserved for the employees within the bargaining unit identified in Article II. As new technologies develop, the parties pledge their best efforts to fully train and include bargaining unit employees in the implementation of such technologies.

Section 2. In furtherance of the parties' intent, a technology committee consisting of two (2) Union and two (2) Company representatives shall be established and shall meet at the request of either the Union or the Company. The committee shall be empowered to investigate and discuss all issues involving the impact of new technology on bargaining unit work. The committee shall reach agreement on issues investigated and discussed.

Section 3. The Company shall provide training, if required, on any new technology used to perform bargaining unit work. The Company will not permit its proprietary or licensed software, data, hardware, equipment or facilities to be used by others to perform work or functions that replace work or functions being performed by bargaining unit employees.

XX. COMPLETE AGREEMENT

Section 1. The parties hereto acknowledge that, during the negotiations which resulted in this Agreement, each had the unlimited right and opportunity to make demands and proposals with respect to any subject or matter not removed by law from the area of collective bargaining, and that the understandings and Agreements arrived at by the parties after the exercise of the right and opportunity are set forth in this Agreement. Therefore, the parties hereto, for the life of this Agreement, each voluntarily and unqualifiedly waives the right, and each expressly agrees that the other shall not be obligated, to bargain collectively with respect to any subject or matter referred to, or covered or not specifically referred to or covered in the Agreement, even though such subject or matter may not have been within the knowledge or contemplation of either or both of the parties at the time that they negotiated or signed this Agreement.

Section 2. The parties hereto expressly agree that this contract is the sole and complete Agreement between them and that any other previous understandings or Agreements, oral or written (inconsistent with the provisions of this Agreement), are superseded and are of no effect during the term of this Agreement (except as elsewhere provided in the Agreement).

XXI. TERM OF AGREEMENT

Section 1. This Agreement shall be effective April 1, 2006, and shall continue in full force and effect to and including March 31, 2009, and from year to year after the latter date, unless and until either of the parties hereto shall give to the other three (3) months' written notice prior to the end of the original term, or three (3) months' written notice prior to the end of any subsequent year, of an intention to modify or terminate at the end of the original term or of the then current year.

XXII.   SUCCESSORS AND ASSIGNS

Section 1. This Agreement shall be binding upon the successors, purchasers, transferees and assignees of the Company.

Section 2. The Company shall give notice of the existence of this Agreement to any successor, purchaser, transferee or assignee. Such notice shall be in writing, with a copy to the Union, at least sixty (60) days in advance of the effective date of transfer. After such notice is given, upon the request of either party, the parties shall bargain in good faith about any matter not covered by this Agreement.

Exhibit A

All incumbent employees shall receive the following wages:

Effective June 1, 2006

Work Level A	Start	$10.71	--$14.06
Work Level B	Start	$11.64	--$15.02
Work Level C	Start	$12.53	--$16.48
Work Level D	Start	$13.01	--$16.96
Work Level E	Start	$15.15	--$19.10

Effective June 1, 2007

Work Level A	Start	$10.88	--$14.34
Work Level B	Start	$11.83	--$15.32
Work Level C	Start	$12.74	--$16.81
Work Level D	Start	$13.23	--$17.30
Work Level E	Start	$15.41	--$19.48

Effective June 1, 2008

Work Level A	Start	$11.20	--$14.84
Work Level B	Start	$12.18	--$15.86
Work Level C	Start	$13.12	--$17.40
Work Level D	Start	$13.62	--$17.91
Work Level E	Start	$15.88	--$20.16

MEMORANDUM OF UNDERSTANDING #1
ABSENTEE CONTROL PROGRAM

Executed by Company and Union on June 1, 1998

The Company shall have the sole option of placing an employee on the absentee watch list by issuing a written notice to the employee, with a copy to the Union. The Company's decision to place an employee on the absentee watch list shall not be subject to the grievance or arbitration provisions of the contract.

Once an employee is placed on the absentee watch list, termination will take place in the event there are two (2) unexcused absences or four (4) tardinesses, or any combination thereof in any rolling 90–calendar day period. An unexcused absence is defined as *any* absence that is not approved by the Company in writing and signed by the Company President or a designee. In the event a termination based upon absenteeism or tardiness is processed to arbitration, the arbitrator shall be limited to determining whether or not an individual had two (2) or more unexcused absences or four (4) or more tardinesses, or any combination thereof, in the rolling 90–day period. It is further understood that an individual placed on the absentee watch list shall remain on that list for 300 calendar days provided there is no intervening unexcused absence or tardiness and otherwise for 365 calendar days from the date of written notice provided for above.

MEMORANDUM OF UNDERSTANDING #2 CHEMICAL SUBSTANCE ABUSE POLICY
Executed by Company and Union on October 15, 2004

1. An employee who is found or reasonable believed to be under the influence of alcohol, drugs or an intoxicant in the employee's system during the course of business on Company premises or when conducting Company business *at any time* will be subject to discipline including discharge, or may be referred to the Employee Assistance Program. Being "under the influence" of alcohol is defined as a blood alcohol content of .04 or higher; and being "under the influence" of an unauthorized controlled substance, illegal drug, prescription, or non-prescription drug is defined as testing positive at specified ng/ml levels.

2. It is the responsibility of each employee to report promptly to the Medical Department the use or possession of any prescribed medication which may affect judgment, performance, or behavior. No prescription drug will be brought on the Company premises or business in any manner, combination, or quantity other than that prescribed by a licensed physician. Failure to comply may result in discipline, including discharge, or the employee may be referred to the Employee Assistance Program.

3. All new hires will be tested for the use of drugs, alcohol, and intoxicating substances. Refusal to submit to testing, or testing positive, will result in rejection of employment by the Company. Applicants who are denied employment because of a positive test result may reapply for employment and be re-tested after one year from the time of initial rejection.

4. If Management has reasonable suspicion (as herein defined) that an employee is under the influence or, impaired by, or unfit for work due to a chemical substance, including but not limited to a drug, alcohol, or intoxicating substance, or in the event of an accident when the cause may be human error, the subject employee shall be required to submit to medical chemical screening, which may include breath, saliva, urine, and/or blood specimen testing. Positive test results may result in the employee being disciplined, up to and including discharge, or the employee may be referred to the Employee Assistance Program.

5. "Reasonable suspicion" means objective belief based upon reasonable, individualized suspicion that can be described with particularity that a specific employee may be under the influence of alcohol, drugs, or other intoxicating substances based on direct observation by a supervisor or management representative.

NATIONAL LABOR RELATIONS BOARD FORMS

(1) Petition for Election.

(2) Stipulated Election Agreement, and

(3) Unfair Labor Practice Charge Against Employer.

(4) Unfair Labor Practice Charge Against Union.

(5) Remedial Notice.

FORM NLRB-502
(3-96)

UNITED STATES GOVERNMENT
NATIONAL LABOR RELATIONS BOARD
PETITION

FORM EXEMPT UNDER 44 U.S.C. 3512

DO NOT WRITE IN THIS SPACE	
Case No.	Date Filed

INSTRUCTIONS: Submit an original and 4 copies of this Petition to the NLRB Regional Office in the Region in which the employer concerned is located. If more space is required for any one item, attach additional sheets, numbering item accordingly.

The Petitioner alleges that the following circumstances exist and requests that the National Labor Relations Board proceed under its proper authority pursuant to Section 9 of the National Labor Relations Act.

1. **PURPOSE OF THIS PETITION** (If box RC, RM, or RD is checked and a charge under Section 8(b)(7) of the Act has been filed involving the Employer named herein, the statement following the description of the type of petition shall not be deemed made.) (Check One)

☐ **RC-CERTIFICATION OF REPRESENTATIVE** - A substantial number of employees wish to be represented for purposes of collective bargaining by Petitioner and Petitioner desires to be certified as representative of the employees.

☐ **RM-REPRESENTATION (EMPLOYER PETITION)** - One or more individuals or labor organizations have presented a claim to Petitioner to be recognized as the representative of employees of Petitioner.

☐ **RD-DECERTIFICATION (REMOVAL OF REPRESENTATIVE)** - A substantial number of employees assert that the certified or currently recognized bargaining representative is no longer their representative.

☐ **UD-WITHDRAWAL OF UNION SHOP AUTHORITY (REMOVAL OF OBLIGATION TO PAY DUES)** - Thirty percent (30%) or more of employees in a bargaining unit covered by an agreement between their employer and a labor organization desire that such authority be rescinded.

☐ **UC-UNIT CLARIFICATION** - A labor organization is currently recognized by Employer, but Petitioner seeks clarification of placement of certain employees: (Check one) ☐ In unit not previously certified. ☐ In unit previously certified in Case No. _____

☐ **AC-AMENDMENT OF CERTIFICATION** - Petitioner seeks amendment of certification issued in Case No. _____
Attach statement describing the specific amendment sought.

2. Name of Employer	Employer Representative to contact	Telephone Number

3. Address(es) of Establishment(s) involved (Street and number, city, State, ZIP code)	Telecopier Number (Fax)

4a. Type of Establishment (Factory, mine, wholesaler, etc.)	4b. Identify principal product or service

5. Unit involved (In UC petition, describe present bargaining unit and attached description of proposed clarification.)	6a. Number of Employees in Unit:
Included	Present
	Proposed (By UC/AC)
Excluded	6b. Is this petition supported by 30% or more of the employees in the unit?* ☐ Yes ☐ No
(If you have checked box RC in 1 above, check and complete EITHER item 7a or 7b, whichever is applicable.)	*Not applicable in RM, UC, and AC

7a. ☐ Request for recognition as Bargaining Representative was made on (Date) _____ and Employer declined recognition on or about (Date) _____ (If no reply received, so state.)

7b. ☐ Petitioner is currently recognized as Bargaining Representative and desires certification under the Act.

8. Name of Recognized or Certified Bargaining Agent (If none, so state.)	Affiliation

Address, Telephone No. and Telecopier No. (Fax)	Date of Recognition or Certification

9. Expiration Date of Current Contract, If any (Month, Day, Year)	10. If you have checked box UD in 1 above, show here the date of execution of agreement granting union shop (Month, Day, and Year)

11a. Is there now a strike or picketing at the Employer's establishment(s) Involved? Yes _____ No _____	11b. If so, approximately how many employees are participating?

11c. The Employer has been picketed by or on behalf of (Insert Name) _____, a labor organization, of (Insert Address) _____ Since (Month, Day, Year) _____

12. Organizations or individuals other than Petitioner (and other than those named in items 8 and 11c), which have claimed recognition as representatives and other organizations and individuals known to have a representative interest in any employees in unit described in item 5 above. (If none, so state.)

Name	Affiliation	Address	Date of Claim
			Telecopier No. (Fax)

13. Full name of party filing petition (If labor organization, give full name, including local name and number)

14a. Address (street and number, city, state, and ZIP code)	14b. Telephone No.
	14c. Telecopier No. (Fax)

15. Full name of national or international labor organization of which it is an affiliate or constituent unit (to be filled in when charge is filed by a labor organization)

I declare that I have read the above petition and that the statements are true to the best of my knowledge and belief.

Name (Print)	Signature	Title (if any)

Address (street and number, city, state, and ZIP code)	Telephone No.
	Telecopier No. (Fax)

WILLFUL FALSE STATEMENTS ON THIS PETITION CAN BE PUNISHED BY FINE AND IMPRISONMENT (U.S. CODE, TITLE 18, SECTION 1001)

UNITED STATES OF AMERICA

9. COMMERCE. The Employer is engaged in commerce within the meaning of Section 2(6) and (7) of the National Labor Relations Act and a question affecting commerce has arisen concerning the representation of employees within the meaning of Section 9(c). (Insert commerce facts.)

10. WORDING ON THE BALLOT. When only one labor organization is on the ballot, the choice shall be "Yes" or "No." If more than one labor organization is on the ballot, the choices shall appear as follows, reading left to right or top to bottom. (If more than one labor organization is on the ballot, any labor organization may have its name removed by the approval of the Regional Director of a timely written request.)

First.

Second.

Third.

11. PAYROLL PERIOD FOR ELIGIBILITY - THE PERIOD ENDING _____

12. DATE, HOURS, AND PLACE OF ELECTION.

13. THE APPROPRIATE COLLECTIVE-BARGAINING UNIT.

_____
(Employer)

By _____
(Name)   (Date)

_____(Title)_____

Recommended:

_____
(Board Agent)   (Date)

Date approved _____

_____
Regional Director
National Labor Relations Board

Case _____

_____
(Labor Organization)

By _____
(Name)   (Date)

_____(Title)_____

_____
(Labor Organization)

By _____
(Name)   (Date)

_____(Title)_____

9. **COMMERCE.** The Employer is engaged in commerce within the meaning of Section 2(6) and (7) of the National Labor Relations Act and a question affecting commerce has arisen concerning the representation of employees within the meaning of Section 9(c). (Insert commerce facts.)

10. **WORDING ON THE BALLOT.** When only one labor organization is on the ballot, the choice shall be "Yes" or "No." If more than one labor organization is on the ballot, the choices shall appear as follows, reading left to right or top to bottom. (If more than one labor organization is on the ballot, any labor organization may have its name removed by the approval of the Regional Director of a timely written request.)

First.

Second.

Third.

11. **PAYROLL PERIOD FOR ELIGIBILITY - THE PERIOD ENDING** _____

12. **DATE, HOURS, AND PLACE OF ELECTION.**

13. **THE APPROPRIATE COLLECTIVE-BARGAINING UNIT.**

(Employer)	_(Labor Organization)_
By _____	By _____
(Name) _(Date)_	_(Name)_ _(Date)_
(Title)	_(Title)_
Recommended:	
_____	
(Board Agent) _(Date)_	
Date approved _____	
	(Labor Organization)
	By _____
Regional Director	_(Name)_ _(Date)_
National Labor Relations Board	
Case _____	_(Title)_

FORM NLRB-501
(11-88)

FORM EXEMPT UNDER 44 U S C 3512

UNITED STATES OF AMERICA
NATIONAL LABOR RELATIONS BOARD
CHARGE AGAINST EMPLOYER

DO NOT WRITE IN THIS SPACE	
Case	Date Filed

INSTRUCTIONS:
File an original and 4 copies of this charge with NLRB Regional Director for the region in which the alleged unfair labor practice occurred or is occurring.

1. EMPLOYER AGAINST WHOM CHARGE IS BROUGHT

a. Name of Employer

b. Number of workers employed

c. Address (street, city, state, ZIP code)

d. Employer Representative

e. Telephone No.

f. Type of Establishment (factory, mine, wholesaler, etc.)

g. Identify principal product or service

h. The above-named employer has engaged in and is engaging in unfair labor practices within the meaning of section 8(a), subsections (1)
and (list subsections) _____ of the National Labor Relations Act,
and these unfair labor practices are unfair practices affecting commerce within the meaning of the Act.

2. Basis of the Charge (set forth a clear and concise statement of the facts constituting the alleged unfair labor practices)

By the above and other acts, the above-named employer has interfered with, restrained, and coerced employees in the exercise of the
rights guaranteed in Section 7 of the Act

3. Full name of party filing charge (if labor organization, give full name, including local name and number)

4a. Address (street and number, city, state, and ZIP code)

4b. Telephone No.

5. Full name of national or international labor organization of which it is an affiliate or constituent unit (to be filled in when charge is filed
by a labor organization)

6 DECLARATION
I declare that I have read the above charge and that the statements are true to the best of my knowledge and belief.

By _____   _____
(signature of representative or person making charge)   (title if any)

Address _____   _____   _____
(Telephone No.)   (date)

WILLFUL FALSE STATEMENTS ON THIS CHARGE CAN BE PUNISHED BY FINE AND IMPRISONMENT (U. S. CODE, TITLE 18, SECTION 1001)

*U.S. Government Printing Office: 1989-241-525/05104

FORM NLRB-508
(11-98)

UNITED STATES OF AMERICA
NATIONAL LABOR RELATIONS BOARD
**CHARGE AGAINST LABOR ORGANIZATION
OR ITS AGENTS**

FORM EXEMPT UNDER 44 U.S.C. 3512

DO NOT WRITE IN THIS SPACE	
Case	Date Filed

INSTRUCTIONS: File an original and 3 copies of this charge and an additional copy for each organization, each local, and each individual named in item 1 with the NLRB Regional Director of the region in which the alleged unfair labor practice occurred or is occurring.

1. LABOR ORGANIZATION OR ITS AGENTS AGAINST WHICH CHARGE IS BROUGHT

a. Name	b. Union Representative to contact
c. Telephone No.	d. Address (street, city, state and ZIP code)

e. The above-named organization(s) or its agents has (have) engaged in and is (are) engaging in unfair labor practices within the meaning of section 8(b), subsection(s) (list subsections) _____ of the National Labor Relations Act, and these unfair labor practices are unfair practices affecting commerce within the meaning of the Act.

2. Basis of the Charge (set forth a clear and concise statement of the facts constituting the alleged unfair labor practices)

3. Name of Employer	4. Telephone No.
5. Location of plant involved (street, city, state and ZIP code)	6. Employer representative to contact

7. Type of establishment (factory, mine, wholesaler, etc.)	8. Identify principal product or service	9. Number of workers employed

10. Full name of party filing charge

11. Address of party filing charge (street, city, state and ZIP code)	12. Telephone No.

13. DECLARATION
I declare that I have read the above charge and that the statements therein are true to the best of my knowledge and belief.

By _____
(signature of representative or person making charge)

(title or office, if any)

Address _____

(Telephone No.)   (date)

WILLFUL FALSE STATEMENTS ON THIS CHARGE CAN BE PUNISHED BY FINE AND IMPRISONMENT (U. S. CODE, TITLE 18, SECTION 1001)

☆U.S. Government Printing Office: 1989-241-525/05107

NATIONAL LABOR RELATIONS BOARD

AN AGENCY OF THE UNITED STATES GOVERNMENT

The National Labor Relations Act gives employees these rights:

    To engage in self-organization;
    To form, join, or help unions;
    To bargain collectively through a representative of their own choosing
    To act together for collective bargaining or other mutual aid or protection;
    To refrain from all of these things.

WE WILL NOT promulgate, maintain or enforce a rule which prohibits employees from posting pro-Union literature on Company bulletin boards without permission.

WE WILL NOT threaten employees with discipline for violating such a rule.

WE WILL NOT promulgate, maintain or enforce a rule which prohibits the distribution of materials related to union or other activity by Section 7 of the National Labor Relations Act in nonwork areas without prior approval.

WE WILL NOT interrogate job applicants about their union affiliation, their feelings about working for a non-union employer or whether their past employers were unionized.

WE WILL NOT request employees to report to management if they are harassed by employees who support [Union], or any other labor organization.

WE WILL NOT refer to employees interested in or engaged in union activity as "trouble" and WE WILL NOT threaten to discharge such employees because of their union activities.

WE WILL NOT in any other manner interfere with, restrain or coerce employees in the exercise of the rights guaranteed by Section 7 of the Act.

WE WILL notify our employees, in writing, by memorandum or letter separate from this document, that the rules referred to above are no longer in effect.

WE WILL allow our employees to wear union and/or other buttons, insignia, stickers, writings or other markings on their clothing. We will not allow our employees to put union or other buttons, insignia, stickers, writings or other markings on their hard hats, except for safety and security items specifically required by the Company.

WE WILL amend our rule with respect to hard hats to specify that the only items permitted to be put on the hard hats are safety and security items specifically required by the Company. WE WILL NOT promulgate, maintain or enforce a rule which allows any other items.

XYZ COMPANY, INC.
(Employer)

Dated: _____   By _____
                               (Representative)   (Title)

THIS IS AN OFFICIAL NOTICE AND MUST NOT BE DEFACED BY ANYONE

This notice must remain posted for 60 consecutive days from the date of posting and must not be altered, defaced, or covered by any other material. Any questions concerning this notice or compliance with its provisions may be directed to the Board's Office.

615 Chestnut Street, One Independence Mall, 7th Floor,
Philadelphia, Pennsylvania 19106 (215) 597-7601

†